UNIX® System Architechure

UNIX® System Architechure

Prabhat K. Andleigh

Prentice Hall, Englewood Cliffs, New Jersey 07632

Library of Congress Cataloging-in-Publication Data

Andleigh, Prabhat K.
  UNIX systems architecture / Prabhat K. Andleigh.
    p. cm.
  ISBN 0-13-949843-5
  1. UNIX (Computer operating system) 2. Computer architecture.
I. Title.
QA76.76.063A534   1990
005.4'3—dc20

Editorial/production supervision: *bookworks*
Cover design: *Wanda Lubelska Design*
Manufacturing buyer: *Marianne Gloriande*

UNIX® is registered trade mark of AT&T.

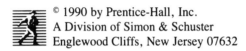 © 1990 by Prentice-Hall, Inc.
A Division of Simon & Schuster
Englewood Cliffs, New Jersey 07632

The Publisher offers discounts on this book when ordered in bulk
quantities. For more information write :

  Special Sales/ College Marketing
  Prentice-Hall, Inc.
  College Technical and Reference Division
  Englewood Cliffs, New Jersey 07632

Printed in the United States of America
10 9 8 7 6 5 4 3 2

ISBN   0-13-949843-5

Prentice-Hall International (UK) Limited, *London*
Prentice-Hall of Australia Pty. Limited, *Sydney*
Prentice-Hall Canada Inc., *Toronto*
Prentice-Hall Hispanoamericana, S.A., *Mexico*
Prentice-Hall of India Private Limited, *New Delhi*
Prentice-Hall of Japan, Inc., *Tokyo*
Simon & Schuster Asia Pte. Ltd., *Singapore*
Editors Prentice-Hall do Brasil, Ltda., *Rio de Janeiro*

To my parents for their caring and encouragement, to my sons, Vaibhav and Vipur, for their support and interest, and to my wife, Deepa, for her love, patience, and understanding.

Contents

Preface

UNIX operating systems, commonly known as UNIX systems, have made significant strides, moving out of the engineering labs and into the business data processing environment. A number of books and papers have described overviews of the UNIX system architecture and various parts of the system. A wide majority of the books have concentrated on user programming and system administration aspects of UNIX systems.

The first extensive description of the internal algorithms and the design of the UNIX system appeared in the book *The Design of the UNIX Operating System* by Maurice J. Bach. The Bach book is an authoritative treatise on the system design and is an excellent reference and study tool for the experienced UNIX system programmer. It discusses the complex algorithms and the perplexing and obscure processes that take place within the kernel. Bach's book is aimed at advanced undergraduate or graduate level students, as well as system programmers.

This book, on the other hand, presents a straightforward description of the architecture, including the internal algorithms, essential for a clear and detailed understanding of the operating system. I have conveyed a different and, I believe, a simpler perspective than the Bach book. It is an architectural perspective. The organization of this book is designed to be equally useful for a reader new to the operating system, or a reader who is very familiar with the UNIX system and is ready for a detailed discussion of the internal algorithms. This book will be valuable as a textbook for undergraduate as well as graduate-level students when used as the basis for an operating systems course. It is also useful for system programmers intending to enrich their own understanding of the system internals, either for new system applications development or for system administration tasks. The material covers issues like porting UNIX systems and applications portability, system performance, multi-processor and distributed computing issues, and potential areas of enhancing UNIX. This book is also very useful for developing a level of understanding of the operating system as a lead-in to the Bach book. This preparation would provide a better appreciation of the complex issues discussed in the Bach book.

While access to source code is not essential, and this book can be studied independently, readers will benefit the most if they have access to the source code. I have assumed that the reader is generally familiar with some higher level programming languages. To facilitate programmers who are not *C* language literate, the descriptions of algorithms avoid *C* language specific contructs. Instead, I have used indenting to depict procedure blocks or complex statements. The algorithms are generally based on AT&T UNIX System V Release 2; features of System V Release 3 have been covered where applicable. Key areas of differences with the Berkeley Software Distrubution releases 4.2bsd and 4.3bsd have been pointed out. A separate chapter discusses the issues of UNIX Operating System standardization issues.

I have used figures and charts throughout the text to illustrate concepts and relationships among components of the UNIX system. Examples are used as needed to further enhance the understanding of the system. A number of exercises, designed for undergraduate and graduate level students, have been included. These exercises are as useful for system programmers; all readers are encouraged to work at them. The bulk of the kernel architecture description is contained in Chapter 3. An experienced UNIX system programmer may find it worthwhile to skim through Chapter 2, and start serious study with Chapter 3. The following paragraphs describe the organization of the book in detail.

Chapter 1 provides an overview of multi-user and multiple process operating systems as an introduction to this class of operating systems. It introduces some concepts that are important for the understanding of timesharing operating systems in general, and the UNIX operating system in particular.

Chapter 2 describes the UNIX system in overview form and attempts to provide a generalized view of the architecture. It describes a layered view of the architecture; the concepts of user space and kernel space; the concept of processes, process creation, and process management; the hierachical directory structure; and introduces the input/output system. This chapter sets in place a good base for the follow-on discussions in Chapter 3.

Chapter 3 is larger than the other chapters and describes in detail the architecture of each major subsystem of the UNIX system. It uses the descriptions of key algorithms for completeness of the discussion; as well as to assist any reader who may intend to work with UNIX source code. This chapter first describes the key tables and structures used by the operating system to maintain the information it needs for managing its resources and user processes. It then proceeds through a presentation of the key concepts and algorithms, and detailed discussions of memory management, system call processing, process management, interprocess communication, file system management, input/output management, and networking. While all of these subsystems are interrelated, I believe that this sequence of discussions is very useful for understanding the operating system.

Chapter 4 presents the concepts of distributed systems. It explores the various options for distributed file systems and network load sharing. It also explores parallel processing. The architectures of some commercial systems are presented as examples of distributed systems.

Chapter 5 is devoted primarily to performance issues. It evaluates potential performance problems and presents a number of options for increasing performance. Performance is always an issue for any system application developed for a multi-user environment. This chapter would be of special interest to system administrators.

Chapter 6 analyzes the types of ports to which the UNIX operating system implementations have been subjected. It is intended to provoke some thought for readers who are likely to port the operating system on new hardware.

Chapter 7 looks at the other porting perspective, that of application programs. It provides an overview of implementation differences; and discusses the key issues of the POSIX and other standardization efforts. It also discusses the requisites for making applications portable.

Chapter 8 evaluates the areas of the operating system that present opportunities for improving the operating system, either in terms of functionality, or in terms of performance.

Appendix A lists the key parameters of a number of system databases, structures, and tables. It is a useful reference tool for readers who do not have access to a UNIX operating system.

Appendix B presents a glossary of terms typical to UNIX systems that have been used in the book.

I am sure the readers will enjoy digging deep into the UNIX system just the way I enjoyed it through a number of system ports and through system application development. It will not only give them a better appreciation for the features and limitations, but will give them the confidence to deal with the system in an effective manner.

ACKNOWLEDGMENTS

It is my pleasure to acknowledge the ready help and assistance of many friends and colleagues who encouraged me while I wrote this book. They took the time to review my ideas and to present their own thoughts on what they would like to see in a book. I would like to thank all of my colleages, and specially the formal reviewers of this manuscript. Their contributions are immense in nipping errors in the bud, and cleaning up the discussions.

Many people gave their time and energy to review drafts of this book. I would like to thank Tom Cheek, Frank Farance, Francois Sicard, and Andy French for their inputs and the numerous technical discussions that led to the basic structure and presentation perspective. This book owes a lot to Mike Gretzinger's detailed review and comments. I would also like to thank Massood Zarrabian for giving me the opportunity to work on some very interesting UNIX port projects. And, I would like to thank the management at LOBB Systems, Inc. for their understanding and encouragement for completing the manuscript.

I would also like to thank my editors at Prentice Hall, Ed Moura and Patricia Henry. Pat spent a lot of time and gave me immense encouragement to start the project.

Ed's support has helped me continue and complete the project. They, along with their staff, have provided much valuable help and guidance for accomplishing this book in its final form. Karen Fortgang provided help in preparing this manuscript for type-setting.

Last, but not least, I would like to thank my wife, Deepa, for her understanding and emotional support throughout, without which I would not have completed this. I would also like to thank my sons, Vaibhav and Vipur, for patiently enduring wasted weekends and idle evenings while I worked on this book.

UNIX® System Architechure

1

Introduction to Multi-User Operating Systems

The early 1960s are credited with the birth of time-sharing systems. The Compatible Time-Sharing System, first operational and in production use at M.I.T. from 1964 to 1974, has influenced the design of the modern operating systems. These first generation systems provided a subset of the machine for use by normal batch programs. MULTICS, also developed at M.I.T. as a component of Project MAC is a second generation system and is widely recognized as the model for the modern multi-user time-sharing operating systems. The concept of splitting memory into fixed page frames resulted from work at the University of Manchester in the late 1950s on the Ferranti Atlas machine project, and was used for the design of the MULTICS Operating System. MULTICS was the first commercial implementation of the concept of virtual memory segments, where each segment is like a single contiguous chunk of memory broken into pages.

The initial work on the UNIX operating system was performed in 1969 by Ken Thompson on a PDP-7 minicomputer. The primary application for the computing environment created under the new operating system was programming research. As such, the operating system developed was both general and simple. The spartan nature of the operating system resulted in a proliferation of development tools. This proliferation of tools is the primary reason for the popularity of the UNIX operating system. The timing of the original development work and the environment in which it was developed influenced the design of the operating system. A close scrutiny of the architecture of UNIX shows the influence of the MULTICS concepts, its time-sharing base, and its memory management schemes. Over the years, UNIX has grown in size as well as in its repertory of tools and utilities. It has been ported to a number of computer systems and now covers the range from micro-computers to super minicomputers and mainframes.

The architectural features of UNIX, typically found only in very large mainframe operating systems, are the primary reasons for the current standardization of UNIX on micro- and minicomputers. These features include:

1. A multi-process architecture.
2. Ability to initiate asynchronous processes.
3. A hierarchical file system that features dismountable volumes.
4. Compatible file, device, and inter-process input output.
5. System user command language selectable on a per-user basis.

The UNIX operating system supports program development as well as real-time interactive applications and general data processing applications for businesses as well as personal computers for use in homes.

1.1 CONCEPT OF A VIRTUAL MACHINE

Modern multi-user interactive operating systems implement a collection of virtual machines. These virtual machines are similar to the base machine except that some hardware-dependent and potentially hazardous instructions are not available. In a sense, for the user a virtual machine is an image of the base machine.

These virtual machines share a number of system hardware resources including disk drives, memory, communications lines, and most importantly, the central processing unit (CPU). A time-sharing operating system is designed to set up virtual machines for each user. The resources are shared according to the algorithm set up for resource sharing and CPU scheduling. These algorithms combine *priority, readiness to run,* and *round robin* selection for allocating the CPU and system resources to a virtual machine.

The development of the virtual machine concepts also provided a level of indirection to programs that made the virtual machines largely insensitive to the changes in the actual hardware. This level of indirection is the key to the portability of applications programs written for the UNIX environment. Additionally, this provides the means of simulating hardware features that may not even exist on the real hardware to allow applications to run unchanged.

1.1.1 Processes

The UNIX system allocates resources to users and programs by way of processes. A process executes in a virtual machine environment. While this sounds strange, let us take a look at what this really means. This virtual machine environment consists of *memory, priority,* a *terminal* for *user interface,* and shared access to other system resources. This set of resources is associated with a process. The process is also given a user identification. A program runs within a process, much as it would if it had a dedicated single user CPU. The program may use all resources available to the process.

A process may create sub-processes, may terminate its own existence, and may put itself to sleep temporarily, only to wake up on completion of a pre-determined event. Multi-tasking is achieved through scheduling of processes where different processes perform different tasks. Activities of the processes are coordinated through the use of interprocess communications.

We have just seen that a virtual machine is a subset of the full system resources that we call an image of the system. When we start operating this subset to run programs, we call it a process. When a sub-process is created, a virtual machine is created for it. Let us now take a look at multi-user systems and further develop the concept of virtual machines and processes.

1.2 MULTI-USER AND MULTI-PROCESS OPERATING SYSTEM FUNCTIONS

Multi-user operating systems manage a number of virtual machines. The virtual machines support user processes that represent user tasks. The virtual machines also perform the major functions of managing resources such as the following:

1. Processor (CPU) on a timesharing basis.
2. Main memory and secondary memory (memory management).
3. Disk storage (mass storage management).
4. Input/output devices (peripherals and communications interfaces).

These machines also provide the orderly allocation and sharing of these resources among the user processes.

The personality of the virtual machine is determined by the System Call Interface, i.e., the collection of system calls available to an application for interacting with the operating system. The main features of the virtual machines are the following:

1. Capability to interact with the system to perform a large number of tasks through the system call interface. A system call conveys a user request to a routine within the operating system to perform a specific task, for example, to read data from a disk.
2. Processes running in these virtual machines are isolated and protected from one another.
3. The virtual machines have their own memory space.
4. A virtual machine provides access to all devices (this access is controlled by the operating system).

The virtual machines are slower than the base machine due to sharing of CPU, memory, disk storage, and device resources with other virtual machines. The virtual machines compete for these resources via system calls set up as requests for the operating system to perform a function on behalf of the virtual machine. A program needs to know only the manner in which this request is to be made and is not concerned with the actual device access mechanisms. This feature allows portable programs to be written that can run on different machines with different devices.

From the discussion above, we can see that a virtual machine defines the resources that a process can use. The operating system is dynamic, and schedules the resources of the system in an orderly manner to allow processes to run. For our study of the operating system architecture we will concentrate on processes rather than on virtual machines.

1.2.1 Device Interrupts

A major function of the operating system is to read from or write to disk drives, terminals, printers, communications lines, and other peripherals. The operating system can (1) start a transfer to a device and wait for it to complete, or (2) start a transfer and attend to other tasks and check back later, or (3) start a transfer to a device and attend to it only when it requests service. The third mode of operation is more efficient than the first two because the operating system does not spend any time making repeated checks to see if the device transfer has completed. The third mode of operation requires a mechanism for the device to communicate with the processor to request service.

The mechanism used for the third mode of operation is called *interrupt processing*. All device controllers used for hardware running a UNIX operating system have the capability to send a signal to the bus, a *device interrupt,* indicating that the device requests attention. A number of such signals can be waiting at any one time depending on the number of devices that have requested service. Each device interrupt is assigned a priority level. For example, the system clock is at the highest priority level and the printer is generally at a low priority level. The operating system addresses these requests in an order based on the priority of the interrupt and the priority level of the current process. A higher priority interrupt causes the operating system to temporarily suspend its current operation and attend to the interrupting device. We have simplified the device interrupt management description here considerably for the sake of clarity of the concept.

1.2.2 Concepts of Tasks, Processes, and Users

A *task* is the name given to a sequential execution path through the code. Simple applications use a sequential execution path. Applications that perform multiple tasks in parallel, for example, an application that prints while it communicates with a remote system, use separate execution paths for each task. All of these execution paths are a part of the same program and are controlled by the main execution path.

A program runs within a *process*. A process can, therefore, be single-tasking or multi-tasking. An operating system can be designed to run multiple processes. The operating system can be designed such that all processes can be assigned to only one user or application, *single-user*. A more complex implementation of the operating system can assign processes to multiple users, *multi-user,* where each user is independent from other users. The user can create sub-processes to perform multiple tasks at the same time.

1.2.3 CPU Usage and Process Management

The CPU is the primary resource that not only runs user programs, but also runs the operating system code to manage resources and schedule processes. The operating system employs an orderly procedure for scheduling the CPU among the operating system, system peripherals, user applications, and system functions called by the user application programs. There are a number of schemes used by operating systems for scheduling CPU resources. Some notable ones include the following.

1. Sequential operation.
2. Event polling.
3. Multiple-process, interrupt-driven.
4. Preemptive, interrupt-driven scheduling.

Please note that the terminology used, while common for UNIX operating systems, is not standard and may be considered the author's terminology.

Sequential operating systems are generally the simplest; the CPU performs one task at a time. On completion of a task, it switches to the next task. These operating systems are called single-user and single-tasking systems and do not typically support multiple tasks or users.

Event polling is a significant step above sequential operating systems in a sense that it can support multiple tasks or multiple users. Very briefly, the scheduling is performed in a round robin or pre-set order of priority. The task that has an event posted (e.g., a keyboard input, printer completion, etc.) is scheduled. Once scheduled, the task continues until it is blocked for an event (e.g., input from keyboard or a communications line, printer becoming free, etc.). A task that takes too long can prevent the system from responding to users within a reasonable time. For example, the system will not respond to the user keyboard entry until a print job that is running is completed. This is a significant disadvantage of an event polling system. Very careful design is required for system applications where quick and predictable response is essential, for example in communications or process control applications. Despite these disadvantages, the event polling scheme has been used even for large multi-user systems due to its simplicity and processing speed for specific applications.

Interrupt driven systems overcome the disadvantages of the event polling systems noted above by providing the capability to respond to device interrupts quickly. These systems also provide priority and state driven scheduling of processes on an interrupt basis. The real time clock usually provides the interrupt to schedule the CPU. An event, for example completion of disk output, may also cause re-scheduling.

Preemptive interrupt driven systems are generally required for critical real-time applications. The term *preemption* as used in the context of interrupt driven operating systems means the temporary suspension of a lower priority task and scheduling of a higher priority task when an interrupt or an event occurs. The UNIX operating system falls in this class of operating systems but it does not provide full preemption. The UNIX operating system allows preemption only of a process running user code but not a process that has executed a system call and is running operating system kernel code. Full preemption implies the capability to preempt a process running kernel code. Full preemption is especially useful for applications like process control where the interrupts or higher priority processes that become unblocked must be able to preempt a kernel process to provide a rapid response to a process control device. Operating systems of this nature are considerably more complicated than the rest.

1.2.4 Memory Management

Memory management becomes a complex issue in multi-user systems because the total requirements of the users and the operating system generally far exceed the available system memory. Even the rapid price reductions of memory chips and consequently increasing main memory capacities have not overcome the need for larger and larger memory requirements. The theme common to all solutions for more memory is the use of a part of the disk as an extension to main memory. Called *virtual memory,* this storage provides memory space for all users and can be expanded as needed if the number of users the system is configured for increases. Since the CPU can use only main memory for executing code and accessing data, the code and data components of a process have to be copied in to main memory for execution. Among the schemes used for managing these are the following:

1. Swapping.
2. Demand paging.
3. Demand paging and swapping.

Swapping systems swap in or swap out complete processes (text, data, stacks, and other system tables needed to manage the process while they are in main memory). A process resides on disk until it is ready to run again. It is then swapped in to main memory and gets scheduled based on priority. The larger the size of available main memory, the larger the number of processes that can stay resident in memory.

Demand paging systems, on the other hand, do not swap in a complete process. They copy the minimum needed to run the process and use the concept of *page faults* to indicate the need to bring in another page of the process from virtual memory on disk to physical memory. A page fault occurs when the required page is not in physical memory, and the actions for reading it into physical memory from virtual memory are started. Every process is partially in memory at all times.

Demand paging and swapping systems on the other hand, not only use demand paging but have the capability to swap out complete processes if necessary to make room for partially swapping in other processes. This scheme benefits from the advantages of both of the first two schemes.

1.2.5 Mass Storage Management

Hierarchical multi-level (inverted tree) directory structures is the rule for multi-user operating systems. The key issues in multi-user systems are the following:

1. Sharing of files and file protection.
2. Asynchronous operation of processes and peripherals.

The need for sharing of files and protecting the data in the files is obvious. Schemes to manage sharing of files include access control (passwords), and file or record locking. The term asynchronous operation requires some explanation. In a multi-user system, the request by a process for a disk block and the availability of that block in memory are asynchronous. Typically, a request for a disk block causes re-scheduling and the the process may not even be in memory when the disk block is read into memory. Therefore, temporary storage (buffering) and management of system buffers is a major function performed by mass storage management.

1.2.6 Input/Output Device Management

Input/output (also called I/O) devices, including mass storage devices, are shared resources that are used by a number of user processes. Unlike mass storage devices that are shareable, most I/O devices are temporarily dedicated to one user, for example printers or communication lines. A device becomes available to another user only after the current task of the current user is completed. All peripheral devices convey their need for attention via interrupts. Some devices, (e.g., disk drives or clock) are critical to the performance of the operating system itself and need quick attention. The I/O device management function addresses the needs of devices and treats disk storage as a special I/O device. Managing and handling interrupts are key functions for I/O management.

1.3 SYSTEM SERVICES

As we have just seen, managing system resources is the first major function of an operating system. These system resources include the CPU, memory, mass storage, and other peripheral devices. The second major function provided by an operating system are the system services. These are provided via the system calls and consist of the following:

1. I/O services.
2. File/data access services.
3. Networking and communications services.
4. System maintenance services.
5. System usage accounting services.

1.3.1 Input/Output Services

The I/O services consist of start-up, control, data transfer to and from devices, and shutdown of peripheral and terminal devices. The I/O services include the following:

1. Device addressing.
2. System buffers for data transfer.
3. Device interrupt handling.
4. Handling of device errors.
5. Spooling to magtape & printer/plotter devices.

The I/O services provided allow for the sharing of the devices across a number of users and provide a uniform procedure for accessing different kinds of devices. The operating system recognizes the characteristics of the device and optimizes its access mechanisms, (e.g., data buffering schemes) for the most efficient option from an overall system perspective. For example, the operating system differentiates between block data transfer devices like disks and magtapes, and character data transfer devices like serial I/O.

1.3.2 File/Data Access Services

The operating system file/data access services provide the user, or an application, access to the disk file system in a generalized and simple manner. The user or application needs to know only the logical address rather than the physical address, and the file access services perform the address translation from logical to physical disk block address. The services provided by multi-user operating systems include the following:

1. Ability to create and delete files.
2. Ability to access files by a symbolic name (logical address and not by precise physical location on disk).
3. Provide a means of grouping files by user or task in a directory structure.
4. Control access to data and provide for controlled sharing of data.
5. Reliability and integrity of data and relative immunity from system failure.
6. Expansion of the file system.
7. Addition and removal of disk drives from the file system.
8. Means for archiving and back-up.

The disk file system is generally treated as a special case of the overall I/O system, because the disk file system provides a much larger array of services than are typically provided by the I/O services.

1.3.3 Networking and Communications Services

These services consist of sharing the communication facilities across users, providing the control and handshaking signals, buffering data, and programming the controls for different protocols.

1.3.4 System Maintenance Services

System maintenance services include the following:

1. Installation and start-up of the system.
2. User login and password control.
3. Verification and repair of the file system.
4. New device drivers and system rebuilds.
5. Disk backup and restore.
6. Communications link setup.

System maintenance services are designed to automate the task of maintaining a multi-user system; and providing central control of the operational aspects and day to day maintenance of the system.

1.3.5 System Usage Accounting Services

Multi-user systems are a resource shared by a number of users and departments in an organization. As such, information for equitable billing or sharing of costs may be a requirement. The cost sharing or billing may be on the basis of some combination of log-in time, CPU usage time, peripheral usage, communication line usage, print output, etc. Most multi-user operating systems provide functions for collecting, summarizing, and reporting this information.

1.4 SUMMARY

In this chapter, we have been introduced to the concept of multi-user and multi-tasking operating systems, and we have looked at some of the characteristics of these systems. We looked at the key issues of system functions, process management, memory management, input and output management, and file and directory management. We also touched on the issue of system services.

1.5 EXERCISES

1. Describe the differences between single-user single-tasking, single-user multi-tasking, and multi-user multi-tasking operating systems.
2. How would you classify MS-DOS, OS/2, and UNIX?
3. What is an interrupt driven operating system?
4. What is a process?
5. Describe swapping and demand paging.

2

UNIX Architecture Overview

While the terminology used for UNIX is very similar to that used for most contemporary operating systems, readers not familiar with UNIX are encouraged to go to Appendix B and read through the Glossary of UNIX terms provided. This chapter provides an overview of the UNIX operating system architecture and is a good base for the detailed architecture discussions in Chapter 3. It describes the relationship between the sub-systems and provides an overall perspective for the study of each sub-system of the UNIX kernel.

The overview in this chapter describes the subsystems of the UNIX kernel *functionally* as well as *architecturally*. It is important to understand the difference between the two perspectives. The functional perspective describes the capabilities of each sub-system. The architectural perspective, on the other hand, describes the manner in which the modules of the sub-system are laid out, and also describes their interactions with other modules.

The reader is encouraged to refer to Chapter 3 at any time the need is felt to go deeper into the subject matter to understand it. In-depth explanations have been deliberately avoided in this chapter to maintain the narrative at an overview level.

2.1 SYSTEM OVERVIEW AND MAJOR SUB-SYSTEMS

A typical computer system consists of the hardware, the operating system, and applications programs. A typical operating system includes a user command interpreter or equivalent user interface. Almost all operating systems are distributed with *text editors,* language compilers, linker/loaders, and other system utility programs. The operating system also provides a programming interface that allows a user to develop application programs that manipulate system resources.

The UNIX operating system is somewhat unique in that the user command interface is not integrated with the operating system. It is a separate program and can be changed like any other utility program. Figure 2-1 describes the system structure of a computer system running the UNIX operating system.

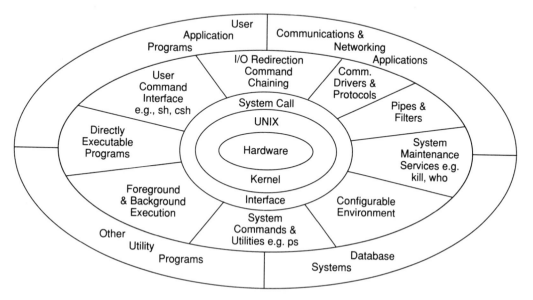

Figure 2-1.   System Architecture

The commands or directly executable user application programs interact with the UNIX kernel via the system programming interface. Programs that call other programs are shown in the top layer. For example, the C compiler calls the C pre-processor (cpp), the two-pass compiler (comp), the assembler (as), and the loader (ld). Some applications may go through two or more such levels, for example, a user application program that in turn calls the C compiler.

Even though UNIX is a complete operating system, it does not implement some usual O/S features that are typically found in most multi-user operating systems. These features are the following:

1. Job accounting for billing purposes.
2. Command language interpreter.
3. File access methods (e.g. ISAM).

These features were not implemented originally to contain the size of the UNIX kernel. However, due to consistent requests for these functions from developers of commercial applications these functions are now being considered for later revisions of UNIX.

The UNIX operating system consists of the following five major components:

1. The UNIX kernel (also called the Base Operating System).
2. The UNIX user command interface (generally called *shell*).
3. Commands and utilities.
4. UNIX system services.
5. UNIX programming interface.

This book will concentrate on the architecture of the UNIX operating system kernel and the system programming interface. However, before proceeding with the UNIX kernel architecture discussion, let us take a quick look at the other components of the UNIX operating system. It would be beneficial to consult the UNIX distribution documentation and user-level texts for a detailed discussion of these components.

2.1.1 The UNIX User Command Interface

The UNIX user command interface is a separate program, commonly referred to as a *shell*. It is a somewhat cryptic user interface to the operating system functions and has not undergone a major change since its original implementation. Indeed, UNIX shells are well liked by system developers due to their built-in programming capability and efficient use of keywords. A number of shells, *e.g. csh, Bourne shell,* and *kshell* are in use. The shell is often replaced by application level interfaces that interact directly with the UNIX kernel. Some systems integrators have replaced the shell with enhanced versions of shells using window management techniques (e.g., SUNtools) that use cursor movement and pointing devices, along with pop-up and pull-down menus.

2.1.2 UNIX Commands and Utilities

UNIX commands and utility programs, like the *shell,* are separate programs. They are a part of the UNIX distribution, but are not considered a part of the kernel. The total number of commands and utilities ranges from over 100 for AT&T UNIX System V to over 150 for Berkeley UNIX 4.3bsd.

2.1.3 UNIX System Services

The UNIX system provides a number of services, such as systems administration, system reconfiguration, and file system maintenance. In addition, the UNIX operating system also provides a file transfer service for copying files across local area or wide area networks of UNIX systems. Called UUCP (for UNIX to UNIX file copy), it features file transfer and electronic mail capability. Other services include the following:

1. Customization of system parameters.
2. Rebuilding the operating system with user drivers.

A description of these services is beyond the scope of this text. These services and the supporting functions are described only to the extent that they form a part of the kernel architecture (for example, configuration parameters). These services are generally well documented in UNIX distribution literature and the reader will find the user manuals to be a good source of information.

UNIX system administration services consist of the following activities:

1. Creation and definition of user accounts.
2. Setting up of access control parameters for files and peripherals.
3. Maintenance of the file systems.

The system administration services are built in the UNIX system as system calls as well as commands. File access control issues have been addressed throughout the architecture description of Chapter 3. Again, system administration services are not really a separate resource of the UNIX kernel, and as such, are not described separately.

2.1.4 UNIX Programming Interface

The programming interface provides user programs access to system functions. UNIX has a very well defined system call interface. There are over 75 system calls in AT&T UNIX System V (some implementations have a much larger number) that perform the various functions that manage the system resources like memory, disk storage, and peripherals. The shell provides functionality equivalent to most of these system calls. The system calls are defined in a run-time library. The run-time library provides the mapping of the programming level system call interface to the kernel routines that service the system calls and perform the system functions.

2.2 UNIX KERNEL FUNCTIONAL OVERVIEW

The UNIX kernel has always been recognized as the base operating system that supports user programs and utility programs like compilers, linkers, source code control system, nroff, etc. The functions provided by the UNIX kernel include the following:

1. Process scheduling.
2. Memory management.
3. Device management.
4. Disk and file management.
5. System call interface.
6. Operator console interface.

These functions are spread over a number of modules within the UNIX kernel. The utility programs and UNIX commands are not considered a part of the UNIX kernel. As we saw in Figure 2-1, the kernel consists of the layers closest to the hardware that are for the most part protected from the user. The kernel may be viewed in a functional layer model as described in Figure 2-2.

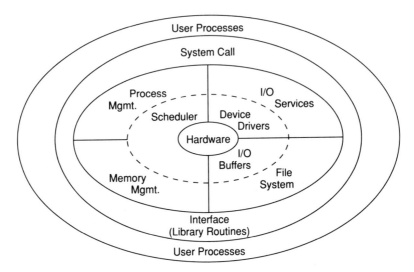

Figure 2-2.   Functional Layer Model of the UNIX Kernel

At the lowest level of this model, the level closest to the hardware in Figure 2-2, there are basic hardware interface modules. These modules provide process scheduling, manage and acquire memory for processes to run, and perform low-level input/output functions. The following is a more complete listing of the functions:

1. Process representation (structures), scheduling and dispatching.
2. Memory allocation and de-allocation.
3. Interrupt handling.
4. Low level device control.
5. Disk storage system management, data buffering.
6. Process synchronization and inter-process communications.

Every time a process is loaded and started up, a chunk of main memory is allocated for program code and data. Additionally, main memory is required for buffers, system databases, and for stack space. The device management routines in this layer start and stop devices, check and reset status, and read and write data from or to devices. Similarly, the disk management routines access the disk drive and perform the basic block read and write functions.

The next layer consists of all kernel services. This layer provides the mapping between user level requests and device driver level actions. The user system call is converted to calls to the kernel service routines that perform requested services. These services consist of Process Creation and Termination, Input/Output Services, Transmit/Receive Data Functions, File/Disk Access Services (called the UNIX file system), and Terminal Handling Services.

The system call interface layer converts a process operating in the user mode to a protected kernel mode process so that the program code can invoke kernel routines to perform system functions.

The uppermost layer consists of user processes running shells, UNIX commands, utility programs, and user application programs. User programs are protected from inadvertent writes by other users. They have no direct access to the UNIX kernel routines and all access is channeled through the system call interface. Additionally, user programs cannot directly access memory used by kernel routines.

2.3 UNIX KERNEL ARCHITECTURAL OVERVIEW

We just noted that UNIX has been implemented in an "onion-style" architecture model consisting of layers of functionality. Additionally, it features two rings of protection from inadvertent programming errors in applications that may tend to damage other user applications or the operating system databases and program modules. The inner protected ring is called *kernel space* and the outer ring is called *user space*. The following discussion describes these two dimensions and their interactions.

2.3.1 User Space

The user space is the space in memory where user processes run. This consists of memory starting above the kernel and includes the rest of available memory. This memory space is protected and the system prevents one user from interfering with another user, i.e. a user process is protected from interference or damage by another user process. Only kernel processes can access a user process. A process operating in this space, also known as *user process,* is said to be operating in *user mode.*

2.3.2 Kernel Space

The kernel space is the space in memory where all kernel services are provided via kernel processes. Any process executing kernel code operates in this space and is known as a *kernel process.* Kernel space is a privileged area and the user has access to it only through the system call mechanism. Users have direct access to neither machine instructions nor devices. A kernel process, however, does have direct access to both. Similarly, a kernel process can modify the memory map, an operation frequently required to perform process scheduling. A user process becomes a kernel process when it executes a system call and starts executing kernel code. A process running kernel code, also known as *kernel process,* is said to be operating in *kernel mode.*

2.3.3 Data Flow between User Space and Kernel Space

Since user space and kernel space are in different address spaces, the scheme for moving data between them is important. The data can be of the type represented by bits, a byte, an integer, or long integer used for flags and addresses, or it can be of the type represented by arrays used for strings or data arrays.

When a system call is executed, the arguments to the call and the corresponding kernel routine identification (entry number in the syscall table) are passed from user space to kernel space. Figure 2-3 describes this event.

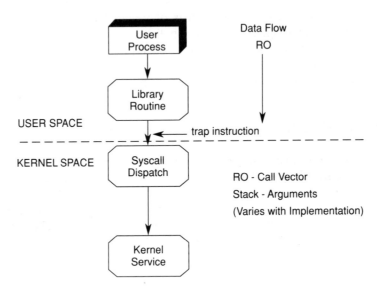

Figure 2-3.   User Space and Kernel Space Relationship

Depending on the UNIX implementation, the entry number of the kernel routine corresponding to the system call (call vector) is passed either in *register 0* or in the stack. The system call arguments are passed in the *u area* of the process.

The *u area* of a process (*user structure* and *kernel stack*), contains control information for the process that the kernel needs while the process is running (i.e., it is the currently scheduled process). This includes the following:

1. Information about the process, such as files open, root, and current directories, arguments to current system call, and process text, stack, and data sizes. (Please refer to Appendix A for a detailed description of the contents of a *user structure*.)
2. A pointer to the *process table entry* containing information required for scheduling a process, such as scheduling priorities.
3. User file descriptor table with information about the files the process has open.
4. The kernel stack for the process (some implemenations exclude the kernel stack from the *u area*) containing information about system calls made by the process in kernel mode. The kernel stack is empty while the process is in user mode.

Very small amounts of data, primarily flags and addresses, not exceeding the size of a long integer can be passed to the user via the return value mechanism of the *C* language used for the system call interface, e.g.

l = lseek(fd,0l,0);

where *l,* a long integer, is the return value from the *lseek* call.

Data like strings or arrays that cannot be returned as values of functions must be passed via pointers, e.g.

ret = read(fd, cnt, &buff);

where the argument 'buff' is a pointer to a buffer area in the user's address space for the data to be returned and 'ret', the value of the function, is used to return the number of bytes read.

In addition to these methods, most UNIX implementations support a handful of routines used by kernel processes for transferring data between the kernel space and the user space. While user processes cannot access kernel memory, kernel processes can access user memory.

2.3.4 Entry Points Into the UNIX Kernel

The entry points into the UNIX kernel, described in Figure 2-4, provide access to the functions and services provided by the kernel. There are three classes of entry points that access or activate kernel services. These are - (1) *system calls* by user application programs or system utilities, (2) *hardware service requests* from device handlers, and (3) *error conditions*. All entry points use mechanisms that *interrupt* the kernel activity.

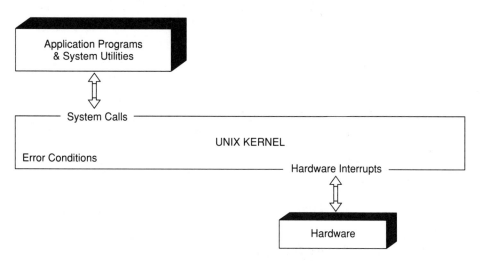

Figure 2-4.   Kernel Entry Points

System calls are handled by a *trap* instruction that switches a system call from user mode to kernel mode. *Interrupts* are used by peripherals to request service from the *device handlers* in the kernel. Abnormal processing conditions, or *error conditions* are also handled through *trap* instructions.

2.4 UNIX KERNEL SUB-SYSTEMS

The UNIX kernel itself is divided into a number of major modules or sub-systems that provide the operating system functions. Each subsystem has the responsibility to manage its own resources, and has a clear interface to the other modules. A subsystem may span a number of functional layers described in the previous section. These sub-systems are the following:

1. Process *0*—the process and CPU scheduler (called the *swapper*).
2. System call dispatch service.
3. The kernel level file services sub-system.
4. The kernel level I/O services module.
5. The disk sub-system.

Figure 2-5 displays the architectural relationship between the different sub-system of the UNIX kernel. It also shows at a very high level the flow of information within the UNIX kernel space.

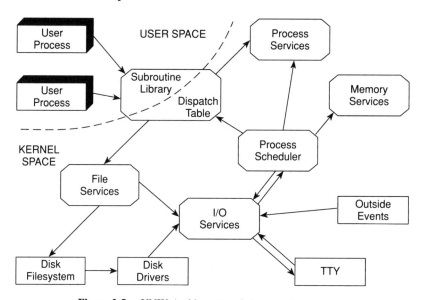

Figure 2-5. UNIX Architecture—Subsystem Interactions

2.4.1 Interactions Across Subsystems

Figure 2-5 demonstrates the interface between the user space and the kernel space. The *process scheduler* (known as the *swapper*) performs as a traffic cop for all processes in the system. The *file services* sub-system presents a common system call interface for disk files as well as other peripherals. The *disk file system* defines the format of data storage in disk files and manages all disk input/output. The *input/output services* sub-system manages all input/output devices, including the operator console.

2.4.2 UNIX Kernel Operational Loop—The Process and CPU Scheduler

The UNIX system uses processes to divide up system resources among a number of tasks. A system of programs or an application runs using one or more processes. Every process created in the system contends for system resources. Resources are allocated to a process based on its priority as well as its ability to use system resources.

The UNIX system uses virtual memory to accommodate a large number of processes. Processes that are not likely to be scheduled immediately are temporarily copied to a *swap device*. A swap device is generally created on a configurable section of a disk. The kernel typically uses a combination of physical memory and swap device (virtual) memory to run a number of processes larger than would be possible in just physical memory. This scheme can succeed only if a scheduling strategy is employed that makes efficient use of system resources.

The *ps* (process status) command with the *e* and *f* options brings up a display that includes the following fields:

UID	PID	PPID	C	STIME	TTY	TIME	COMMAND
sched	0	0	3	Dec 31	?	0:01	swapper
init	1	0	0	Dec 31	?	0:03	/etc/init
root	301	1	0	10:16:45	co	0:21	-sh
mack	302	1	0	10:17:10	02	0:13	-csh
proja	313	1	0	10:17:13	05	0.05	/users/proja/proja
bill	315	1	0	10:17:24	06	0:23	sh
cron	329	1	0	10:17:34	?	0:04	/etc/cron
john	340	1	0	10:17:45	09	0:12	/users/bin/wp
lp	352	1	0	10:17:53	?	0:03	/usr/lib/lp/lpsched
mack	360	302	0	10:34:20	02	0:13	cat /etc/passwd
bill	372	315	0	10:55:45	06	0:24	ps -ef

Process number *0* is running the *swapper* and belongs to the *root* (PID = 0). It is the first process created in the system when the system is booted. The second process created, process *1*, runs the program */etc/init*. All other processes, including all system and user processes, are created as sub-processes of process 1, the *init* process.

The *swapper* process, process *0,* is responsible for process scheduling. Scheduling of processes consists of three main activities. These three activities and the kernel routines that perform them are as follows:

1. Determining which processes are ready to be swapped into memory from or out of memory to swap device (*sched* routine).
2. Swapping a *runnable* process into memory (*swapin* routine).
3. Scheduling the CPU to a process (*swtch* routine).

The first two activities are concerned with ensuring a pipeline of processes that are ready to run and have transferred to physical memory from the swap device if not already in memory. The third activity is concerned with an equitable distribution of system resources as well as providing a timely response to all processes. A process can run only when the CPU is scheduled to it. Let us take a look at how this scheduling takes place. It is important to note here what impels these routines into action.

The *swtch* routine schedules the CPU to the highest priority runnable process. The *swtch* routine is triggered by the *trap* routine in the kernel. The *trap* routine is called by all interrupts and by all system call requests. The real-time clock interrupt also calls the *trap* routine. A clock interrupt happens once every clock-tick (set at 50 to 100 clock ticks in 1 second for most UNIX implementations). A system call request or a real-time clock interrupt almost always cause re-scheduling to take place. However, a process that can continue to run and is not preempted, is allowed to run for a full 1 second. A user process can be interrupted by a higher priority user or kernel process. A kernel process, on the other hand, cannot be preempted by a user process or another kernel process. The kernel process can set up a priority mask register (*spl* routines) that prevents preemption by interrupts from devices up to the priority level set by the mask, but not from devices at a higher priority level. A kernel process can completely lock out preemption by interrupts while it is executing critical sections of system code.

The *sched* routine (also called the *swapper*) is illustrated in the flow-chart in Figure 2-6. This routine contains the main operational loop of the UNIX system. The *sched* routine uses two flags and the *sleep/wakeup* mechanism to determine when processes are ready to be swapped in from or swapped out to swap device. Routine *sched* calls the routine *swapin* to read into memory a copy of the process code, data, and stack of a process that is ready to run but is swapped. If *swapin* does not find enough memory to swap in this process, *sched* searches for a process that can be swapped out. If no process can be swapped out, *sched* sets the *runin* flag. The *sched*

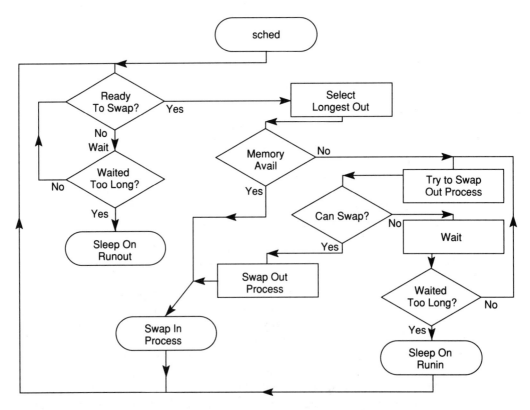

Figure 2-6. Main Operational Loop of UNIX

routine then executes the *sleep* routine; and the *swapper* process gives up the CPU to a process that is scheduled to run, and waits for an event to happen that makes it possible to swap out a process. Such an event is a *wakeup* call issued by another process on completion of the required event.

Sched sets the *runout* flag whenever it can find no process that can be swapped in, and *sleeps* on *runout* waiting for an event that makes a process swappable. A system call request is frequently the event that makes a process swappable. The *sched* routine is activated at clock ticks or at least once every second by a clock interrupt, if the currently running process finishes (completes its time quantum), or due to a *wakeup* call that resets the *sleep* conditions. The algorithm for the sched routine is described in Figure 2-7.

```
sched:
arguments: None

Loop:
    Turn off Interrupts
    Look for a user process ready to be swapped in
        (is ready-to-run, has been out the longest)
    If none found,
        Set runout flag
        Sleep (on event of runout being reset, sleep resets interrupts)
        goto Loop
    Turn on interrupts (found user to be swapped in)
    Call swapin to swap it in
        If memory found
            Swap in user
            goto Loop
        Else (look for process sleeping at low priority or is oldest)
            Turn off interrupts
            Search process table entries
            If found
                Turn on interrupts
                Swap it out
                goto Loop
            Else, Turn off interrupts
                Set runin flag
                sleep (on event process becomes swappable)
                goto Loop
```

Figure 2-7.   Algorithm for the *sched* Routine

2.4.3 System Call Propagation

It is important to note the manner in which a system call propagates across the boundary between the user space and the kernel space. Servicing a system call is a major activity of the operating system.

2.4.3.1 System Call Interface

The UNIX system call interface, at the topmost layer in our model of the kernel space, provides the user with a corridor into the UNIX kernel. This allows the user to access devices and memory as system resources and request the operation of other system functions, e.g. creating a process. As we saw in the earlier section, a system call is the primary gateway between user space and kernel space. Percolation of a system call through the kernel provides a perspective on the link between the various sub-systems of the kernel.

The UNIX system has a large number of system calls. This number varies from one implementation to another. The AT&T UNIX System V (Version 5.3) has over 75 system calls and Berkeley UNIX 4.3bsd has over 150 system calls. The POSIX interface standard in its current form has over 100 system calls.

System calls are assembled in user libraries as function calls. This in itself is an interesting concept, since it allows the user to potentially customize the system call interface. The kernel uses *user id* (actually effective user id) to determine the identity of a user, and uses different levels of identification wherever access permissions checks require checking identification. The sequence of operations for setting up a system call to be executed from a *C* language program is illustrated in Figure 2-8.

System Call Processing
    The argument list is built for the system call
    The library routine sets up arguments in user structure or stack
    Executes *trap* instruction to switch from user mode to kernel mode
    syscall is called and that in turn vectors to the kernel routine
    The process switches to kernel mode
    The kernel services the system call
    The return value is obtained from the kernel
    'C' version of return value is developed
    Return

Figure 2-8.   System Call Processing Sequence

The first three operations are fairly straightforward. The next three operations, i.e. what happens from the time *syscall* is called until the return value is obtained after completion of the system call at the kernel level are of real interest. The *syscall* module uses a dispatch table that provides the mapping between the user library function routines and the kernel services. For example, for AT&T UNIX System V,

    getuid( ) is mapped as *syscall 24* &

    setuid( ) is mapped as *syscall 23*

Syscall is also responsible for performing a number of other functions before it dispatches a system call to the appropriate service routine or module. The arguments are passed from user space to kernel space. Depending on the implementation of UNIX, these arguments are passed either through a data structure called the *user structure,* or via the kernel stack. The routine also converts the user virtual addresses to kernel virtual addresses or physical memory addresses. The *syscall* routine also determines from the call or an entry in the dispatch table (or on some implementations is programmed with) the number of arguments associated with that call. *Syscall* fetches all arguments and passes them on to the service routines. There are some system calls that require no argument, for example *fork*.

2.4.3.2 Dispatching a System Call to a Service Routine

Figure 2-9. summarizes the functions performed by the *syscall* routine for system call processing.

```
syscall routine functions:
    Saves general purpose registers
    Sets up the user structure to be mapped in
    Looks up the index in the syscall dispatch table
    Copies the arguments into the user structure
    Sets up the stack and frame pointers, etc.
    Vectors to service routine in the UNIX kernel.
```

Figure 2-9.   Functions of the *syscall* Routine

The kernel uses the *user structure* to maintain information about the user process that it requires while the process is in memory. This information includes *user id*, *privileges*, etc. about the user that originated the call. The location of the user structure for the current user is fixed in memory for most implementations. The user structure area, also known as the *u area*, consists of the *user structure* for that process and the *kernel stack* (for many implementations, the kernel stack is included in the user structure). In addition, register *0*, the *kernel stack pointer* and the *user program counter* have fixed locations.

The service routines perform the actions required, e.g. input and output, *exec*, *fork*, etc. and on completion return status or return a value via registers *0* and *1*. The registers are restored and the *user structure* is unmapped. In case of an error, an error code is returned in *errno*, register *0* is set to -1, and an abnormal return is taken to the system call error handler.

2.4.4 Input/Output Services

A very unusual feature of the UNIX system is the manner in which I/O devices are treated. Each I/O device is associated with a *special file*. Special files are a part of the UNIX File System and are read and written like user data files. Reading from or writing to a device is accomplished by reading from or writing to the *special file* for that device. Even main memory is accessible through a special file. Other devices that can be accessed through the use of special files include disk drives, tape drives, printers, plotters, communications lines, etc.

The feature that separates special files from other files is that special files reside in the directory */dev*. Links may be made to these files from other directories. An advantage of this overall approach is that the target device need not be hardcoded and program file links can be used to redirect the target device. While standard protection mechanisms are available to all special files, the kernel provides additional protection to special files for memory and the active disk.

2.4.4.1 I/O Device Types

The UNIX system treats devices as character or block devices. Typically, character devices include display terminals, printers, and other character-oriented devices. Mass storage devices like disk drives and tape drives are treated as block devices. The I/O subsystem provides system buffers to pass blocks of data between user programs and block devices, and facilitates moving large amounts of data rapidly.

2.4.4.2 Device Handlers

Device drivers are a part of the UNIX kernel. There are two parts to a device driver. The lower part is called the *device handler*. Device interrupts are vectored to the device handlers. A device handler controls a device and manages all data transfers to the device.

User programs interface with devices via system calls. The system calls are vectored to the kernel service routines via the system call interface. The kernel service routines call the upper part of the device driver, the *device service routines,* to set up the device interface and to interface with the rest of the kernel services.

2.4.4.3 Interrupt Service

All devices, including the system clock and system disk, communicate with the UNIX kernel via interrupts. The clock interrupt (50 to 100 times every second for most implementations) triggers the process scheduler so that processes have an opportunity to compete for resources several times every second. A process is, typically, allowed to complete its time quantum (up to 1 second for most implementations) unless interrupted. The interrupts have a priority associated with them. Since the operating system uses the clock and the disk very frequently, these two devices operate at high priority levels. Devices operate at priorities ranging from 0 to 7 (0 is highest). A kernel mode process assumes a priority level associated with the device it *sleeps* on for a system call and retains that priority until the next system call.

The UNIX system is non preemptive at the kernel level, i.e. a kernel mode process does not preempt another lower priority kernel mode process. A kernel mode process can, however, be interrupted by a higher priority interrupt unless it chooses to lock out all or specific interrupts. Even if a high priority interrupt takes place, a process may be allowed to complete a certain function before it gives up control. This happens if the process is operating in a critical region, i.e. it is performing a function that, if interrupted, may cause undesirable consequences or may confuse the operating system. Servicing a higher priority interrupt results in scheduling at less than the normal clock derived scheduling.

2.4.5 File/Data Access Services

Known as the *file system* in UNIX systems, the file/data access services sub-system provides a logical data storage facility on mass storage devices. Unlike most time-sharing systems that impose a record structure on stored data, e.g. Indexed Sequential Access Method, the UNIX system treats files as either text files or as binary files. *Text files* are a string of characters that use *newline* as a separator between lines. There is no built-in record structure other than the line. A *binary* file is a sequence of binary words. Executable files for example are created as binary files by the compilation process and include the additional structure to map the binary coded program in main memory. Filename extensions are used to identify some of the common types of files used by utility programs.

2.4.5.1 File Types

The UNIX system recognizes four types of files: *ordinary disk files, directories, special files*, and *first-in-first-out (FIFO or pipe) files*. Ordinary files are used for a large majority of the disk storage. Directory files are used to catalog these into a hierarchical grouping of files. Special files are used for device I/O. FIFO files are fixed length sequential files used for pipes, a mechanism for passing data from one program to the next; for example, redirecting output from a *cat* command to the line printer spooler.

2.4.5.2 Directory Structure

The directory structure, illustrated in Figure 2-10, resembles an inverted tree with a single root node. Called *root*, this node is referred to as "/". The operating system uses the directories /*dev*, /*users*, /*etc*, /*bin*, and /*usr* as the basic set. Typically, these directories contain,

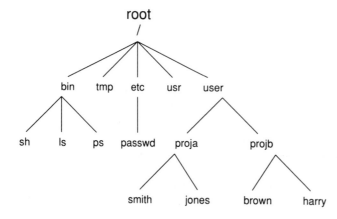

Figure 2-10.   Directory Structure of UNIX

/dev —Special files for device I/O
/usr —System command and program files
/etc —User information files
/bin —Utility programs
/users —Mounted file systems with user files

The /usr directory is the primary directory for commands, program files, and user data. Typically a file system, for example /users, is mounted under the /usr directory. Users can create further levels of directories under it to logically catalog their own groups of files, by project, username, or type of file (e.g. source, data, executable, etc.).

2.4.5.3 Disk Layout and Inodes

Directory files associate filenames with *inode* numbers. The UNIX system builds and maintains a sequential list of inodes on disk. The inode number is the relative position of the inode in the disk inode structure. An inode associated with a file is copied into an inode table in memory when that file is opened. The kernel uses the inode number for all further access to the file.

The disk, known as a UNIX file system, is set up in four sections. The first section or block, called the *boot block*, is used for system bootstrap. The second section or block, called the *superblock*, is used to maintain current user status of the file system. The third section is a contiguous sequence of disk blocks containing sequential inode records. The relative position of the record in the sequence is the inode number. The system always allocates the next available inode to a new file. The total number of inodes is a configurable parameter and is set when the file system is created (*mkfs*). The last section consists of data blocks that make up the files. The data blocks are allocated on a random basis and space is allocated only when it is written into. The exception to this rule is the initial space allocation for a file when it is created. The file is allocated 13 blocks (differs on implementations) where the first 10 blocks are directly addressable data blocks and the last three blocks provide indirect block addressing (up to three levels of indirection) to address very large files.

2.5 ARCHITECTURAL CONSTRAINTS

The UNIX system architecture has been set up to support multiple users and multiple processes in a time-sharing mode. As such, there is a fair amount of overhead at the kernel level for managing multiple users and multiple processes (for example, the set up and usage of user structures and process structures). This overhead is noticeable in both the size and the performance of UNIX.

Due to the multi user architecture, UNIX is not known for high performance real time operation for process control applications. However, due to its standardization and availability on a number of different computer systems, it is often used for real-time applications. The architecture needs to be understood clearly to set up UNIX to provide the best possible performance for real-time applications.

Parallel processing hardware is starting to play an important role in the data-processing environment. While the UNIX kernel was not designed for parallel processing architectures, it has been successfully extended to run on parallel processing hardware.

The UNIX architecture also allows users to write and integrate their own device drivers into the system. This is one route that allows users to inadvertently circumvent the kernel protection built into the UNIX system. It is important to understand this aspect before device driver integration is undertaken. This will help prevent jeopardizing the integrity of the operating system.

2.6 SUMMARY

Two views of the UNIX system are presented in this chapter. The first view is functional and the second is architectural. An overview of the different sub-systems of the UNIX system and the interactions among them presented in this chapter, provide a broad understanding of the architecture. For readers who wish to delve further into specific areas of the UNIX architecture, this chapter provides a frame of reference for understanding the discussions in different sections of Chapter 3.

2.7 EXERCISES

1. Describe the hardware configurations of the system you use. What operating system runs on the hardware?
2. Describe the functions of the UNIX kernel.
3. Draw and describe the main operational loop of UNIX.
4. Study the directory tree on the UNIX system you have access to and draw a picture of it.
5. Describe the sequence of events that take place for servicing a system call.

3

Unix System Architecture

3.1 SYSTEM CONTROL STRUCTURES, TABLES, AND ORGANIZATION

The UNIX System uses a number of control structures and tables to retain important user, process, file, and status information on disk and in memory. Every activity in the operating system involves a number of sub-systems and no sub-system can be studied in isolation from the others. The overview of some of the more significant databases and tables presented in this section will assist in understanding how the operating system manages its information base. The rest of Chapter 3 describes the use of these databases and tables in the operating system architecture for performing the different functions within the kernel. The databases and tables described in this section are compiled with the UNIX kernel as data elements and structures in the header files.

The infrequent user of the UNIX system may find it beneficial to read through this section quickly and refer back to it later. Appendix A lists the variables and parameters, contained in these databases and tables, that are essential for understanding the operation of the UNIX kernel. An experienced user of the UNIX system may find it worthwhile to read through Appendix A or to print out the *header* files in the */usr/include/sys* directory of the standard UNIX distribution and refer to these header files throughout the discussions in Chapter 3. Readers who are new to the UNIX system may find it beneficial to skim through this section quickly and refer back to it as needed.

3.1.1 Page Table Entry

The memory management architecture of the UNIX system is based on dividing the total physical memory in segments of equal size called pages. The typical size of these pages ranges from 512 bytes to 16K bytes depending on the implementation. The page table entries specify the usage of the memory pages. The components of a page table include a page frame number (the number of the physical memory page frame), the type of page (swap device, file, fill0, demand fill); whether the page has been modified;

page protection modes (kernel readable, kernel writable, user writable, kernel writable user readable, and user and kernel readable); and whether it is a valid page. The usage of these parameters is described in the Memory Management section (Section 3.2).

3.1.2 Virtual Address Structure

Virtual memory used by a process is divided into three regions, *text, data,* and *stack.* These regions are mapped in the *User Mode Region Table* for user processes and in the *Kernel Region Table* for the kernel. Virtual memory pages are the same size as physical memory pages. An address in virtual memory is specified in virtual address structures, and is identified by region; virtual page number in the region table; and byte offset in that page.

3.1.3 User Structure

The *user structure* is a database used by the kernel to locate all required information about a user process while the process is swapped into memory. The user structure is described in the header file *user.h.* This is a large structure and is used throughout the discussion in this chapter. We will look at it in greater detail in the section on process management (Section 3.4). For now, let us look at some of the noteworthy components of this structure.

- Error code returned by a system call *(ERRNO).*
- Effective user and group IDs as well as real user ID to determine file access parameters.
- Pointer to the *proc structure* (the process table entry for this process).
- System call return values.
- Buffer address and byte counts for I/O operations.
- Pointers to inodes for current directory, root directory, and parent directory.
- User file descriptors of files *opened* by the process.
- Arguments of the current system call.
- Sizes of text, data, and stack segments for this process.
- An array describing how SIGNALS received will be handled by this process.
- Time spent executing in user mode and kernel mode by the process itself as well as by all its children combined.
- Addresses and sizes of system buffers allocated to the process.
- Mask for files created by this process.
- User *login* data for setting up login terminal.
- Kernel stack for this user.

3.1.4 Process Table Entries

The process table entries, called *proc structures,* are described in the header file *proc.h.* The *proc structure,* one per process, is used by the kernel to determine scheduling priorities, scheduling states of processes, and the resources required for the process to run. Some of the components of proc structures worth noting here include the following:

- Process state (sleeping on an event, running, being created, and so on).
- Process flags (in-core, being swapped out, cannot be swapped out, and so on).
- Process priority and priority adjustments (*nice* call).
- Scheduling parameters to determine the time duration the process must remain in memory before running.
- Signals pending for this process. The signals are saved as a mask.
- Name of the highest level process in the process group hierarchy, and the process ID of the parent process.
- Address and size of swappable image.
- Pointer to the *user structure* to locate it in main memory or alternate storage.
- Pointer to a linked list of running processes.
- Time left for an alarm clock signal set by the process.

3.1.5 Shared Memory Headers

Shared memory headers are used for identifying shared memory segments and their current usage parameters. The contents of the shared memory header structure *shmid_ds* are the following:

- Operation permissions (for creator and for other users by user and group ID).
- Size of memory segment.
- Pointer to associated region table entry.
- Number of processes sharing the memory segment and the number of these actually in memory (not swapped out).
- Times for last attach, detach, and change operations on the shared memory segment.

Shared memory can be set up such that only the creator can write into it and others can read from it. The kernel ensures that as long as an in-memory process is using a shared memory segment, that segment is not swapped out. If only swapped out processes need it, the kernel attempts to retain shared memory segments in memory to avoid reloading them frequently.

3.1.6 Message Queue Header

Processes can communicate using message queues. Messages are posted in the sequence they are written in by the sender process, and receiver processes recover the messages from the queue. Messages are an important mode of interprocess communications in the UNIX system. The components of a message queue header structure are the following:

- Operation permissions (for creator and for other users by user and group ID).
- Total number of messages and the total number of message bytes in the queue.
- IDs of processes that last sent and last received messages.
- Pointers to start of linked list of message headers, next available message header slot, and the last message header slot.
- Times for the last send, receive, and change operation for the message queue.

3.1.7 Message Headers

Message headers form a linked list where the first component of the header points to the next message header. Other components include message type (a field used to uniquely identify the message), the size of the message in bytes, and a pointer to the message data pool.

3.1.8 Semaphore Structures

Flags employed for synchronizing or coordinating two or more processes are called *semaphores*. A process can *sleep* on the event that a semaphore value changes in a pre-defined manner. *Semaphore structures* define semaphores and consist of the following:

- Value of the semaphore.
- ID of the process that made the last change to the semaphore.
- Number of processes waiting for semaphore value to become greater or to become 0.

Semaphore structures are set up as sequential arrays. A *semaphore data structure* points to each array.

3.1.9 Semaphore Data Structure

Semaphore data structures are used to organize semaphores such that an array of *semaphore structures* is set up for each process creating semaphores. Semaphore data structures consist of the following components:

- ID of the semaphore.
- Operation permissions (for creator and for other users by user and group ID).
- Pointer to base address of semaphore array and number of semaphores in the array.
- Time of last operation and last semaphore change.

3.1.10 Superblock

The superblock is always block 1 of the logical disk of a UNIX file system. It contains information that defines the current state of the file system. Key components of this information are the following:

- Size in blocks of the inode list as well as the complete file system.
- Number of free blocks in the file system and a linked list of free blocks.
- Total number of free inodes and a linked list of free inodes.
- Flag to indicate that the superblock has been modified (and should be written back to disk).
- Time and date of last superblock update.
- Name of the disk and the file system.

3.1.11 Disk Inodes

A file is identified internally in the UNIX system via its inode number. The inode is copied into memory for every file that is being accessed. The disk inode includes the following information about the file:

- File type and mode (ordinary, directory, special, etc.).
- Number of links to the file.
- Owner's user and group ID and file access permissions.
- File size in bytes and addresses of ten direct blocks and three indirect blocks.
- Time and date of last access (read or write) and time and date of last modification (write).
- Time and date the file was created.

3.1.12 In-core Inode

In-core inodes are built by copying the disk inode and then adding more fields for additional information. Some of the key additional fields include the following:

- Inode access status (i.e. inode is locked, a process is waiting for inode to become unlocked, the in-core inode has been modified, the contents of the file have been changed so the inode has also changed, and so on).
- Number of processes using the file and the inode.
- Device ID of the disk where the inode is located and the disk address of the file.
- Last logical block read from the file (current file position).

3.1.13 File Structures (or Kernel File Table Entries)

While the inode is used on a per file basis, a file table entry is used on a per file open basis, i.e. a separate file entry is used if the same file is opened by another process. This takes care of the file being accessed under different access permissions. The file table entry includes file access flags describing the file lock status and the file modify status; the number of processes using the file; a pointer to the in-core inode; and a read/write pointer to the current byte offset in the file.

3.1.14 User File Descriptors

A *per-user file open table* is maintained for each process in its *u area* (the *u area*, defined earlier in Chapter 2, consists of user structure information including process table entry pointers, user file descriptors, and kernel stack for the process). Each user file descriptor entry in this table points to the corresponding file structure in the *kernel file table*.

3.1.15 Buffer Headers

The UNIX system employs a number of internal buffers that form the buffer cache (also called the buffer pool). These buffers are used for block device data transfers, for example, disk device data transfers. The kernel also uses buffers to temporarily store information it is likely to need frequently. The kernel checks the buffer pool to determine if the required block is still resident in a buffer before attempting to read the block from disk. This improves system performance. The headers attached to these buffers provide information about the availability and use status of the buffers. Inodes have only information but no data. Buffers on the other hand, have header information, necessary for determining their current usage and data. The buffer header includes the following fields:

- Status flags (that describe if the buffer is busy, i.e. in use, or if it is free).
- Pointer to the queue of buffers allocated and in use by a device.
- Forward and backward pointers in the free buffer list. The kernel can re-use the buffer information if needed as long as it remains on the free list.
- Forward and backward pointers on hash queue (if the buffer is in use or had been used).
- Major and minor number of device currently using the buffer.
- Block number on disk that has been copied into the buffer.

The buffer header includes other information that we will look at later. For now, this information gives us a useful perspective.

3.1.16 Driver I/O Buffers

The driver I/O buffers are dedicated to device drivers for data input. The information included in the headers used for these buffers is as follows:

- Status flags (that describe if the buffer is busy, i.e. in use, or if it is free).
- Device ID of the device currently using the buffer.
- Controller busy flag (if set, indicates that a data transfer or device control function is in progress).
- Device register data.
- Error code, set if error is encountered in an I/O operation.

3.1.17 Block Device Switch Table

The block and character device switch tables are created when the kernel is compiled. The device configuration file *conf.c,* compiled with the kernel, contains no code; it contains arrays of structures that define these tables. These structures are described in */usr/include/sys/conf.h.* This table is indexed by major device number; and each block device has an entry that includes the names of the device *open, close,* and *strategy* routines and a pointer to the buffer allocated for data transfers.

3.1.18 Character Device Switch Table

This table is also indexed by major device number. Each device has an entry that includes device *open, close, read, write,* and *ioctl* routines. The address of the terminal structures is also included.

3.1.19 C-lists and Cblocks

While system buffers are used for block devices, *C-lists* are used for buffering data for character devices. C-lists consist of a linked list of *cblocks* used for storing character I/O and raw I/O data temporarily. C-list headers contain a count of characters in the c-list, a pointer to the first cblock entry, and a pointer to the last cblock entry.

Cblocks, ususally 24 to 32 bytes long, are a linked list of buffers and consist of a pointer to the next cblock entry, the positions of the first and the last characters in the cblock data area, and the data characters. The positions of the last and first characters change as data is entered at the end of the data area and is read off from the beginning of the data area. The section on Input/Output (Section 3.6) has a more detailed explanation of this process.

Typically two or more c-lists may be used for I/O to any device. Separate c-lists are used for input and output.

3.1.20 TTY Structure

A TTY structure is needed for each UNIX character device that is used for normal terminal I/O. It consists of addresses of c-lists, input and output routines, line discipline routines and other parameters required for character I/O. Some noteworthy components of the TTY structure include,

- Pointers to c-list structures for raw I/O, canonical queue, output queue, and control queue.
- Pointers to the routines to start input and output.
- Device number and device address.
- Mode flags that can be set by an *ioctl* call.
- Internal state (timeout, device open, device busy, and so on).
- Name of original parent process of the process group.

- Line discipline for the device.
- Erase and kill characters, and other device characteristics.
- Transmit and receive speeds.

3.2 MEMORY MANAGEMENT

The UNIX operating system is supported on a wide variety of hardware architectures ranging in physical memory capability from 512K bytes to 32M bytes. The UNIX system uses the concept of pages to operate as a virtual memory system. Physical memory is divided into segments of equal size, for example, segments of 1K bytes each, called *pages*. With this kind of mapping, every page of memory can be addressed by a page number.

At any given time, there may be a number of UNIX processes in the system. Only a limited number of processes can be resident in available physical memory at any time and the rest are swapped out to disk. This situation gives rise to the virtual memory concepts. A process is stored on disk as a full or partial image of the process in memory. Page tables map virtual memory to physical memory and facilitate rapid loading of a process into physical memory. There are three notable schemes employed by a majority of the UNIX implementations. The *swapping* scheme, introduced in Chapter 1, was used in AT&T UNIX Version 7 through System V. Berkeley added *demand paging* in UNIX 4.2bsd. AT&T UNIX System V has been enhanced to provide a *combination* of swapping and demand paging. This chapter describes the general concepts of these schemes and the overall memory organization of the UNIX System.

3.2.1 Physical and Virtual Memory Organization

Before we go into a discussion of the memory swapping or demand paging schemes for memory management, let us look at how the UNIX kernel organizes and allocates physical memory. Let us first, in this section, understand the key differences in *physical memory, virtual memory,* and *swap memory.* In Section 3.2.2 we will look at the architecture of the Memory Management sub-system.

The basic concepts of organizing and addressing physical memory and the associated data structures are largely independent of the memory management scheme. The data structures for managing physical memory are designed to provide four significant capabilities, listed below:

1. Addressing of large physical memory spaces (up to 32M bytes or more).
2. Rapid allocation and deallocation of physical memory.
3. Use of large Virtual memory spaces (gigabyte range).
4. Protection of kernel as well as individual process memory.

A UNIX system typically supports a large number of users. The memory required by these users is generally much larger than the physical memory in the system. A process that is not scheduled to run is stored temporarily on disk in a special area called a *swap device*. A swap device is a configurable partition on disk treated in a manner similar to memory. We will go into the details of the swap device later in the chapter, but for now, let us look at the concepts of *swap memory, process virtual address space,* and *physical memory.*

Programs running in a process are compiled and linked on the basis of certain assumptions about memory address ranges. Processes swapping in and out of memory on a recurring basis fragment physical memory and make it impossible to guarantee that exactly the same physical memory blocks will be available to a specific process every time it is swapped in. Without this guarantee, the kernel would have to recalculate all addresses in the programs every time the process is swapped back in, unless an alternate scheme is employed. The use of *process virtual address space* solves this problem by assigning contiguous virtual memory blocks to a process. These blocks are mapped to *physical memory* when a process is swapped in, and to *swap device memory* when the process is swapped out. As we see, the crucial kernel tasks we have to understand are the following:

1. Rapidly tracking free physical memory.
2. Allocation and de-allocation of physical memory.
3. Mapping process virtual address space to physical memory.
4. Allocation and de-allocation of swap memory (on swap device).
5. Mapping process virtual address space to swap memory.

The kernel achieves the first two goals by maintaining bit arrays to determine rapidly if a page of memory is in use. A *memory free list structure* tracks free physical memory. We will look at this in detail shortly. For now, let us continue with understanding how the mapping of virtual memory to physical memory and swap memory is accomplished and the data structures associated with it. A *page table* is an important database in this mapping.

Page tables are used to map virtual memory pages to physical memory pages. A page table contains a sequential list of data structures called *page table entries*. A page table delineates the virtual memory space for the *text, data,* and *stack* segments, called *regions,* of a process. Let us take a look at the effects on memory management from running user code and kernel code.

A UNIX process is said to be in *user mode* while it is executing user code or code from a runtime library for setting up a system call. Executing the *trap* instruction switches the process from user mode to *kernel mode*. The code for the kernel service routines is called kernel code. While a process is executing kernel code it is protected. As we saw in Chapter 2, there are very few entry points into the UNIX kernel. User mode processes can neither activate any code directly in the kernel, nor can they access any data in the kernel. However, the kernel may access data from a user mode process. This distinction between user and kernel is maintained by grouping page tables for the kernel in a *kernel page table* and grouping page tables for the user in *user mode page tables*. Let us now look at these concepts and structures in greater detail.

3.2.1.1 Data Structures

A *page table entry,* briefly described in Section 3.1, consist of the following elements:

1. Page frame number.
2. Age.
3. Page modified bit.
4. Page protection.
   a. Kernel mode readable only
   b. Kernel mode writable only
   c. User mode writable
   d. Kernel mode writable, user mode readable
   e. User and kernel mode readable only.
5. Page valid bit.

The *page frame number* pertains to the physical memory page. The rest of the page table entry describes the attributes of the current assignment of that memory page.

A *region table entry* consists of the following elements:

1. Pointer to inode of file loaded in this region.
2. Region type (e.g., text, data, and stack).
3. Region size.
4. Location of region in physical memory (pointers to page tables).
5. Region status (e.g., locked, in demand).
6. Reference count.

3.2.1.2 Virtual to Physical Memory Mapping

Figure 3-1 describes how a virtual address structure is mapped to physical memory via region tables and page tables.

Virtual address space of a process is divided into *text, data, stack,* and *shared memory regions.* For each process, *region table entries* are attached to the common region table corresponding to text, data, stack, and shared memory regions. The region table entries contain a sequential list of virtual addresses that map into *page table entries.* Page table entries contain physical page numbers (corresponding to physical memory pages). This mechanism translates the contiguous virtual address space of a process to randomly addressed pages of physical memory. An address in the virtual address space consists of three components: a pointer to the region table entry, a virtual page number, and a byte offset within that page. These three components provide sufficient information for virtual to physical address translation.

A *virtual address structure,* described below, completely defines a memory address.

- Byte Offset

- Virtual Page Number
- Region

Figure 3-2 describes the region tables for a process and the mapping of virtual memory to physical memory via the page tables.

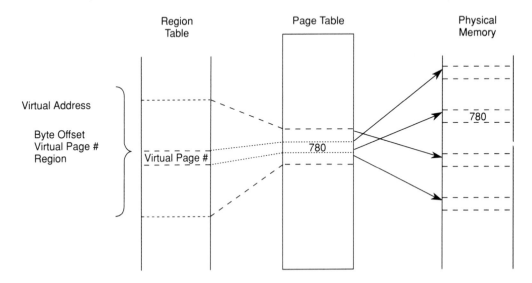

Figure 3-1. Example of Virtual to Physical Address Translation

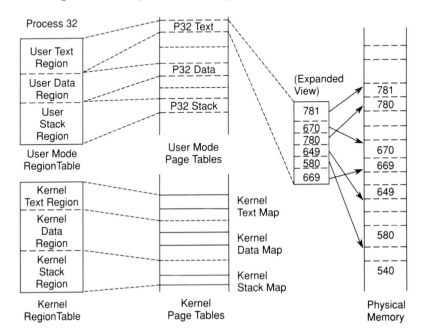

Figure 3-2. Example of Memory Mapping

Region tables, as shown in Figure 3-2, assume contiguous *virtual* memory for a process. The text, data, and stack regions are mapped to the respective entries in the page tables. There is one page table entry for each block of memory specified in the region table. The page table provides an interrelation between the virtual address and the physical address. The physical memory page number occupies the page frame number field as long as that page of virtual memory is mapped into physical memory. Even though kernel space is common to all processes and simpler and more direct addressing can be used for the kernel regions, most implementations use the same mechanisms for user processes and the kernel. The mapping of processes swapped out to disk is achieved by tracking disk block addresses corresponding to their virtual addresses. Depending on the implementation, either page frame numbers are replaced by disk block addresses for the pages of a process that are swapped out or an additional disk block descriptor field is used.

3.2.2 UNIX System Memory Organization

The proliferation of UNIX System implementations on a variety of computer systems has stimulated a wide variation in the physical organization of memory for the UNIX operating system. The operating system has been designed largely to optimize use of available memory. If a system has a large physical (or primary) memory space, most of the operating system code and in-core data structures may reside in physical memory. If the memory space is not quite as large, the operating system resides partially on disk in virtual memory and is overlaid as needed.

Figure 3-3 describes a typical memory layout of the UNIX operating system. The memory used by processes is generally known as user memory and the memory for the three major system components is known as system memory.

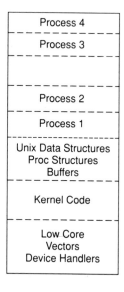

Figure 3-3.   UNIX System Memory Map

The UNIX System memory consists of the following components:

1. Low core components
   - Interrupt vectors
   - Device handlers
   - Physical memory mapping routines.
2. Kernel code
   - Memory management
   - Process management
   - Disk management
   - I/O management
   - Interprocess communication.
3. System data
   - Process table (*proc structures*)
   - User structure
   - Kernel stacks
   - Buffer pool
   - In-core Inodes.
4. In-core processes.

3.2.2.1 Memory Allocation Architecture

The *memory free list structure* records page frames of available memory. The free list structure is used in conjunction with another data array, a sequential array of bits for free memory called *memvad*. Each bit in this array, called a *page frame bit,* is mapped to a page frame of physical memory. A *page frame bit* is set to *1* if the frame is in use, or it is set to *0* if the frame is free. The memory free list structure includes the following components:

1. Count of free memory pages in *pnum array.*
2. Pointer to first free memory page frame in *pnum array.*
3. Pointer to last memory page frame in *pnum array.*
4. Pointer to last memory allocated.
5. Total page frames of memory available.
6. *pnum array* (up to 100 page frame numbers stored).

On system initialization, the free list structure lists the first page frame number, last page frame number, and the total number of available page frames. It also lists up to NICMEM (coded as 100 for UNIX AT&T System V) page frames in the free list structure, the *pnum array.* After operation for a certain duration, memory starts to fragment as processes are swapped in and out. The *pnum array* is used for quick access to free memory. This array is replenished when exhausted from the *memvad* array if the number of *total available page frames of memory* is still positive. Every time a batch of free page frames numbers is allocated and entered in the *pnum array,* the pointer to the first page frame address and the count of available page frames parameter are adjusted. Any time memory is freed up, the page frame numbers are attached at the tail of the array in the free list structure. The last page frame address is updated, and the count of available page frame parameters is adjusted. Let us now take a look at the algorithms of routines that allocate and free memory.

3.2.2.2 The *Memall* and *Memfree* Routines

The physical memory allocation routine *memall*, is called with the arguments *base* (starting page frame address) and *size* (number of page frames specifying the size of memory to be allocated). If there is no memory available, a *0* is returned. Otherwise, memory is allocated and the *size* value is returned.

The routine first checks if the requested *size* is *negative* or exceeds available memory, and in either case, returns a *0*. If it already has free blocks in the *pnum array*, it removes them from the free list array and adjusts the pointers until it reaches the required size. The available page frame count parameter is decremented each time a page frame is removed.

If the number of free memory pages in the *pnum array* winds down to zero, the *memall* routine rewinds the pointer to *last allocated memory page frame* to the beginning of the *pnum array*. It then searches through the memory table *memvad* to locate free blocks, sets their in-use bit, and enters their page frame numbers in the *pnum array*. It also increments the free page frame count. This is continued until the array is filled. Figure 3-4 describes the algorithm for the *memall* routine.

```
memall:
arguments: Pointer to return array for allocated page frames
           size—Number of page frames required

    If size negative or greater than available memory
       return 0
    For (loop until value of size decremented to 0)
       If no more free page frames
          While number of free page frames < NICMEM
             Enter next free page frame address in pnum array
    Reset last page frame allocated pointer
    Set up appropriate frame mask
    Enter page frame number in return array
    Decrement available memory number
    Return (size)
```

Figure 3-4.   Algorithm for *memall* Routine

The *memfree* routine is also called with the arguments *base* (pointer to array containing the page frame numbers of physical memory pages to be freed) and *size* (the number of memory pages to be freed). The routine uses a *while* loop until *size* decrements to 0. The free list *pnum array* is filled one page number at a time and the corresponding in-use bit in *memvad* is reset. As it increments the pointers to the *pnum array,* it checks to see if the array is filled up. If so, it empties out the *free list* (adjusts all pointers to the *pnum array*) and starts filling it up again.

3.2.3 Memory Swapping

AT&T UNIX systems, right up to the first release of System V, used only one *swap device*. We noted earlier in this section that a swap device is defined as a contiguous block device on disk reserved for swapping processes. Later releases of System V supported multiple swap devices and demand paging. The structure of the swap device differs from the structure of the normal disk in the following ways:

1. The size of the swap device is a configurable parameter.
2. The disk space is allocated on file system initialization.
3. Disk transfers occur in large blocks.

These features require a mechanism different from that used for accessing data blocks for disk files. Indeed, swap devices are managed through *maps* that track blocks of free page frames on the swap device.

3.2.3.1 Memory Map Allocation Architecture

Memory maps are used for swap devices and for certain special I/O functions. As we just saw, swap devices are treated essentially like memory. A memory map, called *swap map* for a *swap device,* consists of *map structures* that have two parameters - a *map address* and a *map size.* Each *map structure* defines the start of a contiguous block of free *swap units* of memory. A swap unit is 512 bytes for AT&T UNIX System V for type 1 swap devices. It may vary in other implementations and swap units of 1024 byte are used in many implementations. The kernel starts with one map structure that points to the start of the memory (that is, the starting page on the swap device), and specifies the size as the total size of the device. The kernel then uses sections of contiguous blocks from this memory for rapid unloading of processes. Fragmentation is reduced by combining memory fragments every time some memory is released.

The *malloc* routine allocates swap memory. It should be noted that the *malloc* routine allocates memory on the swap device, not physical memory. Physical memory is allocated only when the process is re-scheduled. When swap memory is allocated, the memory map table is checked for the required size. The first structure that provides a sufficiently large size is used, and the required number of swap units are allocated at the beginning of this block. The *size* parameter in the map structure is reduced by the amount of the swap units allocated, and the start address is set to the new start address of the free block of swap units. If no memory is found, a *0* is returned.

When swap memory is freed up, blocks of swap units being freed up are added to the *memory map table*. However, the *mfree* routine first sorts the *swap map table* by swap unit start address for each map structure entry, and checks if the map structure for the freed block can be combined into the previous structure or the following (*next*) structure. It can combine with the previous structure if the start address of the first swap unit address in the freed up block is one greater than the last swap unit address in the map structure. The size parameter in the *previous* map structure is increased to combine them. Combination with the next block can take place if the address of the last swap unit in the freed up block is one less than the start swap unit address of the next map structure. If so, the start address in that map structure is set to the start address of the freed up block and the size parameter is increased by the number of swap units freed. Figure 3-5 illustrates the mapping between map structures and swap device blocks.

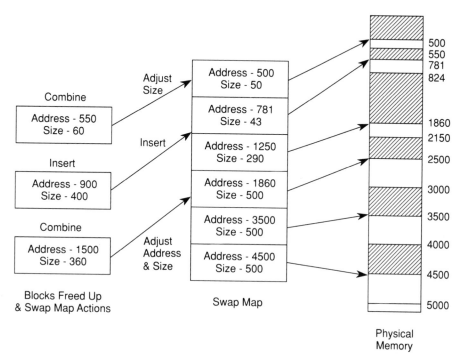

Figure 3-5. Swap Device Memory Example

3.2.3.2 The *Malloc* and *Mfree* Routines

The *malloc* routine, allocates *swap* memory from the *swap map,* and the *mfree* routine frees up *swap* memory and restores it to the swap map.

The *malloc* routine, described in Figure 3-6, is called with the arguments *map address* (pointer to the map) and *size* (number of swap units to be allocated). If successful, it returns the address of the block of swap units allocated. On error, it returns *0*. The routine uses a *for* loop to check all map structure entries in the map table until it finds one with *size* large enough to satisfy the request. It saves the address of that map structure to return it as the address where memory is allocated. It then increases the address parameter in the map structure by the *size* value and, adjusts the size parameter in the map structure. If the new value of the size parameter in the map structure is 0, it deletes the map structure and all map structures are bumped up; the map is always maintained as a contiguous list ordered by the start address parameters

and terminated by a structure with a size parameter of value 0. It returns the original
address saved if successful, or a *0* if it cannot find a block of swap units large enough
for the request.

```
malloc:
arguments: Address of map (base)
           Number of units requested (size)

    For (every map structure in map)
        If size in map structure is greater than or equal to requested size
            Increase address in map structure by size
        If size is equal to size in map structure
            Delete map structure and move up other structures
            Change map size parameter
        Return original map address (base)
    Return 0 (none found)
```

Figure 3-6.   Algorithm for *malloc* Routine

The *mfree* routine is called with three arguments - *map address* (pointer to the
map), *size* (number of swap units to be freed up), and *base* (the address where the
block of swap units is to be freed up). As noted earlier, this routine not only reverses
the operation of *malloc,* but also checks to see if it can combine the space being freed
up into an existing structure to achieve a larger contiguous block.

3.2.4 Demand Paging Systems

Berkeley UNIX 4.2bsd provided the first major re-design of the UNIX kernel to
support demand paging. The later releases of AT&T UNIX System V also supported
a version of demand paging. First, let us look at some general concepts used in demand
paging systems.

3.2.4.1 Demand Paging Architectural Concepts

As the term implies, the demand paging architecture requires loading of pages of
memory from disk to physical memory on demand. Instead of swapping in the entire
process, only parts of it that are actually required are loaded. An advantage of this
approach is that a large number of processes can actually be swapped in at any given
time. On the other hand, the operation of demand paging causes a process to be
blocked if the required page is not in memory. The benefits of keeping a large number
of processes in memory appear to outweigh the disadvantages of more frequent
resource blocking. Certainly, the volume of disk swapping is reduced significantly in
demand paging systems.

The two most significant notions in demand paging are *page faults* and *cache
memory*. The page fault mechanism is used to determine when the code crosses page

boundaries and the next page is not in physical memory. A page fault generated as a result of this, sets in motion the following activities:

1. Adjusting in-core page tables to accept a new page.
2. Setup for a page to be read in from disk.
3. *Sleep* until page is loaded.
4. Start execution at start of new page when re-scheduled.

Cache memory is employed by some implementations to anticipate required pages and bring them into memory before they are required by the CPU to avoid page faults to the extent possible. This is especially true in very high performance multi-processor systems. A *free page pool* is also used just like the buffer pool to buffer demand paged memory.

The concept of regions and page tables is very similar to that described for swapping systems. However, the components of the page table entries differ. Two additional fields are required for demand paging. The *age* field is used to track the duration for which the page has been retained in memory, and is used in the algorithm to reclaim memory. The *reference* flag indicates whether the page was accessed by a process. Each page table entry is associated with a *disk block descriptor* that describes the block of disk storage for that virtual page. The *page table entries* and *disk block descriptors* are combined into page tables similar to the page tables used for swapping systems.

Demand paging systems use an additional data structure called a *page frame data structure*. A *page frame data table* consists of one page frame data structure entry for each page in use and contains information about the state of the page, reference count, and corresponding disk storage. The page frame data table maintains a list of page frame data structures, called the *free list,* for structures with a reference count of *0*. In case the same page is needed again, the free list of page frame data structures is checked to see if the page frame is still available. If so, it is re-allocated and there is no need to copy it back from the disk. The operation of page frame data tables is analogous to the buffer pool mechanism described in Section 3.7.2. A study of the operation of the buffer pool is recommended for a better understanding of the operation of the page frame data structure free lists. Figure 3-7 describes the manipulation of these tables in the demand paging architecture.

Another data structure required specifically for demand paging systems is the *swap-use table* that tracks the number of page table entries that point to the swap device storage units.

3.2.4.2 Data Structures for Demand Paging

While similar structures exist for other implementations, the descriptions presented here apply to the AT&T UNIX System V releases. The *page table entry structure* consists of the following components:

1. Page frame number (physical memory page address).
2. Age.

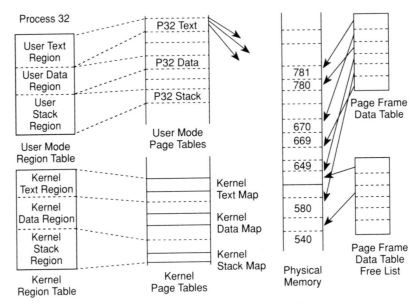

Figure 3-7.   Use of Page Frame Data Tables

3. Copy on modify (make another copy if modified by one process).
4. Modify (has been modified, need to be written back).
5. Reference (count).
6. Validity.
7. Protection.

The *disk block descriptors* are used as an extension of the page table entries and one descriptor is associated with each page frame table entry. The components of the disk block descriptors are the following:

1. Swap device (logical device name).
2. Swap device storage unit number (e.g. block number).
3. Type of storage unit.

The *page frame data structures* contain information about the usage of the memory page frame. This usage information includes the following:

1. Status of page
   a. On swap device
   b. In executable file
   c. DMA in progress
   d. Available for use.
2. Reference count (number of processes actually using it).
3. Logical device and storage unit number.
4. Pointers to page frame free list.

The *swap-use* structures, one for every page or storage unit on swap device, contains use information for every page consisting of the following:

1. Reference count (page table entries pointing to it).
2. Page/storage unit number.

Figure 3-8 describes the tables used for demand paging.

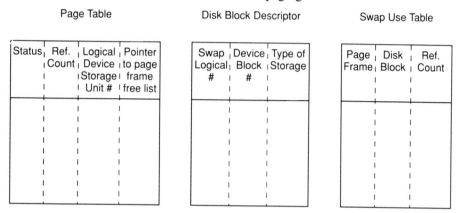

Figure 3-8.   Use of Tables for Demand Paging Systems

3.2.4.3 Page Frame Management

As noted earlier, the page frame fault mechanism is used in most demand paging implementations to bring in new pages. A page fault can occur if a page being modified is set for *copy on modify*. This situation is generally called a *protection fault* since the protection bit for the memory indicates *copy on modify* status if no separate bit is assigned for this status. Another kind of page fault can occur if the page required is not in memory, or it is outside the virtual address space for that process. The *valid* bit is used to indicate this kind of page fault. A page that is within the *valid* virtual address space for the process can be found at one of the following three locations:

1. On the free page list (free pool) in memory.
2. On a swap device (has been loaded once but is swapped out).
3. Still in the executable file (has not been loaded at all so far).

The disk block descriptor defines the type of page, i.e., does it require clearing to zero (e.g. for uninitialized data) or it can be loaded without clearing. Figure 3-9 illustrates the logic behind page fault management.

The page fault handling routines are called with the address of the page that caused the process to cause a page fault. The key points to note here are the usage of different tables and the operation of the *valid* bit and the *copy on modify* bit.

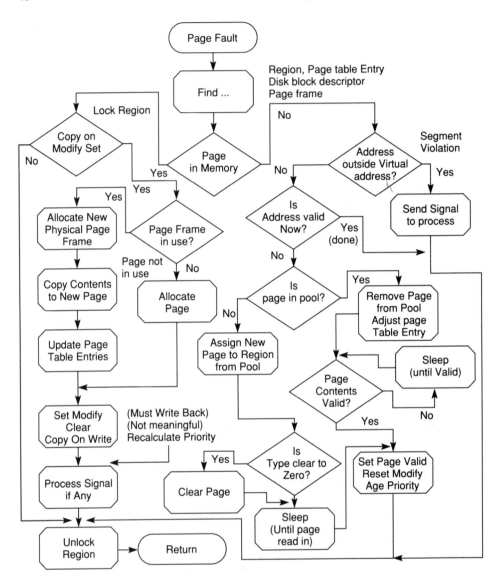

Figure 3-9. Flow Chart of Page Fault Mechanism

3.2.5 EXERCISES

1. Describe the differences between swapping systems and demand paging systems.

2. Explain the operation of swap space. How big should the swap space be in relation to physical memory? What is the impact of the size of the swap space on system performance?

3. Is it possible to swap out any part of the kernel? What parts of the kernel cannot be paged out? Why?

4. Describe memory management strategies for a *fork* system call and for a *vfork* system call.

5. The validity fault algorithm swaps in only one page at a time. Can this algorithm be improved to avoid rescheduling on a page fault? Can the next page be brought in before it is needed?

6. Design potential architectures for a system that pre-fetches required pages.

7. What should the fault handler do if the system runs out of free memory pages?

3.3 SYSTEM CALLS

3.3.1 Definition of System Calls

A system call is a request by a user or application program to the UNIX kernel to perform a specified function. System calls provide a mechanism for user programs to access kernel services such as device access, program execution, file transfers, etc. System calls provide user programs a channel to communicate with the kernel and execute routines in the kernel that are identified by entry points within the kernel.

3.3.2 C Language Interface

The *C* Library provides a mapping between a system call, structured within the semantics and syntax of the *C* Language, and the assembly level library routines. The library routines provide the mapping vectors used to access the service routines in the kernel. The *C* Language interface is designed for the convenience of the programmer and provides a means for accessing system functions of the operating system from a higher level language application program.

3.3.3 Types of System Calls

The types of system calls may be viewed from two perspectives. The first perspective includes the following aspects:

1. System calls that return no values.
2. System calls that return bit/int/long values.
3. System calls that return byte or word arrays.

Another perspective is based on the functions performed by the system calls. These may be classified as system calls to perform the following:

1. Process management.
2. Memory management.
3. File system management.
4. Device input/output management.
5. Miscellaneous functions.

3.3.4 UNIX System Call Interface

The UNIX system call interface exists at two levels: the subroutine library, and service routines in the kernel.

The *subroutine library* is a library of functions, mostly in assembly language, that corresponds to the *C* Language level calls. The system call is converted to a set of parameters as the arguments to the call, and a number that is passed to the kernel as an index to the table of the kernel service routines.

The system calls are vectored to *service routines* in the kernel via the *syscall* routine. The service routines are also provided with the arguments to the system call by the *syscall* routine. The service routines call the appropriate routines within the kernel to perform the required functions.

3.3.5 System Call Processing

System calls are processed at four levels in UNIX. These levels include the *C* Language programs, the corresponding subroutine library modules in user space, transfer of the call from user space to kernel space (system call dispatch), and servicing of the call by the kernel routines. Figure 3-10 describes these four levels generically.

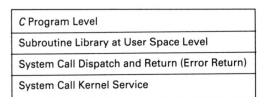

Figure 3-10.   System Call Levels

Let us look at the levels of the *fork* system call as an example, and follow it through for an understanding of the operation of system calls.

3.3.5.1 Levels of *Fork* System Call

As we just saw, the *fork* system call operates at these four levels of the UNIX operating system. The case of the *fork* system call is interesting because it has two normal returns instead of one return usual for most system calls. These four levels or stages for the *fork* system call are described as follows:

1. *C* Language level.
2. Assembly language routine calling kernel service.
3. System call look-up and dispatch.
4. *Fork* kernel service operations.

The following discussion describes the stages that the *fork* system call progresses through and the subsystem relationships as they pertain to the processing of a system call.

3.3.5.2 Example of *Fork* System Call at *C* Level

A *fork* system call takes no arguments. An interesting point to note is that a *fork* system call produces two returns. It returns the *pid* value of the child process to the parent and a value of *0* to the child process. It may return an error condition instead if it is unable to create a child process. Figure 3-11 is an example of the *C* code for a fork call. The appropriate code sections denoted by the curly brackets '{}' are executed for the parent or the child process according to the return value. A process *id* of -1 is returned if the fork fails. The discussions of call processing in the following sections elaborate on the internal operations of system call processing.

```
pid = fork ();
if (pid == -1)
     { error, fork failed } else
else
if ( pid ! = 0)
     { parent }
else
     { child }

fork returns 3 classes of values

−1 error
     No more process slots in process table or
     No more process slots for process group

0 child

>0 parent
```

Figure 3-11.   Example of *fork* Call and Return from it

The *fork* call returns an error if no more process slots are available for that *process group*, or if there are no more process slots available in the *process table* (also called *proc table*). The process group is defined as all processes associated with a particular user. The maximum number of processes in a process group is a configurable number. The last slot in the proc table is reserved by the kernel and is left free for use by a superuser in case other processes get deadlocked and do not exit normally. The last slot ensures that a superuser can start a process to kill locked (or hung) processes.

3.3.5.3 Calling Kernel Service

Figure 3-12 describes the subsystem relationships for system call processing. The *C* Compiler uses pre-defined libraries of functions to map system calls in a user program to the UNIX library routines. On program execution, the library routines set up the call arguments to be passed to the kernel. A system call entry routine number is then set up

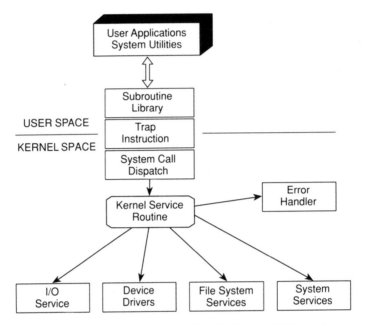

Figure 3-12. Subsystem Relationships for System Call Processing

in *register 0* or the stack (depending on the implementation), and a *trap* instruction is executed. The *trap* instruction switches a system call from user mode to *kernel mode*. The low order byte of the *trap* instruction defines the system call type.

The execution of the *trap* instruction causes a number of changes to take place, including the following:

1. The *mode* changes from *user* to *kernel* mode.
2. The *user process* is converted to *kernel process*.
3. Special privileges become available to the process, such as:
   a. Ability to change kernel memory pages
   b. Ability to change priority.

The exact nature and extent of these privileges is hardware dependent. The *trap* instruction is treated as an interrupt and the execution of the *trap* instruction causes the start of the *trap* routine. The system call information, including location of arguments to the call, number of arguments, and the system call routine name and address in the dispatch table are passed to the *trap* routine. The *trap* routine identifies the trap types as system calls or as system exception (error) conditions. For system calls, the routine extracts the type of the call from the trap instruction. It then calls the *syscall* routine, which collects the system call arguments from the *user mode stack* or the *u area* and vectors through the system call dispatch table to the kernel service routine for that call.

Another point to note here is that the trap instruction provides very strong protection for the kernel from inadvertent user interference. Users have no direct control at or access to the kernel level and are restricted by the trap instruction. The kernel is in full control and protects itself while system code is in operation in the kernel mode.

3.3.5.4 System Call Look-up and Set-up in the Kernel

The *syscall* routine sets up the parameters for the system call on the user stack, or in the *u area* (i.e., user structure and kernel stack) depending on the implementation. The appropriate kernel service routine address is looked up in a table located in the *sysent* module, and the routine is started up.

Some system calls provided for the same basic function may be called with different parameters. They are frequently named with slight variations and a routine is set up for each system call in the subroutine library. However, the library routine maps them to the same kernel service routine after appropriately handling the parameters. The *exec, execv,* and *execl* calls are a good example of this.

The major functions performed for handling a system call include the following:

1. Mapping of system calls to library routines.
2. Setting up of the user structure and the system call parameters.
3. Saving current context for abnormal return.
4. Calling kernel service (*trap* instruction).
5. Handling normal or error return.

The sequence of operations performed by the *syscall* routine consist of a number of steps and a number of other modules are called to complete the tasks. The *syscall* algorithm is described in Figure 3-13.

```
syscall:
Input: System Call Table Index

       Set User Structure to be mapped in.
       Save appropriate registers
       Look-up index in table in sysent module
       Copyin arguments in user structure.
       Save context for abnormal return
       Call kernel service routine
       Unmap user structure (copy it back)
       If error return (carry bit set?)
           Set register in saved context to error number
           Turn on carry bit in saved PS (Processor Status)
           Return to user space
       else (no error)
           Restore saved registers 0 and 1 to return values
           Return to user space
```

Figure 3-13.   Algorithm of *syscall* Routine

3.3.5.5 Kernel Service Operations

The dotted line in Figure 3-14 separates the user space from kernel space. As we noted earlier, the trap instruction switches the process from user mode to kernel mode, the system call dispatch table is used to locate the kernel service routine, and the selected routine is then called for further processing.

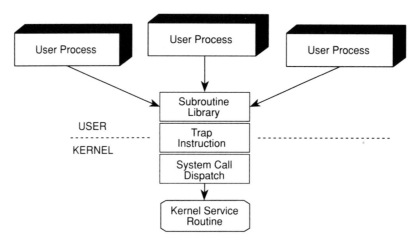

Figure 3-14. Kernel Service Processing

Exactly what happens to a system call in the kernel depends on the type of system call, the state of processes and of the system, and the state of the CPU and the peripherals. This question will be addressed to a large extent in the detailed discussion of each sub-system (Section 3.4 onwards). In fact, the *fork* system call is described in Section 3.4.2 and briefly visiting that section at this time may be worthwhile. For the present, let us assume that the required system call function is handled in the kernel and a normal return or an error return takes place.

On return from completion of the *system call*, the process switcher, the *swtch* routine is called if the pre-emption flag is set. It cleans up the kernel stack and restarts the interrupted process. In case of the *fork* system call, there are two processes instead of one, the parent process and the child process. On completion, the parent process performs a normal return. The child process is set up for a *pseudo* return; that is, it is set up as if it had also executed a system call.

The system call may request a kernel service that is not immediately available (e.g., *open* a device). In a situation like this, the process *sleeps* until it is scheduled to run again.

3.3.5.6 System Call Completion

On completion of the system call at the kernel level, the instruction after the *trap* instruction is executed. The carry bit of the *PS* register is checked for an error condition. In case of no error, the return values from the call are returned to the user.

3.3.5.7 Successful Return

The *registers 0* and *1* of the user context are set to the return values from the system call in case of a normal return. Register *0* contains the return value of the system call if the system call is used as a function call.

3.3.5.8 Error Return

If the carry bit is set in the *PS* register the returned register *R0* is checked for the error code. This is the error code word copied from the *user structure* (as part of unmapping of the user structure) by the *syscall* routine. The error code is moved to *errno* by the library routine, register *0* is set to -1, and an abnormal return (*jump*) is taken to the system call error handler.

3.3.6 EXERCISES

1. Look at the system call mapping on your system and list the kernel routines called for each system call.
2. Trace the path for *fork* and *read* system calls through the kernel.
3. On executing a *fork* call, which process gets scheduled first—the child or the parent? Why? Can this be changed?
4. Determine the complete algorithm for the *syscall* routine on your system. Flow chart this routine.

3.4 PROCESS MANAGEMENT

The UNIX system is a time-sharing operating system in which processes compete for system resources. Every process is scheduled to run for a period of time called its time slice. On completion of the time slice, or on blocking due to an I/O request, another ready process is scheduled. The selection criteria for a process to run is based on priority and readiness to run. This section describes the creation, scheduling, operation, and termination of processes.

3.4.1 Definition of a Process

A UNIX process is portrayed as the execution of an image (or the current state) of a virtual machine. The virtual machine remains in memory until it is displaced by a higher priority process or terminated by executing an *exit* call or by a *kill* signal from another authorized process. An image is characterized by the following:

1. Memory in use.
2. General register values.
3. Status of files opened.
4. Default directory.

A process competes with other processes for CPU and system resources. A process first competes for memory to be swapped in. Once loaded or if already in memory, a process competes for the CPU. When it gains temporary control of CPU and necessary resources, a process executes a program in its memory space. One process does not interfere with another process and cannot read or write data into the memory space of another process.

To the user it may appear that several processes are operating concurrently. This illusion is created by the system through process scheduling by the kernel. The kernel allocates systems resources to the highest priority *ready-to-run* process not waiting for completion of an event, for example, completion of a disk block input.

The following major components are associated with a process and they govern its operation. The data structures describe the characteristics of the process. The kernel utilizes the following characteristics to schedule and manage the process:

1. *Text*—program instructions in machine code.
2. *Data*—machine language representation of data.
3. Kernel *stack*.
4. Process table entry (*proc structure*).
5. User *stack*.
6. *User structure*.

Let us now study how these components are used for process management. Figure 3-15 describes one use of these structures.

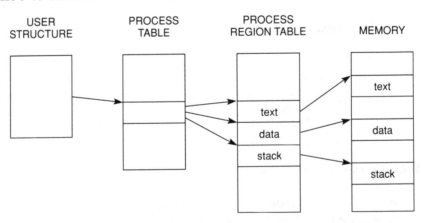

Figure 3-15.   Structures Used by a Process

The *user structure* points to the entry for the process in the *process table*. The process table entry, called *proc structure*, points to a region table, which maps the process memory image to physical memory.

The *user stack* is used to store the parameters of a system call including the arguments for the call, the return address on completion of the call, and local variables. The *kernel stack* stores similar information for kernel service routines for that system call. Figure 3-16 describes the components of user and kernel stacks.

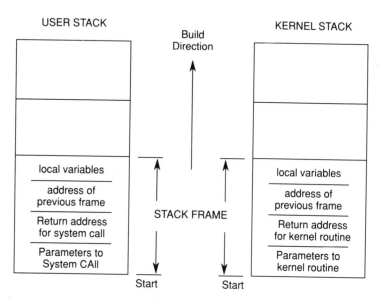

Figure 3-16.   Kernel and User Stack Images

3.4.2 Process Creation and Initialization

In the UNIX System *process 0*, called the *swapper*, is always assigned to the *process and CPU scheduler*, which manages the complete operation of process scheduling and swapping. The associated routines are *sched, swapin, swtch, sleep*, and *wakup*.

Process 0 is created as a part of system boot-up. Every other process in the system is created as the result of a *fork* system call. The *fork* system call splits a process into two processes. The process that invokes the fork system call is called the *parent* and the new process created as a result of this operation is called the *child* process. But first, let us study the creation of *process 0* and initialization of the UNIX system.

The UNIX system initialization, described in Figure 3-17, consists of the following activities:

1. User memory is cleared and is set (marked) free.
2. System real-time clock interrupts are turned on.
3. *Process 0* is hand crafted.
4. All system tables are initialized, including:
   a. message tables
   b. Semaphore tables.
5. *Root's* superblock is read in and current date is set to last modified date.
6. System buffers are marked free.
7. *Process 0* is created by a *fork* call and scheduled.
8. *Process 1* is created by a *fork* call to execute bootstrap.

The creation of *process 1* is the final activity of system boot and initialization.

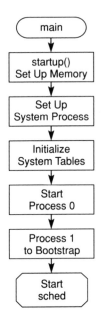

Figure 3-17.   System Initialization Flow Chart

Process 1 is created by *process 0* as the *init* process. The *init* process, in turn, manages all user *login* activity and creates the initial user process for each user.

3.4.2.1 The *Fork* System Call

The *fork* system call creates a new process that duplicates the characteristics of the parent process. The original process, called the parent process, and the new process, called the child process, maintain the *parent-child* relationship, with a few exceptions, throughout the life of the child process.

This method of creating a process, illustrated in Figure 3-18, is frequently called *spawning* a process. Figure 3-19 describes the stages of process creation. A process may spawn one or more child processes. The child processes may, in turn, spawn their own child processes. Processes spawned in this manner become limbs of a hierarchical inverted tree structure.

3.4.2.2 Sibling Processes

The *fork* system call, as we see, creates a child process in the image of the parent process. This image includes the following:

1. Shared text.
2. Data.
3. User stack.
4. User structure.
5. Kernel stack.

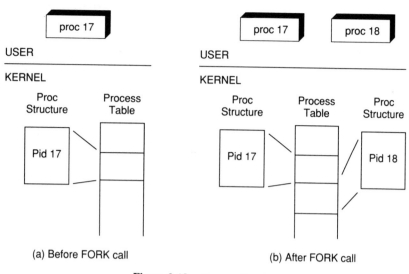

(a) Before FORK call

(b) After FORK call

Figure 3-18. Process Creation

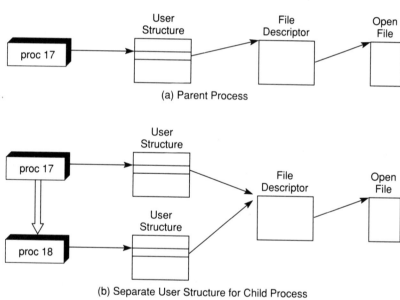

(a) Parent Process

(b) Separate User Structure for Child Process

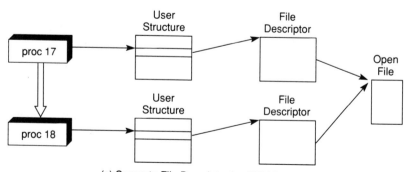

(c) Separate File Descriptor for Child Process

Figure 3-19. Stages of Process Creation

A combination of *fork* and *exec* system calls is employed to create a new process and start another program under the new process, for example, starting a new shell or running an *ls* command under the current shell. The *exec* system call overlays another program in the child process image, and the child process invokes its own *text* component for the new program. Child processes are also called sub-processes. Processes at the same level that have descended from the same parent are called *siblings*. Figure 3-20 describes the creation of siblings. Siblings created within a short duration of one another tend to have very similar characteristics on creation. Like parent-child process relationships, siblings also have a special relationship. The creation of siblings is illustrated below.

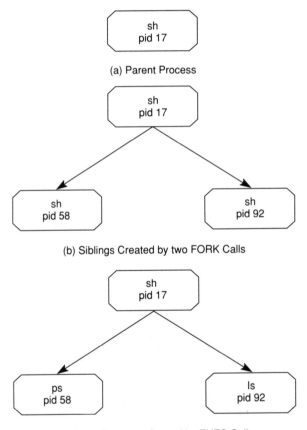

(a) Parent Process

(b) Siblings Created by two FORK Calls

(c) Other Programs Started by EXEC Calls

Figure 3-20.   Sibling Process Creation

As we noted earlier, siblings start with similar characterstics, because *fork* creates the child as a duplicate of the parent. Two siblings created one after another have the following in common:

1. Same text (shared text or code).
2. Identical data segment.

3. Identical stack segment.
4. Same file descriptors of open files.
5. Same signals (preserved for each sibling).

The only difference between the two processes is that on return from the system call, the *pid's* are different. Not only are the open files passed on to the child process, but because the file descriptors are passed on intact, the child process retains the same position in the open file. Figure 3-21 illustrates the file relationships.

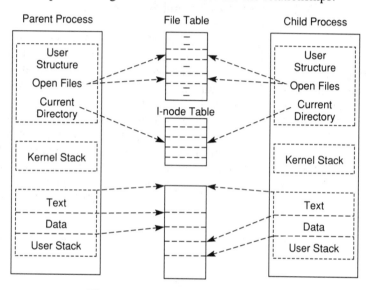

Figure 3-21.   Parent and Child Contexts

3.4.2.3 Example of *syscall* Mapping of *Fork* system call

Let us revisit the *fork* system call processing, this time concentrating on the kernel service aspects of it. Figure 3-22 describes the system call vector to the kernel service routine.

```
syscall 2 (fork)
On return
    if carry bit is on (error)
        Set register in saved context to error number
        Turn carry bit on in saved PS
        Set R0 to −1
        Jump to subroutine for error handling.
    Else (no error)
        Restore saved registers 0 & 1 to return values
        Return
```

Figure 3-22.   Example of *syscall* Mapping

3.4.2.4 *Fork* at Kernel Service Level

Continuing further in our example, let us say we have made the system call and we are in the kernel. Before the fork system call is executed, the parent process has an entry in the process table and its user structure is mapped in kernel space as the currently scheduled process. On execution of the system call, the system switches to kernel mode, system text and data are mapped in, and the *fork* kernel routine starts executing.

3.4.2.5 Algorithm for *fork* Kernel Service

The *fork* routine first ensures there is enough memory, that a process table slot is available, and that the user has not reached the configured limit on the number of sub-processes. If successful, a unique *ID* is assigned, usually the next available ID number. If not, an error is returned. A child process cannot be created if there is no available process slot, if the user has exceeded the limit for the number of processes in the process group, or if there is insufficient swap memory. Even though *newproc* creates the child process in physical memory, the kernel first calls *malloc* to allocate swap memory. The reason for this will become clearer when we look at the memory allocation strategies for process creation a little later in this section. If no swap memory is available, the kernel searches for processes that can be removed and calls *mfree* to free swap memory. Figure 3-23 describes the algorithm of the *fork* kernel service routine.

```
fork:
arguments: None

        Are kernel resources available for spawning a process
            If not, return error
        Allocate memory, if none available call mfree to free swap memory
        Call newproc to create child process

    swtch (on return value from newproc)
        Case 1: (child created—return is from child)
            Reset user structure for child (parent process id, times, size, etc)
            Return

        Case 0: (child created—return is from parent)
            Reset child process id
            break

        default: (unsuccessful fork)
            Set user error
            break
    Return
```

Figure 3-23. Algorithm of *fork*

The *newproc* routine, described in Figure 3-24, is the kernel service routine that creates a new process for *fork*. While the *fork* routine ensures that a process table entry slot is available, the *newproc* routine actually locates and assigns a slot for the process. A *proc structure* entry is created for the new process and information including process status, timing, user ID, process group ID, the *nice* number, pointers to and sizes of text, data, and stack are *copied in*.

The files associated with the parent process are automatically associated with the child process by copying in the inode numbers into the child process user structure. These files include the current directory, the *root* directory, and any open files known to the process and referenced in the file descriptor table. The reference counts of the associated *inodes* are also incremented. Only open files are reproduced for the child process.

The *user structure area* (also known as the *u area*) consists of the user structure and the kernel stack. The user structure of the parent is copied to the *u area* of the child process and its *proc table* pointer is changed to point to its own (child's) *proc structure* in the process table. The final steps in the context set-up sequence are setting up of shared text, copying of data stack segments of the parent process to the child process, and setting up the child process parameters as if the child process had been executing previously and was swapped out.

Allocation of the *proc structure* makes the new process operational. In most implementations the parent winds up getting scheduled first. Generally, this action is made more explicit via the *wait* call issued for the parent.

```
    newproc:
    arguments:

        Is there a free proc structure (i.e. free process slot in the proc table)
        Allocate a process table slot (new proc structure)
        Copy parent proc structure parameters to child proc structure
        Set-up new information, e.g. process ID, CPU time
        Set-up inodes for sharing between two processes
        Call shmfork to set up shared memory for child process
        Partially set up new (child) process to resume
        Split into two kernel processes
        Allocate new memory for child process
            if no memory, and no swappable processes
                Swap out current process as child process
        Copy text, data and stack
            Reset shared memory page tables
        Copy user structure.

        If parent process executing,
            Set child ready to run (SRUN)
            Return 1 (with ID of child process)
```

If child process executing after fork,
    Reset timing in User Structure of parent
    Return 0

Figure 3-24.   Algorithm of *newproc* Routine

On completion of the child process context set-up, it is set *ready to run,* and the child process ID is returned to the user by the parent process. When the child process is scheduled to run, its first task is to complete its part of the *fork* system call and it returns a *0* to identify itself as the child process.

3.4.2.6 The *vfork* Call

The *vfork* is a fast *fork* that does not copy the text and data segment of the parent process to the child process on an assumption that the fork will be followed immediately by an *exec* call, and the *exec* call will load new text and data segments.

3.4.2.7 Memory Allocation Strategies for *fork* Call

We touched briefly upon memory allocation for a new process. Let us take a closer look now. The algorithm for *newproc* described the memory allocation sequence for *fork* in a swapping system. The sequence for locating physical memory for the child process consists of the following steps until it finds enough.

1. Look for sufficient available memory.
2. If no memory available, start swapping out any swappable processes.
3. If still not sufficient, swap out a copy of parent process as child process.
   (Note: The parent retains its currently allocated memory; the
   child needs the same amount of memory as the parent)

The child process is set *ready-to-run* and, if it had to be swapped out, will get swapped back in whenever there is sufficient free memory. Figure 3-25 illustrates swap memory mapping and allocation for a child process.

Figure 3-26 describes the algorithms for the *fork* routine for memory swapping systems. The *fork* in a demand paging system differs primarily in the manner of allocation of memory. In UNIX System V, initially the child process shares all text pages and has its own set of data and stack pages. The shared text pages are set for *copy-on-modify* and if either the child or the parent modify a shared text page, their own separate pages are allocated. In UNIX 4.2bsd, all pages including text pages are duplicated so that the child has its own complete memory set. Figure 3-27 describes the algorithms for *fork* and *exec* for a demand paged system.

The *exec* is a little different in demand paging systems in that it does not copy the full image at once. It brings in only a part of it and the rest is brought in as needed via the page fault mechanism.

Parent Process
Virtual Addresses

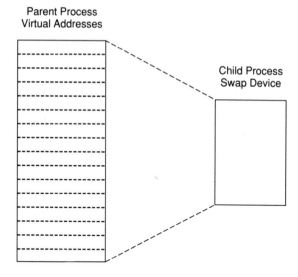

Child Process
Swap Device

Figure 3-25. Memory Allocation on Swap Device for Child

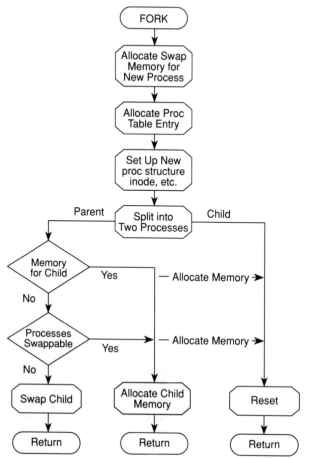

Figure 3-26. Memory Mapping Algorithm for Swapping Systems

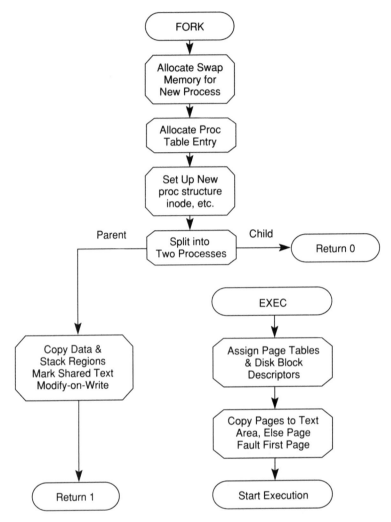

Figure 3-27. Use of *fork* and *exec* in Demand Paging Systems

3.4.3 Starting a Program—*Exec* Kernel Service

The *exec* system call overlays a new program into a process. As we saw earlier, a child process duplicates the parent process on creation except for the *process ID*. The characteristics duplicated also include the program running within the parent process. The *fork* and *exec* combination is used very frequently in UNIX to spawn a new process and to overlay a new program. A common example is typing *ls* at a *shell* prompt. The shell *forks* a new process which starts with a shell image, and then makes an *exec* call to overlay the *shell* image with the *ls* image. Figure 3-28 shows how *fork* and *exec* combinations are used in code for spawning a process and starting a new program.

```
/* This program reads a command line from the terminal and executes it */
#include <stdio.h>
main()
{
    char line[128];
    char *command;
    char **argv;
    int pid;

while (1) {
        printf("%%");
        if (gets(line) == 0) exit(0);                   /* exit on EOF */
        if (strlen(line) == 0) continue;                /* no command */
        parse_command(line,command, &argv);             /* get argument list */
        pid=start_command(command,argv);                /* start the command */
        if (pid > 0) wait(0);                           /* wait for process to exit*/
    }
}
start_command(command, argv)
char *command;
char **argv;
{
    int pid;

/* Create child process. */
    pid = fork();
    if (pid == 0) {

/* Code here is for child. */
        child(command, argv);
    } else if (pid < 0) {
        perror("fork");
    }
    return pid;
}

child(command, argv)
char *command;
char **argv;
{
    int status;

/* EXEC new command in child process. */
    status = execvp(command, argv);

/* If exec was successful, this code will not be executed. */
    if (status < 0) {
        perror(command);
    }
    exit(0);
}
```

Figure 3-28. Example of *fork* and *exec*

An *exec* call can also be used by itself, as illustrated in Figure 3-29, to overlay a new program within the current process. The main characteristics of the *exec* call are the following:

1. Files are not closed or affected across *exec*.
2. Process ID and position of the process in process hierarchy does not change.
3. Arguments are passed to the main routine of the program.
4. Signals are preserved.
5. Environment variables may be passed to the new program.

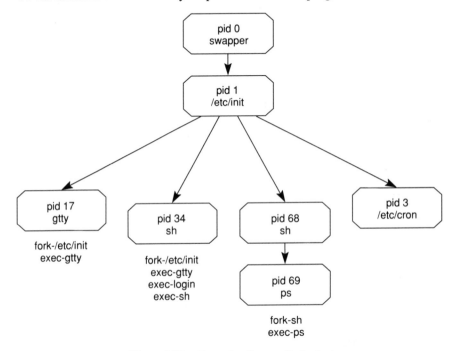

Figure 3-29.   Example of *exec* calls for *login*

The environment variables are typically inherited by the process through a *fork* system call that precedes the *exec,* or are set up explicitly. The *exec* call passes the variables automatically in calls to *execl, execlp,* and *execvp,* or explicitly in calls to *execle* and *execve.*

There are two distinct parts or operations in an *exec* call. The first operation, described in Figure 3-30, consists of validation of memory requirements and file access permissions. The second operation, described in Figure 3-31, consists of setting up the process to run the new program.

3.4.3.1 First Part—Validation (Access & Memory)

The kernel service routine for *exec* first reads in the header information in the program executable file to complete the first part of the validation process. It calls *gethead* to read in the header.

The *gethead* routine calls the *namei* routine to get the inode for the file name that is to be overlaid. It then reads in the header information and validates if for type, access permissions, memory requirements, and availability to run it. It also confirms that the file is an executable image, and calculates the memory requirements. If there is insufficient memory available, an error is returned. Otherwise, it proceeds to the second part that consists of the actual process setup.

```
exec:
inputs: File name
        Argument pointer
        Environment pointer
    Call gethead routine that
        Calls namei to access filename by inode
        Access file and read in the headers, validate
            Return error if no swap space for arguments
        If not executable program
            (i.e.'x' bit set on permissions for user)
            (i.e. does have execute access)
            Release inode (iput)
            Return with access errors in user structure
    Examines text, data & segments.
    Checks for memory requirements.
Bad:
    If too much memory required
        Return with memory errors in user structure
        (i.e. larger than system capability)
```

Figure 3-30.   Algorithm for First Part of *exec* call

3.4.3.2 Second Part—Process Setup

An *executable file* consists of a number of headers that define the loading and operating characteristics including the following:

1. Magic number (defines the executable memory and loading characteristics).
2. Start address for process execution.
3. Sizes and virtual addresses for each section of text and data.
4. Sizes and virtual addresses for symbol data if debug information is included.

```
copy in argument list to system space.
copy in environment (environ).
If the maximum # of characters in argument list is exceeded,
    Return error message
else
```

Overlay new Process—new program/executable file over old.
  Detach old regions
  Allocate new regions
  Load regions into memory
Copy in arguments to new user stack
Release inode and buffers
Release swap memory
Return

Figure 3-31.   Algorithm for Second Part of *exec* call

The routine first copies in the arguments from the user level context and saves the arguments to the new program. These may be saved on the kernel stack, unallocated memory pages, or other memory areas depending on the implementation. The old memory areas can now be released (*detachreg*). New memory areas are allocated and attached for text and data (*allocreg, attachreg*). Memory is allocated for the data initialized at compile time and is extended (*growreg*) for the data not initialized at compile time—*bss*. The argument list is then copied to the user stack. The user context is restored and the *inode* is released.

The process remains vulnerable during this second part to load errors from potential addressing conflicts as it has no error return mechanism left and can be terminated only through a signal. On return from the *exec* call, the process starts executing the new program.

3.4.4 UNIX System Administration of Processes

The UNIX System maintains two key tables to track the status of processes and the users associated with processes. These are the process table and the user process table.

The process table is a collection of data structures, called *proc structures*. There is one *proc structure* per active process. Typically, these structures are of the order of 100 bytes in length (this number varies with implementations) and contain data needed about the process even while the process may be swapped out. The process table is retained in memory in its entirety for all processes invoked in the system. The *user process table* is a collection of *u areas* (also known as *user structures*), one per swapped-in process. Each user structure contains process information that needs to be referenced only while the process is swapped in.

3.4.4.1 Process Table

The process table entry for a process contains status as well as control information that characterize the process. Each invoked process uses a slot in the process table. Since processes get created and terminated quite frequently, the process table is not maintained as an ordered structure. The kernel looks for the first empty slot starting at its current position, and rewinds to the beginning of the process table and continues until it finds an empty slot or determines that all slots are in use. If an empty slot is not found, a new process cannot be created and an error is returned. The last slot is reserved for use by a superuser in case locked or hung processes need to be terminated.

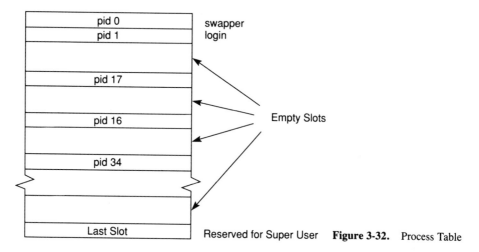

Figure 3-32.   Process Table

3.4.4.2 User Process Table

As we just saw, the User Process Table is a collection of user structures (or *u areas*). There is one user process table entry per user structure of a swapped in process. A user structure is swapped out with the process. Typically, a user structure is 1k to 4k bytes long (this size varies with implementations), and contains all the information not found in the process table structures and not referenced while the process is swapped out. The user structure also contains a structure that is a part of the header of the executable file. This structure contains the following:

1. Magic numbers.
2. Text size (code size).
3. Data size.
4. *bss* size.
5. Symbol table size.
6. Entry location.

The kernel maps the user structure of the currently scheduled process to a pre-defined virtual address that varies with hardware and implementation (e.g., virtual kernel location 0140000 for PDP 11/70 and 0x7ffff800 for VAX 11/780). The size of the space reserved for the user structure is determined by USIZE**click* where *click* is 64 bytes long for most implementations. The example in Figure 3-33 shows *pid 17* as the currently running process.

3.4.4.3 Memory Allocation Within a Process

Processes are organized in three segments, also called *regions*. There are separate regions for user mode and kernel mode. The four basic regions are the following:

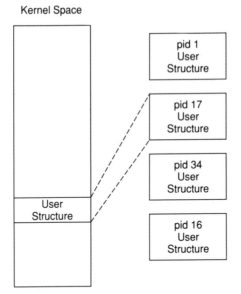

Figure 3-33. Kernel Image of User Structure

1. Text.
2. Data.
3. Stack.
4. Shared memory.

Figure 3-34 illustrates the relative memory locations for the constituents of a process. The text segment is fixed by the program and includes code (instructions) and

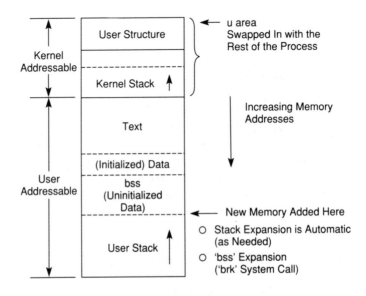

Figure 3-34. Process Image with User Structure

read only data. The *data* segment contains initialized and uninitialized data and its size can be changed with the *brk* system call. The *stack* segments contain the subroutine linkages. The kernel stack is located at the address space above the user structure and is increased automatically. If the expansion of the bss data or the user stack exhausts available memory, the process is blocked and is rescheduled to run the next time with a larger memory space. New memory is added between the data and stack segments.

3.4.4.4 Memory Allocation Strategies for Processes

Figure 3-35 describes the memory allocation for a process on systems that do not support demand paging.

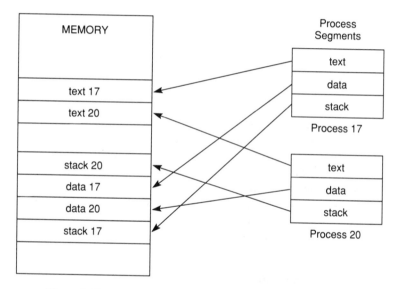

Figure 3-35.   Memory Allocation on Systems Without Demand Paging

On systems where there is no paging hardware, memory is allocated in contiguous segments for text and data to achieve acceptable performance. 'Memory' on swap devices is allocated by the kernel routine *malloc*. The kernel maintains a memory map and *malloc* searches for the first contiguous set of memory blocks large enough to accommodate the text, data, and stack segments. On swap out, only physical memory is copied and saved. Virtual memory is rebuilt from the virtual memory map when the process is swapped back into physical memory. Figure 3-36 demonstrates the components of a user process that are resident and that are used to rebuild the virtual memory image of the process.

It should be noted here that the kernel stack is a part of the system data area, called the *u area* (that includes the user structure). A kernel process cannot be preempted, but may be swapped as a result of a *sleep* call. When a kernel process is swapped out, the kernel stack is also saved. As we noted at the beginning of this sub-section, the *proc structure* remains resident from the creation of the process until

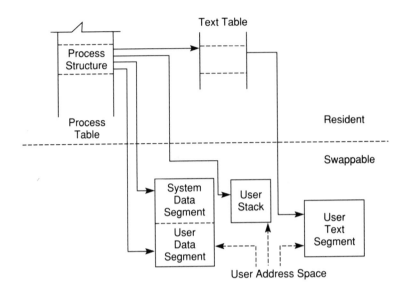

Figure 3-36. Memory Mapping of Pages on Swapping Systems

it *exits* or is *killed*. The *proc structure* has a pointer to the disk address of the swapped image and has the size information for text and stack.

On systems with paging hardware, segments are allocated but, as shown in Figure 3-37, the pages are not necessarily contiguous. The pages actually needed are loaded dynamically and executed even though the complete process is not loaded in physical memory. The process can be an order of magnitude larger than the physical memory used to run it. The virtual process size limit still applies due to overall addressing limitations imposed by hardware or software implementations. For many implementations, this limit is 32M bytes.

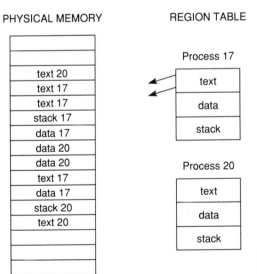

Figure 3-37. Segment Allocation for Demand Paging Systems

The concept of demand paging is based on an expectation that typical programs run small segments of code repeatedly and other small segments of code sequentially. Not all *text* is executed at the same time. The kernel uses sets of table structures to save the following parameters for memory page frames in use:

1. *Age* to indicate duration since last reference.
2. *Modify* to indicate that it has been modified and needs to be written back.
3. *Copy on Modify* if a duplicate page needs to be created before this page is modified.
4. *Reference* to indicate that the process used the page recently.
5. *Valid* to indicate pages actually in use

The kernel can optimize the usage of physical memory to retain code used repeatedly. It writes out only pages that have been actually modified when it needs to free up memory. The page fault mechanism is used when a required page is not in memory, e.g., the page required for the next executable instruction. If all memory is used up, as is very often the case, the kernel uses the *ageing* attribute to determine the least recently used page. It writes this page back if *modified,* otherwise overlays it with the new required page. Execution starts at the beginning of the new page.

While demand paging systems may appear to have performance overhead due to page faults and memory fragmentation, they gain in overall performance as compared to swapping systems by keeping more processes *in-memory*. This makes process scheduling and context changes much faster.

3.4.4.5 Critical Regions

Certain areas of the system code that can be prone to potentially conflicting entries that may corrupt the system, if interrupted, comprise the *critical regions*. The critical regions include data areas that are modified by interrupt handlers and accessed by other processes.

A number of restrictions are used to prevent this kind of system corruption. The restriction on *preemption* of a process operating in kernel mode is one such safeguard for a critical region. This prevents processes from accessing the same user or system data simultaneously. The critical regions are also protected by raising CPU priority to an appropriate level before the critical region is entered. All *interrupts* from devices at that or lower levels are prevented. The CPU priority is reset to normal on exiting from the critical region.

3.4.5 Process Scheduling

There are two kinds of process flags located in the data structure of the process tables that are used to manage process scheduling. These are swap states and process states.

The flag for *swap states* defines the swappability of a process, i.e. it determines whether a process can be swapped out. This flag defines the following states and swap parameters.

1. In core.
2. Scheduling process (not swappable).
3. Locked (process cannot be swapped).
4. Process is being traced.
5. Valid text pointer (shared text).
6. Process partially swapped out.

A process *in-core* is a process that is already resident in memory and can either be scheduled to run, or can be swapped out if blocked or has used up its time, or if memory is required to run a higher priority process. The process can be swapped out if it is blocked or if it has used up its time quantum. The swapper, pid 0, is always the *scheduling process* and it is never swapped out. A process that is operating in the *critical region* cannot be interrupted by an equal or lower priority process or preempted, and it cannot be swapped out. It is set with a swap *lock* until it is out of the critical region. The *tracing* state defines a child process that is being traced by a parent, usually for debugging purposes. This state is tracked because tracing variables that are used to pass trace commands from the parent process to the child process cannot be shared and are locked for each user. *Shared text* segments can also be locked or unlocked for swapping. Shared text memory cannot be released until the usage count for the shared text segment drops to zero. A *partial swap* takes place in the case of shared text in the process.

The flag for *process states* defines the runnability of the process. This flag defines the following states:

1. Sleeping.
2. Waiting.
3. Runnable.
4. Idling (during process creation).
5. Zombie (during process termination).
6. Stopped (being traced).
7. Swapping.

A *sleeping* process is a process that has executed the *sleep* function and is waiting to be awakened by an *event*. A process voluntarily gives up control of the CPU and causes the process scheduler to look for a process that can be scheduled.

A process can be put in a *wait* mode by the *wait* system call to await a signal of termination of a child process.

A *runnable* process is one that is in memory and that is not waiting for completion of an I/O or an event. The process is in memory and can be scheduled. A process that is ready-to-run (runnable) but swapped out and is waiting only for memory allocation before it can be scheduled is called *ready-to-run swapped* to differentiate it from a process that is *runnable* (i.e., ready-to-run in memory).

A process being traced can enter a *stop* state. The parent is informed when that happens and the child process is able to receive commands from the parent. This is frequently used for debugging utilities.

Process state changes can take place at a clock tick or at least once every second (or the time quantum) due to the clock interrupt (this time frequency varies with implemention—Berkeley 4.3bsd allows the programmer to reset it). These changes can also happen earlier in the time quantum as a result of the running process executing a *sleep* function call, as a result of a higher priority interrupt, or if a higher priority process becomes runnable. Note that a kernel process is not preempted when a higher priority process becomes runnable. These state changes for kernel processes are illustrated in Figure 3-38. The four cases described are:

1. Blocked on I/O but retained in memory.
2. Blocked on I/O and swapped out.
3. Finished time quantum and swapped out.
4. Executed an *exit* call.

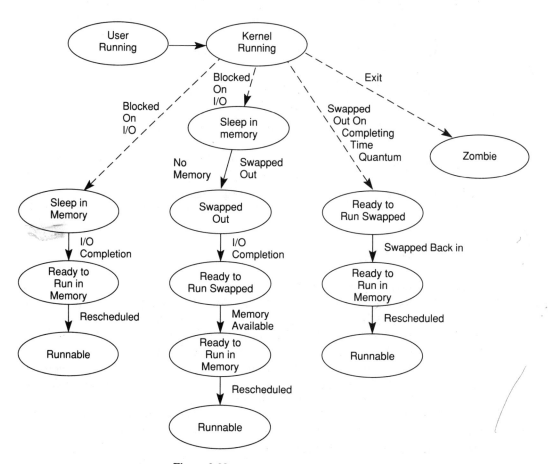

Figure 3-38.   Kernel Process State Changes

Other information in the proc structure and the user structure that helps in determining which processes are candidates for rescheduling includes the following:

1. Duration resident in memory.
2. CPU time used.
3. Process priority.
4. Process priority modifier.

3.4.5.1 Process Scheduling Criteria

Process rescheduling can occur at every clock interrupt, also called a clock tick (typically 50 to 100 per second). Scheduling is basically round-robin. However, that algorithm is modified slightly for a process that becomes compute bound. If a process is running and is able to run without being preempted, it can run up to a complete second (or time quantum according to the implementation) before being rescheduled. The process resumes execution from the point of suspension when it is rescheduled. The following conditions for the executing process cause rescheduling to occur.

1. The process finishes (completes its time quantum).
2. The process terminates.
3. The process has insufficient memory to execute further.
4. The process is blocked (say for I/O).
5. Preemption (a higher priority process becomes runnable).

Processes typically spend a majority of their time in one of two states—runnable or blocked. The highest priority process that is *ready-to-run in memory,* or has been preempted earlier, is selected. If several processes meet this criteria, the process longest in that queue is selected. If no process qualifies, the processor idles until the next clock interrupt.

3.4.5.2 Process Priority

A process is assigned a base priority by the system when it is created. The priority level of a process may be lowered via the *nice* system call. The priority level of a process determines its precedence for being rescheduled, that is, the process with the highest priority of the runnable processes (the process with the lowest priority value) gets scheduled. A process priority may change significantly if it is blocked as a kernel process and sleeps on a queue. This happens because it assumes the priority level of the queue it is attached to, for example, the queue for disk I/O. UNIX features two kinds of priority levels: variable priority and fixed priority.

We just looked at the *variable* priority levels, that is, the base priority modified on the basis of the CPU use and *nice* factor. The process reverts to this priority level on completion of the task that had caused it to block.

The *fixed* priority levels are used to optimize access to block devices and to allow the operating system to respond quickly to system calls. In the order of fixed levels, the *swap device* (disk device for swapping out processes) is at the highest level and the user mode is at the lowest, these levels in order are as follows:

1. Access to swap device.
2. Devices capable of block I/O (disks & tapes).
3. Access to inode list (for file search).
4. Character I/O devices.
5. User mode (user process queue).

Processes at the first three levels are generally non-interruptible and typically operate in kernel mode. These priorities are assigned to a process in the *sleep* routine. For example, a process performing disk I/O is assigned the priority level for disk I/O. Processes are usually preempted on return from kernel mode to user mode if higher priority processes are ready-to-run. Processes in user mode are interruptible and processes performing character device I/O are interruptible due to the intermittent nature of character I/O. Each of the five priority levels has a process queue. Processes at the same queue level follow a round robin algorithm; that is, the process that has been in the ready-to-run state and in memory the longest is scheduled first.

3.4.5.3 Process Priority Changes

The kernel assigns or modifies priority in the following situations:

1. Process calls the *sleep* routine.
2. Process returning from kernel mode to user mode.
3. The clock handler adjusts process priorities at rescheduling intervals.

When a user process is created, it is placed in the *user process queue* and it is linked as a runnable process to the *run* queue. A process can be loaded and scheduled to run only after all higher priority processes in the queue have been scheduled. Since each priority level, 1 through 5 noted above, has its run queue, if a user process gets blocked by disk I/O, for example, it gains the second highest priority level by being moved to that queue. During this period, other processes gain the CPU in order of their priority queue and relative priority within the queue. On completion of the required disk access, the user process is unblocked and flagged runnable at the disk I/O priority level. However, after getting scheduled, it drops to the user process queue priority level before returning to user mode.

A process returning to user mode from kernel mode, as we have just seen, may still be operating at a high kernel level priority due to a *sleep* call. The priority is dropped back to the user process level by the kernel before the process switches to user mode.

The *clock* handler interrupts at every reschedule time quantum (1 second for UNIX System V) and adjusts the recent CPU usage for each process. At the same time, the clock handler recomputes the priority of every user mode process in the "preempted but ready-to-run" state. Higher CPU usage results in lower relative scheduling priority.

3.4.5.4 System Priority

There are some operations during which the priority level of the CPU is raised to make it uninterruptable. This occurs to ensure system integrity while system data areas are being modified, for example, after an interrupt. The CPU priority is dropped back on completion of that activity.

The system also protects itself in another manner. During execution in the kernel mode, preemption (i.e. scheduling of higher priority process) is prevented to ensure that the system does not find itself tangled up in processes blocked that depend on one another for getting unblocked, a situation commonly referred to as deadly embrace.

3.4.5.5 Preemption

The UNIX system does not allow preemption of kernel mode processes. Only user mode processes can be preempted. A kernel mode process is preempted only when it is about to return from kernel mode to user mode. A process at a priority higher than the running process can cause preemption if an event, such as it being awakened due to completion of an I/O request, causes it to become runnable. Preemption can also be caused by the clock handler changing the priorities of all ready-to-run processes. The preemption flag, if set, indicates on return to user mode that another kernel process is *runnable in memory*.

3.4.5.6 Process Priority Modification by Type

All user processes are queued in the user process queue. While all user processes start out at the same priority level, the user process queue separates them into two classes: system-bound processes and compute-bound processes.

Processes that make 17 consecutive system calls without getting blocked are designated *system bound* and are forced to relinquish the CPU after their priority is dropped a notch. Their priority is, however, restored on getting rescheduled.

Compute-bound processes are processes that do not block themselves and use the complete time slice. Their priority is dropped one notch and is not restored until they start blocking themselves.

3.4.5.7 Context of a Process

The context of a process consists of static and dynamic components. The process context is saved completely if a process is not going to be scheduled again for a relatively long period, for example, it has executed a *sleep* call or is being swapped out. Partial contexts are saved in a different manner if the process is likely to be rescheduled soon. The components of a process context are as follows:

1. Static components
   a. Process text, data, user stack, and shared data
   b. Process structure (Process table entry)

      c. User structure
      d. Kernel stack
      e. Per process region table (Memory map).

  2. Dynamic components
      a. Save areas for each *save* layer
      b. Kernel stack for each layer.

The *save* layers referred to above are created as a result of events that interrupt the normal execution of a process. The events that cause the context of a process to be saved are the following:

1. Execution of a system call.

2. Handling of a device interupt.

3. A clock interrupt causing rescheduling.

Process Id	In Memory	Swapped	Comments
pid 12	Running		
pid 17		Ready to Run	
pid 34	Ready-to-Run		
pid 43		Sleeping (Blocked)	;waiting for disk I/O
pid 49	Sleeping (Blocked)		;waiting for disk I/O
Case 1: pid 12 is blocked, pid 34 is scheduled, and pid 43 unblocks			
pid 12	Sleeping (Blocked)		;executed system call
pid 17	Ready to Run		;swapped in
pid 34	Running		;scheduled to run
pid 43		Ready-to-run	;I/O completed
pid 49		Sleeping (Blocked)	;swapped out
Case 2: pid 34 executes a system call, pid 49 unblocks			
pid 12	Sleeping (Blocked)		
pid 17	Running		;scheduled to run
pid 34	Sleeping (Blocked)		;executed system call
pid 43	Ready-to-run		;swapped in
pid 49		Ready-to-run	;
Case 3: pid 12 unblocks, and pid 17 issues a sleep call			
pid 12	Ready-to-run		;in kernel mode
pid 17	Sleeping (blocked)		;executed system call
pid 34		Sleeping (blocked)	;swapped out
pid 43	Running		;scheduled to run
pid 49	Ready-to-run		

Figure 3-39.   Process Scheduling Example

3.4.5.8 Process Scheduling Example

Figure 3-39 illustrates the scheduling of processes in a UNIX system and the sequence of operations performed through a scheduling cycle. The three cases show the changes in the process states through three rescheduling cycles.

3.4.6 Process Events

A process event is a notable happening. Examples of process events include the completion of an I/O operation, an interrupt from a device, and a signal from another process. The mechanisms that create process events include *signals* and *sleep/wakeup* call combinations.

Process events cause a process to go through a different sequence than normal. An event can be anticipated by a process, or it can be initiated by another process. The resolution of a process event frequently results in the process being terminated, rescheduled (*wakeup*), or blocked (swapped out). The following discussion describes the handling of signals and the sleep/wakeup mechanism.

3.4.6.1 Signals

Signals operate through the use of two system calls: *kill* system call and *signal* system call.

3.4.6.2 The *Kill* System Call

The *kill* system call sends a signal to a process. The system call requires the *process ID* of the process to be terminated and the *signal number* to send as arguments. The *signal* system call arranges to catch a signal. It requires the signal number and identification of the signal handling routine as its arguments. The *process* ID specified in the call determines how the signal is handled and which processes it applies to. Figure 3-40 describes the interpretation of the process ID values.

```
>0–Process with process ID = specified ID

0–All processes in the Process Group

−1–All processes with Real User ID = Effective User ID of Sender
<−1–All processes in process group with ID = Absolute value of specified ID
```

Figure 3-40.   Process ID Specification for *kill* System Call

The signal is accepted only by processes that satisfy the criteria set in Figure 3-40. It is ignored by all other processes. Figure 3-41 is a list of some common signals used in UNIX.

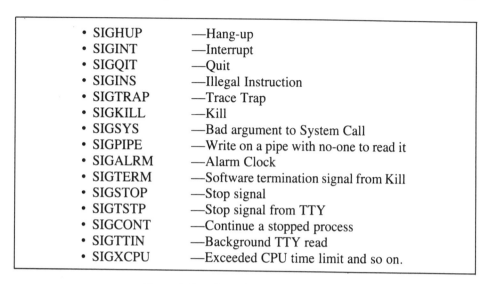

- SIGHUP   —Hang-up
- SIGINT   —Interrupt
- SIGQIT   —Quit
- SIGINS   —Illegal Instruction
- SIGTRAP   —Trace Trap
- SIGKILL   —Kill
- SIGSYS   —Bad argument to System Call
- SIGPIPE   —Write on a pipe with no-one to read it
- SIGALRM   —Alarm Clock
- SIGTERM   —Software termination signal from Kill
- SIGSTOP   —Stop signal
- SIGTSTP   —Stop signal from TTY
- SIGCONT   —Continue a stopped process
- SIGTTIN   —Background TTY read
- SIGXCPU   —Exceeded CPU time limit and so on.

Figure 3-41. Some Common UNIX Signals

3.4.6.3 The Signal System Call

The kernel level routine *psig* performs the action specified by the current signal. The routine *issig* is called before calling *psig* to determine that there is a signal that needs to be serviced. Figure 3-42 describes the algorithm for the *psig* routine.

The *proc structure* pointer is retrieved from the *user structure*. If the trace flag is set in the *proc structure,* then the *stop* routine is called to set the process ready to accept commands from the parent. The *fsig* routine is called with the *proc structure* pointer to get the signal number. If there is no signal, the routine terminates and returns. If there is a signal, it checks to see if the user had made a *signal* system call and is therefore expecting a signal. If the call was to ignore the signal, a normal return is taken. If on the other hand, the *signal* system call was to handle a signal, it checks to see if the signal is a trace trap (SIGTRAP) or a kill signal (SIGKILL). If not, it clears the user signal system call flag and calls the *sendsig* routine to process the signal, and then returns normally. If the user was not anticipating a signal, or if the signal is a SIGTRAP or SIGKILL, the *switch/case* statement checks to see if the signal is of the type that requires the core to be dumped. In any case, the *exit* routine is called to terminate the process. This discussion implies that users have to be careful with signals like SIGKILL that can terminate an unsuspecting process.

Signals can be generated by outside events. Signals can be caught by specifying a signal catching routine. The signal SIGKILL is never caught and always terminates a process.

```
psig:
argument: (Not used)
    Retrieve proc structure pointer from user structure
        If the flag was set for trace
            Call stop and accept commands from parent
        Call fsig to get signal number
        If signal number is 0, return
        Else reset signal number in proc structure
        If user had made signal system call
            Get user virtual address of signal catcher from user structure
            Return if call is to ignore signal
            If not trace trap or kill signal
                Clear user signal system call flag
                Process signal (call sendsig)
                Return
        Else switch on case - signal type
            SIGQUIT:
            SIGKILL:
            SIGTRAP:
            SIGIOT:
            SIGEMT:
            SIGFPE:
            SIGBUS:
            SIGSEGV:
            SIGSYS:
                Call core to dump core
    Call exit to terminate process
```

Figure 3-42.   Algorithm for the *psig* Routine

3.4.6.4 Signal Acceptance

Possible actions that can be taken on receipt of a signal include the following:

1. Ignore it.
2. Process signal.
3. Terminate a process.

Signals cannot be stacked; that is, if a number of signals are received while the process is swapped out, only the last signal in a sequence of identical signals will actually be received. The reason for this is that signals are stored as bit maps of pending signals.

A super-user can send a signal to any process. A super-user can therefore cause a process that is hung to be terminated via the signal mechanism. A user can kill a subprocess owned by the user by logging in at another terminal and sending a SIGKILL signal to the hung process. The processing of signals depends considerably on the state of the process and the priority levels. The reader is encouraged to give special attention to the handling of signals in the following discussions of *sleep/wakeup* algorithms as well as the *swtch* algorithm.

3.4.6.5 Sleep/Wakeup

A special event combination—*sleep/wakeup* is used to unblock processes that are blocked due to unavailability of resources (e.g. disks, memory). A process suspends itself by making the *sleep* call when it is blocked due to I/O or resource allocation. The priority to be assumed on waking up, and the reason for sleeping are specified in the *sleep* call. When an I/O event takes place, the process realizing the event issues a *wakeup* call, and all other processes sleeping on that particular event are awakened and linked with the run queue. On *wakeup,* the process is placed on the scheduling priority queue at a priority level defined by the kernel service required (e.g., disk access results in high priority while character I/O results in low priority). The priority is also based on the applicability of signals, that is, the priority is set at a level at or above the level at which signals are evaluated and acted upon immediately, or below it so that they are enacted after issuing a *swtch* call in an attempt to schedule another process.

```
sleep:
arguments: chan (sleep channel address)
           Priority (to sleep on)


    Set processor level to high, block all interrupts
    Set process state to SSLEEP (sleep)
    Enter sleep channel address in proc structure
    Link process with hash queue for that sleep address
    Reset process time
    Set sleep priority to input priority
    If priority set is below signal level (interruptible)
        If signal received
            Enable interrupts, Link process with run queue
            Set processor level to level at start
            If priority is set to catch signals, return (1)
            goto psig
        Else, enable all interrupts (no signal waiting)
        If runin set, reset it to 0
            Wake up scheduler to start here
        Call swtch to perform a context switch and reschedule
        If signal waiting, goto psig
    Else, enable interrupts (priority set above signal level)
    Call swtch to perform context switch and reschedule
    Set processor level to level at start
    return(0)


psig:
    Call longjmp (non local goto to saved location)
```

Figure 3-43. Algorithm for *sleep* routine

The *sleep* routine, described in Figure 3-43, performs some complicated functions and sets the processor level high to block off all interrupts. It then sets the process state of the calling process to SSLEEP (sleep) and enters the sleep channel address in the *proc structure* (this determines what event will cause a *wakeup*). The process is linked with the hash queue for the sleep address and its process time is adjusted. The priority is an input argument to this routine and is set to the level determined by the function that caused the *sleep,* for example, disk I/O.

The response to signals comes into play at this point. If the priority is such that the process is interruptible by signals, and a signal has been received, the process is removed from the sleep hash queue, linked back to the run queue, and the process state is changed back to SRUN (ready-to-run). If the process sleep priority was set to catch signals, it returns 1, indicating that a signal has to be processed. If not set to catch signals, it performs *longjmp* (long goto) to the return address to re-start where it had left off.

If, on the other hand, it did not receive a signal, the routine enables all interrupts, and if the scheduler has the *runin* flag set (i.e., no processes ready to be scheduled), it resets it to *0* to attempt rescheduling. A full context switch is performed by the *swtch* routine. When the process is resumed, it again checks to see if a signal is waiting.

If the priority was set not to respond to signals, then the interrupts are enabled right away and a full context switch is performed by the *swtch* routine to schedule another process. On being awakened, it reschedules and returns a *0* after setting the processor level to that at start. The algorithm for the *wakeup* routine is described in Figure 3-44.

```
wakeup:
argument: chan (sleep channel address)

    Set processor level to high, block off all interrupts
    Call sqhash to find hash queue for sleep address
    For (every process with state SSLEEP)
        Set state to SRUN (ready-to-run)
        Take process off hash queue
        Link process with run queue
        If process not in memory (swapped out)
            Clear runout flag to wakeup scheduler
        Else, if awakened process has higher priority
            Set runrun (preemption flag) to reschedule
    Reset processor level to the level at start
```

Figure 3-44.   Algorithm for *wakeup* routine

3.4.7 Process Scheduling and Swapping

The *scheduler* (*process 0*), also known as the *swapper,* manages swapping of processes. It is initially started on system initialization as the first process, and then *sleeps* as the highest priority process. It *awakens* whenever memory changes, or at least once per clock tick, for example, about 50 to 100 times every second depending on the UNIX implementation. The *scheduler* synchronizes on two events: *runout* flag and *runin* flag. Figure 3-45 shows the operation of these two flags.

The scheduler uses the process table entries, the *proc structures,* to evaluate the status of processes to determine how to react to events.

```
sched sleeps:
    * Set runout flag and sleep if no runnable processes
    * Set runin flag and sleep if no memory to run processes

sched awakens:
    * If runout flag set:
         Process on swap device becomes runnable
         Waiting process on swap device receives signal
         Runnable process swaps itself out

    * If runin flag set:
         Currently running process enters wait state
         Currently running process ages (once every second)
```

Figure 3-45.   Basic Scheduling Algorithm

The *runout* flag is set by the scheduler if it finds no *runnable* processes. It then *sleeps.* The *runin* flag is set by the scheduler when processes are ready to be scheduled but the scheduler cannot find any free memory, i.e. it cannot do anything until another process can be swapped out. The scheduler *sleeps* after setting the *runin* flag also. The scheduler reacts to different events on the basis of the state of the *runout* and *runin* flags. For a process to run, it must be loaded in memory first. If the *runout* flag is set, the *swapper* will be awakened whenever a process on the swap device becomes runnable, a waiting process on the swap device receives a signal, or a runnable process swaps itself out. The first two events indicate that a process has become runnable and the scheduler needs to go into action. The third indicates that the CPU is idle and the scheduler needs to see if there are other processes ready to run.

If the *runin* is set, the *swapper* is awakened when the running process enters a wait state or a process ages. In either case, the scheduler is in position to swap out the process to free memory for a runnable process.

3.4.7.1 Process Swapping Routines

As we saw earlier, the main loop of process scheduling is contained in *sched.* The key routine it calls is *swapin* which swaps in a process. The *swtch* routine actually reschedules the CPU. *Sched* also calls *sleep* when there is nothing it can do (i.e., it is waiting on the *runout* or *runin* flags). As we also saw, process 0 that runs *sched* never swaps out.

3.4.7.2 The *Swapin* Routine

The *swapin* routine, described in Figure 3-46, is called by *sched* to swap a process into memory if memory is available, whenever it finds a process that is in ready-to-run state (SRUN) but is swapped out.

```
swapin:
argument: Pointer to proc structure
input:      Pointer to user structure

    If shared text already in memory
        Lock it from being swapped
    Calculate memory required, check for partial swap
    If not enough memory, goto Nomem
    Call memall to allocate memory, goto Nomem if no memory
        Set up links to shared text already in memory
        Unlock shared text
    Copy process in
    Return 1


Nomem:
    Link process to run queue
    Return 0
```

Figure 3-46.   Algorithm for *swapin* Routine

The *swapin* routine checks to see if there is any shared text already in memory, and if so it locks it to prevent it from being swapped out before its use count is bumped up. It then allocates memory, sets up the links to shared text, and updates the *proc structure* (process table entry) parameters. It returns a *0* if there is no memory available (and *sched* then looks for a process to swap out) or a *1* if successful.

3.4.7.3 The Swtch Routine

The *swtch* routine is called by *qswtch*, which in turn is called by the *trap* routine. The *trap* routine is called from the *trap handler* when a processor trap occurs, or a system call is being serviced, or an interrupt (including a clock interrupt) occurs. A case statement in the *trap* routine determines the type of trap. It then either resumes an interrupted process, or calls *qswtch* to place the current process on the *run* queue and *qswtch* then calls *swtch*. The *swtch* routine also sets up *process 0* to resume and return to *sched* when it is made runnable by being awakened. Figure 3-47 describes the algorithm for the *swtch* routine.

The *swtch* routine performs the following three main functions:

1. Saves the context of the current process (dynamic).
2. Switches to process *0* (the swapper).
3. Selects and resumes a new process.

```
swtch:
arguments: None
inputs:      proc structure

    If calling process is not process 0 (scheduler)
        Save general purpose registers, user structure & stack (partial context)
        Resume process 0
            (map user structure of process 0 in kernel space)
    If calling process is process 0, enter process search loop

Loop:
    Lock out interrupts
    Clear preemption flag (runrun)
    Search runnable queue for highest priority process
        If none found, idle
        goto Loop
    Else, select highest priority process
    Unlink it from runnable queue
    Enable interrupts
    Set selected process running
```

Figure 3-47.   Algorithm for *swtch* Routine

The *save* routine is used to store general purpose registers. The *resume* routine is called to restore general purpose registers and restart the process from the current kernel level stack frame for that save.

As noted earlier, there are three events that cause process scheduling and switching to be initiated. This implies that the *swtch* routine may be called by interrupt routines (e.g., clock interrupt). It first determines if the calling process is process 0, the scheduler, or not. If not, it saves the partial context including stack and frame pointer (partial since the process is not being swapped out) and resumes process 0. After process 0 is resumed, it disables interrupts (this is a critical region) and clears the preemption flag. The routine then searches the *runnable* process queue (i.e. process ready-to-run and in memory) for the highest priority runnable process. The priority is determined by a combination of *initial priority, CPU usage factor,* and the *nice* factor. Remember that the nice factor is adjusted via the *nice* system call. If it cannot find one, it calls *idle*, and starts the search again. If it finds one, it unlinks it from the runnable process queue, links it to the run queue, and sets it up for a *resume*. The interrupts are then enabled, and the process is set running.

A process can execute in *user* or *kernel* mode. The *trap* routine is used to switch to kernel mode via either a *trap* or an *interrupt*. If an interrupt caused process switching, the interrupt is handled. Before returning to the user mode, the *runrun* flag is checked to see if the CPU needs to be rescheduled again. If not, the interrupted kernel process is made to resume.

3.4.7.4 The *Nice* System Call

The *nice* system call provides the user the means for adjusting process priority. A user can lower the priority of a compute-bound process and be 'nice' to other users. Only a superuser can raise priority. The *nice* system call makes adjustments to the *nice factor* in the *user structure*. As we noted above, the nice factor is just one of the components that affect priority at the kernel level. At the user level, it can have a noticeable impact.

3.4.8 Process Termination

A process terminates itself by executing an *exit* call. It may also be terminated as a result of a *kill* signal from another process. The process flow for termination is shown in Figure 3-48.

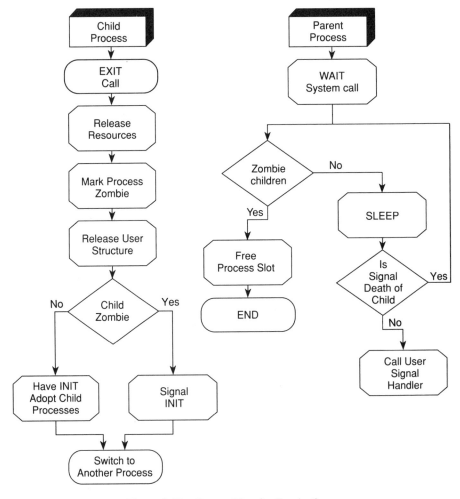

Figure 3-48. Process Flow for Termination

3.4.8.1 The *Exit* Call

A process that executes an *exit* system call is first placed in a *zombie* state. In this state, the process does not exist anymore but it may leave timing information for its parent process and an exit code specifying the reason for exiting. A zombie process is removed by a *wait* system call executed in the parent process.

The termination of a process requires a number of cleanup activities. These include releasing all memory used by the process; reducing the reference counts for all files used by the process, and closing any files that have reference counts of zero; releasing shared text areas if any; and releasing the process table entry, the *proc structure*, for this process. The process table entry is released when the parent issues a *wait* system call. The *wait* system call returns the *process ID* of the terminated child process. It then releases the *proc structure*. The algorithm for the *exit* call is described in Figure 3-49.

```
exit:
Input:
    Release all memory used by the process except user structure
    Reduce reference counts for all open files, close if necessary
    Release any shared text area
    Mark process state as a zombie process
    Copy exit status into process table entry & release user structure
    Search process table for parent process and child processes
        If child is in zombie state
            Signal init process
        Else
            Have child processes adopted by init process
    Switch to another process
```

Figure 3-49.   Algorithm for *exit* Routine

3.4.8.2 The *Kill* call

The *kill* system call is described in Section 3.4.6 under Process Events. The *kill* system call can be used to send a SIGKILL signal to terminate the receiving process. Unless a process has executed a signal system call to ignore signals, the kernel will process signals, typically before switching from kernel mode to user mode on return from a system call. The SIGKILL signal will, in a case like this, cause the *exit* routine to be executed on behalf of the process receiving the signal.

3.4.9 Process States and Events

The process state diagram is shown in Figure 3-50 for a review of the events and activities that cause process state changes. This diagram summarizes the administration of processes.

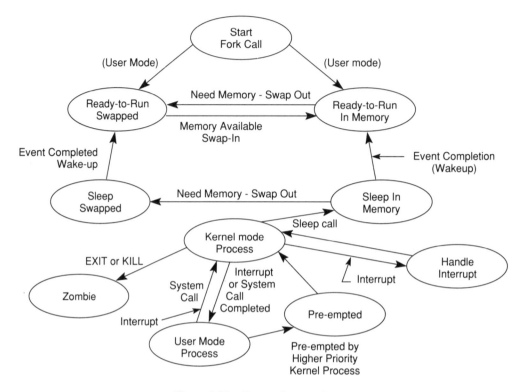

Figure 3-50.   Process States and Events

3.4.10 Performance Issues

A number of architectural issues in the management of processes affect system performance and system response time. These issues include the following:

1. System hardware architecture.
2. Available memory and proportion of processes that can stay resident.
3. Total number of processes invoked at any given time.
4. Swapping/demand paging algorithms.

A more detailed discussion of performance issues is presented in Chapter 5. A study of that chapter is recommended if system performance is a significant issue for the reader.

3.4.11 Summary

In this subsection we looked at the key task of the UNIX operating system of creating, scheduling, operating, and terminating of processes. We looked at the structures, the *proc structure* and the *user structure,* used to manage process scheduling. We also looked at the operations of swap memory for the creation of a process and we looked at the use of the *fork* and *exec* system calls. We further looked at the operation of *sleep/wakeup* system calls and the use of *events* to control the scheduling of processes in an efficient manner. The use of *signals* as a means of communications among processes, and as a means of recovering from a hung process were the other key areas of discussion.

3.4.12 Exercises

1. What is a process? What information is maintained in the *proc* structure?
2. Describe what happens on process creation in a system that has no memory left.
3. How does the *sleep-wakeup* combination work? Explain.
4. When does a process check for signals? How does it handle signals? Can signals be lost?
5. Is there any advantage in retaining the sequence in which signals are received? How would you change the data structures to make that feasible?
6. What would be gained by having a process check for signals at the start of executing a system call, i.e. entering kernel mode? What problems might this create?
7. Note that UNIX does not allow preemption in kernel mode. How would the architecture change to accommodate a preemptive interrupt driven mode of operations?
8. What are the differences in the context switch operations for an interrupt versus a process rescheduling?
9. What functions or routines require a search through the process table? Which routines need to determine the full process group for a particular user? How does the kernel locate the process group?
10. Describe what happens if the kernel issues a *wakeup* call for a particular address when no processes are actually asleep on that address.
11. Describe the mapping of events to addresses for processes sleeping on a particular event. How are these addresses used in a *wakeup* call?
12. Describe the complete algorithm for the *sleep* routine?
13. How do you distinguish a child process from a parent process?
14. What are the critical regions? How does the kernel protect itself during these critical regions?
15. What is a zombie process? What is the importance of a zombie process?
16. Some UNIX implementations allow user definable intervals for clock interrupt handler for rescheduling processes. Is it possible to make this interval system load sensitive? What would be the benefits of such a scheme? How would this be achieved?
17. What level of control does the *nice* system call give you for adjusting process priority on your system? How would you change the UNIX architecture to get better control of process priority?

3.5 INTERPROCESS COMMUNICATION

Applications operating in a UNIX System environment frequently invoke a number of processes to perform different tasks or functions. The processes need a means of communication to exchange data or synchronize execution for completing the tasks in a required sequence. This communication may be required at the *shell* level, for example, to *pipe* a text file from the *cat* command to the printer spooler, or it may be at the kernel level for synchronization of processes. The UNIX system provides the following mechanisms for performing interprocess communications:

1. Unnamed and named pipes.
2. Shared memory.
3. Message queues.
4. Semaphores
5. Signals
6. Sleep and wakeup calls.

It should be noted that the architecture of each of these mechanisms is different, and they are typically used to perform different types of interprocess communications. It is, however, interesting to note that the concepts for *shared memory, message queues,* and *semaphores* bear a resemblance and they are accessed by very similar system calls. AT&T UNIX System V features three kinds of system calls that look alike for shared memory, message queues, and semaphores. These system calls perform comparable functions and have similar suffixes, for example, shm*get,* msg*get,* and sem*get.* These three kinds of system calls are:

1. *-get* Retrieve existing entry or create a new entry.
2. *-ctl* Set or retrieve status of entry, or remove entry.
3. *-op* Set up interprocess links and provide communications.

The usage of these three systems calls appears to be consistent with similar parameters, and they use common concepts of identification, *key* and *id.*
Let us now look at each of these interprocess communications mechanisms in detail.

3.5.1 Unnamed and Named Pipes—
Concepts and Implementation

Pipes are a special implementation of the UNIX file system. Internally called first-in-first-out (FIFO) files, pipes can be read or written only sequentially. The only other difference from ordinary files is that FIFO files (or pipes) use only the direct blocks to minimize performance impact, and do not use any level of indirect block addresses. The direct blocks are used as a ring buffer. (Please note that *direct* and *indirect* blocks are described in detail in Section 3.6.5—Physical Organization of the File Structure). The use of only direct blocks limits the maximum size of pipes. The file byte offset in the user structure points to the current byte position and is adjusted up if data is appended to the pipe, and down if it is read off the pipe. The byte pointer wraps around to the start of the ring buffer if the sequential byte pointer increases beyond the end of the buffer. The *open, read, write,* and *close* file access routines described in Section 3.6.6 demonstrate the special handling for FIFO files.

As we just noted, there is a finite size limit on a FIFO file (directly addressable blocks). At any given time, only one process can access a FIFO file for reading or writing. A *read* function always succeeds on a FIFO file. It returns the actual number of bytes read if the file has less bytes than what the user specified for the read call. If on a *read* call the FIFO file is empty, the process *sleeps* until the pipe is written into by another process. Similarly, if on a *write* call there is insufficient space to write into a FIFO file, the process *sleeps* until the FIFO file is read from by another process and sufficient space is created. If a pipe is closed by all writers without satisfying processes *sleeping* on read requests, the pipe is closed and the sleeping processes wakeup and return with *0* bytes read. Conversely, if there are processes *sleeping* on write requests, and the last reader closes the pipe, the sleeping processes are sent an error signal with a *wakeup*.

3.5.1.1 Unnamed Pipes

Unnamed pipes, also known as just *pipes,* or *ordinary pipes,* provide a channel to pass data between two processes. These processes can use the pipe only if they have descended from the same parent process that invoked the pipe and therefore inherited the file descriptor. An unnamed pipe has no directory entry and is not accessible to other processes. A command of the type

```
ls | pr
```

prints a directory listing by providing a link between the output of the *ls* command and the input of the *pr* command.

The number of unnamed pipes that can be opened at any time is a configurable parameter based on the definition of a *pipe device.* The definition of the pipe device specifies the total number of disk blocks allocated for pipes and the inodes set aside for pipes.

An unnamed pipe is invoked by the *pipe* system call. The kernel service routine for the pipe system call sets up an inode, and it also sets up two file descriptors in the user structure of the process and two file structures in the file table, one of each for reading from the file and the other for writing to the file.

3.5.1.2 Named Pipes

A *named pipe* is a special file of type FIFO that is opened using the normal *open* system call. The inode is allocated from the normal inode pool and is returned to it after the last close (unlink) of the FIFO file. There is one significant difference between named pipes and ordinary files. Since either a read or a write can be in process at any given time, the kernel keeps track of the reads and writes and ensures that a *read* does not *wait* on an empty pipe, nor a write on a full pipe. The processes *sleep* in such cases and a *wakeup* is issued when the required event takes place.

3.5.2 Shared Memory—Concepts and Implementation

The use of *shared memory* as a means of communication between two processes requires a mechanism for identifying common blocks of memory that can be accessed by two or more processes. This is achieved by the use of two data structures—*per process region tables,* and the *shared memory headers* (Figure 3-51). Per process region table consists of *page table structures* (detailed in Section 3.2.11) that describe physical memory pages as follows:

1. Page frame number.
2. Type of page.
3. Page modified flag.
4. Page protection flag.
5. Valid page flag.

Shared memory headers are used for identifying shared memory segments and their current usage parameters. These headers are combined in a list called the *shared memory table.* The contents of the shared memory header structure *shmid_ds* include the following:

1. Operation permissions structure
   a. Creator user ID
   b. Creator group ID
   c. User ID
   d. Group ID
   e. Mode.
2. Segment size.
3. Pointer to associated region table.
4. ID of process that performed last shared memory operation.
5. Current number attached.
6. In memory attached.
7. Last shared memory attach time.
8. Last shared memory detach time.
9. Last shared memory change time.

These data structures are accessed by a number of routines that intialize, allocate, attach, detach, and cleanup shared memory segments. There are four system calls—*shmget, shmctl, shmat* and *shmdt* (*shmop*)—that perform shared memory functions. The main kernel routines that service and support these calls are the following:

- *shmget*   —Allocate and initialize new shared memory segment.
- *shmat*   —Attach specified shared memory segment to calling process.
- *shmdt*   —Detach specified shared memory segment from calling process.
- *shmctl*   —Shared memory control and remove operations.
- *shmfree*   —Decrement use count. Free segment and page table if last free.
- *shmconv*   —Convert user supplied shared memory id into a pointer to shared memory header.
- *shmexec*   —Called by *setregs* to handle shared memory *exec* processing.
- *shmexit*   —Called by *exit* to clean up shared memory on process exit.
- *shmfork*   —Called by *newproc* to handle shared memory fork processing.

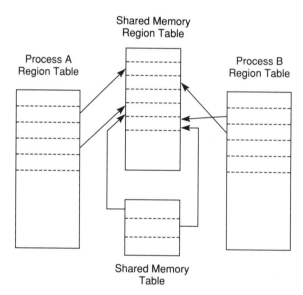

Figure 3-51. Shared Memory Architectural Relationships

There are three arguments to the *shmget* call—*key, size,* and *flag*—where key is the identifier of the shared memory segment in the shared memory table, size is the number of bytes in that segment, and the flag sets the operation permissions. The *shared memory table* is searched for the key. If an existing segment is found that matches the key, and if the *flag* was set for proper permissions, its shared memory id (*shmid*) is returned, or else a new segment is created. For creating a new segment, its header information is formulated and memory is allocated to the segment. The total memory required is set to the user specified segment size plus the shared memory header plus the page table entry size. The shared memory segment can be accessed in a manner similar to accessing other virtual memory. However, before this can be done, the shared memory segment has to be mapped into the data segment of the virtual memory of the process intending to access shared memory. A process executes a *shmat* call to attach the shared memory segment. The location of the mapping as a result of the attach operation can have a significant impact on potential growth of the *bss* or the stack. The *shmat* system call takes the segment id (*shmid*), the shared memory start address, and flag as the three arguments. If the shared memory address is specified as *0*, the kernel maps the segment at the first available page aligned location in the data segment. Otherwise, it is located at the address defined by the system call. If any valid memory segments (i.e. segments already in use) may be overwritten, an error is returned. If needed, the size of the process page table is increased. The shared memory segment is then mapped into the attached data segment.

The *shmdt* kernel routine services the *shmdt* (*shmop*) system call. The *shmat* call, discussed above, returns an address argument that the user supplies as input to the *shmdt* call. The instance of the shared memory segment located at the specified address is detached. The kernel routine then calls *shmfree* to decrement the shared memory attachment count, and frees up segment memory. Page tables are also freed if applicable.

A process uses the *shmctl* system call to perform various shared memory control operations, including some wildcard operations based on the memory segment id.

3.5.3 Message Queues

The concept of message queues is very similar to the concept of shared memory. There are four system calls *msgget, msgctl, msgsnd,* and *msgrcv* that create message queues and manipulate them, and read from them or write to them.

The main data structures used for message queue management include *msgmap*—message allocation map, *msgque*—message queue header, and *msgh*—message header. The message queue header, also called the message queue structure, consists of a pointer to a linked list of message headers. The message queue header structure includes the following:

1. Operation permissions structure
   a. Creator user ID
   b. Creator group ID
   c. User ID
   d. Group ID
   e. Mode.
2. Total number of messages in queue.
3. Maximum number of bytes in queue.
4. ID of process that last sent message.
5. ID of process that last received message.
6. Pointer to first message on linked list.
7. Pointer to next available message slot.
8. Pointer to last message slot in linked list.
9. Time of last message send.
10. Time of last message receive.
11. Time of last message change (control).

Message headers form a linked list. The following describes the components of the message header structure:

1. Pointer to next message header.
2. Message type.
3. Message byte count (text size).
4. Message pool allocation spot.

Figure 3-52 describes the architectural relationships among the structures used for message queue management. The message queue id, *msqid,* is converted internally to a pointer to the entry in the message queue header list.

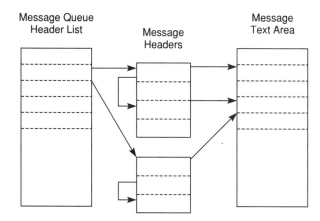

Figure 3-52. Message Queue Memory Architectural Relationships

Any access to any message queue requires updating the parameters in the queue headers. The message headers change only if messages are added or deleted. The routines, *msgget, msgsnd, msgrcv,* and *msgctl* are the main kernel routines that service system calls. The following are the main routines that support the message queue functions:

- *msgget*   —Retrieve an existing message queue or create new one.
- *msgsnd*   —Send the specified type of message to the specified queue.
- *msgrcv*   —Retrieve a message of the type specified from the specified queue.
- *msgctl*   —Various message control operations.
- *msgconv* —Convert user supplied queue id into a pointer to message queue table.
- *msgfree* —Free up space and manage headers, relink pointers on queue.

All arguments to the system calls are provided to the kernel routines as data structures. The *msgget* kernel routine checks the *key* argument against the message queue header list for a match. A number of message queues can be set up, identified, and accessed using keys specified in a *key* argument. Depending on the *flags* set, an existing queue is located, a new one is created, or an error is returned. If a queue associated with the specified *key* is found, the message queue id (*msqid*) is returned. If the flags were set for creation, and no existing queue is found, a new queue is set up and initialized. The *msqid* returned is used as input for the other three system calls.

As we just noted, the message queue identifier *msqid* is also an argument to the *msgsnd* system call. The *msqid* is converted to a queue pointer. Other arguments to the call include the pointer to the structure containing the message, the size of the message, and the condition flags. The kernel routine for *msgsnd* checks if the message size is larger than the system wide limit. It further checks validity of the other arguments and ensures that the queue has not been removed. It then allocates space on the queue, allocates a message header from the free chain, and allocates buffer space. If the queue has insufficient space, or there is no message header available, and the IPC_NOWAIT flag is set, it returns an error. If the IPC_NOWAIT flag is not set, the process *sleeps* until space is freed up. If everything is fine up to this point, the message text is copied in, the header parameters are updated, and the message is placed on the queue.

The *msgrcv* system call arguments include the message queue identifier *msqid*, a pointer to the structure where the message text will be returned, the total number of bytes to read in (can be less than the message size if MSG_NOERROR is TRUE), the message type (0 for first message in queue, -1 for first message of lowest type, or actual type number), and message flag. The *msqid* is converted to a message queue pointer. The *msgrcv* routine checks the queue number, access permissions, and validity of the specified message length. It then determines the action required for the *type* parameter and searches through the message headers for the message. Note that the type parameter is a very effective means of uniquely identifying a message or a sequence of messages and, in effect, creating a unique communications path between two processes. The routine then checks the size of the message and returns an error depending on the MSG_NOERROR flag. If the message is not found and the IPC_NOWAIT is set, an error is returned, else the process *sleeps* until a message of the appropriate type is sent. If everything is fine at this point, it copies the message text. The message is then removed, the space is freed up, the message header is returned to the free list, and the queue parameters are updated.

The *msgctl* system call arguments include the message queue id *msqid,* a *cmd* that describes the control operation, and the address of the buffer where the output of the operation will be returned to the user. The kernel routine *msgctl* services this call. It can be used to remove a queue, or to get the status of the members of a queue. The routine is set up as a *switch-case* statement that switches on the value of the *cmd* argument. It handles the cases for IPC_RMID (remove specified queue), IPC_SET (set the values, e.g. permissions for specified queue members), and IPC_STAT (retrieve status values for each member in specified queue).

3.5.4 Semaphores—Design and Uses

The root of this word is the Greek *sema* meaning *signal*. The expanded meaning of the word is—a system to convey information by visual signaling. In the UNIX system, semaphores are used by processes to send signals, rather than data, to other processes.

These signals determine synchronization of processes, for example, cooperating processes can lock out each other during critical code segments such as updates to shared data segments or common data bases.

The *semaphore* implementation uses a number of data structures. These include the *semaphore allocation map, semaphore structures, semaphore data structures,* and *undo table pointer* chains. The semaphore allocation map, set up at system initialization time, provides a means of rapidly locating free memory for creating semaphores. All memory released by cancelled semaphores (*semctl* system call) is marked free in the semaphore allocation map. The *semaphore structure* defines the semaphore itself and consists of the following:

1. The value of the semaphore.
2. Process id of last operation.
3. Number of processes awaiting semaphore value to become greater.
4. Number of processes awaiting semaphore value to become *0*.

The semaphore data structure consists of the following components:

1. Semaphore id.
2. Operation permissions structure
   a. Creator user ID
   b. Creator group ID
   c. User ID
   d. Group ID
   e. Mode.
3. Pointer to semaphore arrays—base address (lists).
4. Number of semaphores in this set.
5. Time of last operation.
6. Time of last message change (control).

The semaphore undo structure pointer consists of the following parameters:

1. Semaphore set ID.
2. Semaphore number.
3. Adjustment (decremented).

The *semaphore data structure table* (also known as the *semaphore table*) is a linked list of *semaphore data structures*. The semaphores themselves are built as an array of *semaphore structures* that are accessed sequentially (Figure 3-53). Each semaphore data structure is identified by a semaphore id *(semid)* that is associated with the user specified *key* (from the *semget* call).

The kernel routines that service the system calls to create and manipulate semaphores are the following:

1. *semget*   —Retrieve a semaphore data structure or create new one.
2. *semctl*   —Perform specified control operations on selected semaphores.
3. *semop*   —Perform specified operations on selected semaphores.
4. *semconv*   —Convert user supplied queue id into a pointer to a semaphore data structure.
5. *semaoe*   —Create or update adjustment on exit from *semop*.
6. *semundo*   —Undo work done since operation cannot be completed.
7. *seminit*   —Called by *main* to initialize semaphore map.

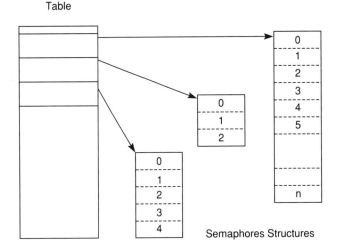

Semaphore
Data Structure
Table

Semaphores Structures

Figure 3-53.   Semaphore Architectural Relationships

The arguments to the *semget* system call include the *key*, the number of semaphores to be set up in this semaphore array, and a flag specifying permissions. The key is associated with a *semid*—a semaphore array identification number. The *semconv* routine converts the *semid* to a pointer to a semaphore table header (*semaphore data structure*). This routine also checks the permissions. As in other *-get* calls, the arguments are passed to the *semget* kernel routine as a data structure. The *semget* routine checks to ensure that the maximum system limit for the number of semaphores will not be exceeded. It then allocates memory. In case any errors are encountered, the permissions in the semaphore data structure are cleared before returning a user error. If there are no errors, the semaphore data structure is initialized and the base address (the pointer to the semaphore array), the number of semaphores in the array, and the current time are entered in the semaphore data structure just initialized. If it is an existing semaphore, then the initialization consists of checking that the total number of semaphores in the array is equal to or greater than the requested number. The current time is also updated. If there are no errors, the *semid* is returned.

The *semctl* kernel routine is similar to the other—*ctl* routines, in that it also uses a *switch-case* statement that switches on the command *(cmd)* value. The routine handles the following cases:

1. IPC_RMID —Remove semaphore array (set).
2. IPC_SET   —Set ownership and permissions.
3. IPC_STAT   —Get semaphore data structures.
4. GETCNT   —Get number of processes sleeping for greater *semval*.
5. GETPID   —Get process ID of last process to operate on semaphore.
6. GETVAL   —Get *semval* of one semaphore.
7. GETALL   —Get all semvals in an array (or set).
8. GETZCNT   —Get number of processes sleeping on semval becoming zero.
9. SETVAL   —Set semval of specified semaphore.
10. SETALL   —Set semvals of all semaphores in a set.
11. default   —User Error (EINVAL).

The *semop* kernel routine services the *semop* system call. The arguments to the *semop* call include *semid* (semaphore id), *sops* (a pointer to an array of structures where each structure describes an operation and consists of the *semaphore number, semaphore operation,* and *operation flags*), and *nsops* (the number of structures in the *sops* array). The *semconv* routine is called to convert the *semid* to a pointer to the semaphore data structure. It makes sure that the total number of *sops* structures does not exceed the system limit. It also verifies that the semaphore numbers are in the correct range for this semaphore array, and that the permissions are granted. The loop starts at this point. A close scrutiny of Figure 3-54 is important for understanding the algorithm for the semaphore operations handling. The value *sem_op* is the calculated value of the semaphore operation and *semval* is the value of the semaphore.

```
semop:
arguments: None
Inputs:     semid (semaphore array ID)
        Pointer to structure of sops
        nsops—Total number of sops structures

    Convert semid to pointer to semaphore data structure
    If # of sops greater than system limit, return error
    If permissions not okay for any sops operation, return
    If semaphore count not in range for array, return error

Loop: (first time)
    If semid (semaphore data structure) invalid (semaphore removed)
        return error
    Copy user operation list

    (for loop for each sops structure)
for (each structure)

    if sem_op is positive,
        Add sem_op to semval
```

If new semval is greater than system limit OR
If SEM_UNDO flag set & *update* set on exit,
    Set user error
    If not first operation, call *semundo,* undo operations
Wakeup processes waiting for increased *semaphore value*

if *sem_op* is negative,
    If *sem_op* less than *semval* (*new semval* will be positive)
    Add *sem_op* to *semval*
    If new semval is greater than system limit OR
    If SEM_UNDO flag set & *update* set on exit,
        Set user error
        If not first operation, call *semundo,* undo operations

    If *sem_op* = *semval* (i.e., new *semval* = 0)
    Wakeup processes waiting for zero *semaphore value*
        Continue

    If not first process,
        If SEM_UNDO flag set & *update* set on exit,
            Set user error
            If not first operation, call *semundo,* undo operations
        If IPC_NOWAIT flag set, (cannot sleep), return user error
        else sleep on event of increased *semval*
        Goto Loop.

if *sem_op* is 0
    If *semval* is 0
        Call *semundo* and reverse all actions
        If IPC_NOWAIT flag set, (cannot sleep), return user error
    else sleep on event of *semval* = 0
    Goto Loop

End of Loop: (all operations succeeded)
    Update all *sempids* for accessed semaphores

Figure 3-54.   Algorithm for *semop* Routine

The operations specified in the *sops* structures are performed sequentially, one at a time (atomically). However, it is required that the complete set be performed in one pass without *sleeping*. If all operations cannot be completed in one pass, the *semundo* routine is called to revert the effect of all operations performed on the semaphore values in this try. The main loop is a *for* loop ranging from *0* to *nsops* (the total number of *sops*). The loop tests three main conditions based on the calculated value of the semaphore operation. These three conditions are,

1. sem_op > 0 (calculated value is positive).
2. sem_op < 0 (calculated value is negative).
3. sem_op = 0.

Further processing is based on testing the new value of the semaphore after adding the calculated value of the semaphore operation. Depending on the SEM_UNDO flag, the processes waiting for the change that occurred in the semaphore value are issued a *wakeup*. These processes include some that are sleeping on the semaphore value becoming greater and some that are sleeping on the semaphore value becoming zero.

Another important point to note here is the operation of the *semundo* routine. It is essentially a cleanup routine that has to do a lot of backtracking. To perform this backtracking, it requires a database of actions performed on the semaphores up to that point in the *semop* call. The structures it uses are called *undo headers* (or *undo data structures*). There is one *undo data structure* per process in the *undo table*. The *semaoe* routine builds the undo structures. The undo data structure includes the following components:

1. Pointer to next undo data structure entry.
2. Pointer to start of undo structure array.
3. Total number of undo structures in the array.

Figure 3-55 describes the architecture of the *undo structure arrays*. The undo structures consist of the following three components:

1. Semaphore ID *(semid)*.
2. Semaphore number.
3. Adjustment on exit value.

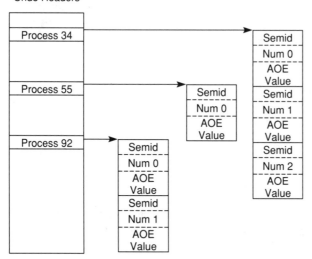

Undo Headers

Figure 3-55. Semaphore Undo Structure Architecture

The SEM_UNDO flag provides a safeguard against potential locking of processes due to actions of other processes that no longer exist. This architecture allows the kernel to call the *semexit* routine to clean up semaphore actions that a process left on the undo structures before *exiting*. The *adjustment on exit* value is a running adjusted value of *semval* as updated by *semaoe* routine for every calculated *sem_op* value for that semaphore. Whenever the adjusted value becomes zero (i.e., the final semaphore value is equal to its value before the start of this try), the undo structure is freed.

3.5.5 Signals

While pipes, shared memory, and message queues provide a means of communicating data across processes, semaphores, signals and sleep/wakeup calls are used to trigger certain actions by other processes. Signals are used to convey to another process the occurrence of an event that is asynchronous, or to convey to another process the need to take a certain action. A signal is communicated via the signal field in the *proc structure* (process table entry). A signal usually has a delayed reaction because it is not checked *(caught)* until the process receiving the signal is ready to switch from kernel mode to user mode.

Some common examples for the use of signals include process termination (process *exits* or death of a child process); continuing a stopped process; using the clock as an alarm; signals caused by unexpected errors during system calls (e.g. bad arguments or bad dispatch table entry number, and writing a pipe that has no processes reading it).

The operation of signals is described in detail in Section 3.4.6 and a review of that section is encouraged for a better understanding of the implementation of signals.

3.5.6 Sleep & Wakeup Calls

The *sleep* and *wakeup* call mechanism is an excellent means for conserving CPU resources and for making the most effective use of process scheduling. Any process that cannot proceed further due to unavailability of a resource or due to synchronization with another process, voluntarily relinquishes the CPU and *sleeps* in memory on an event. It may get swapped out while sleeping. When the event takes place, the process enters a *ready-to-run* state swapped or in memory, and is made eligible to be scheduled at the next normal scheduling sequence.

An example of the usage of the *wakeup* call is provided a few pages back in the algorithm in Figure 3-54. We notice that the process issues a *wakeup* call to all processes *sleep*ing on the event that the semaphore value increases. The processes that were sleeping on this event receive information that the event they anticipated has happened. Other examples of *sleep* and *wakeup* calls are a process sleeping on the event of a buffer becoming available for a disk block or a disk block in use becoming available for a write. Similarly, a process can sleep on the event of a device in use by another process becoming available.

Section 3.4.6 describes the *sleep* and *wakeup* routines in detail and the reader is encouraged to refer to that section for a better understanding of the implementation of these calls.

3.5.7 Summary

In this section we looked at the six different means for interprocess communications. We learned that unnamed or named pipes, shared memory, and message queues communicate data. Semaphores, signals, and the sleep/wakeup mechanisms, on the

other hand, are designed for specific kinds of process coordination and synchronization. It is interesting to note the similarity in the architectures of shared memory,
message queues, and semaphore mechanisms.

3.5.8 Exercises

1. Describe the different mechanisms for interprocess communication in the UNIX
   operating system.
2. Can two processes use the same named pipe for exchanging data? Explain.
3. Under what conditions would you use a signal? How does this differ from the use
   of a semaphore?
4. Explain the operation of shared memory. How does this differ from message
   queues?
5. What is the undo structure used for? Why is this function required?

3.6 FILE SYSTEM

The file system is one of the major subsystems of the operating system. It is responsible for storing information on disk drives and retrieving and updating this information
as directed by the user or by a program. The file system is accessed by the user or an
application through system calls such as *open, creat, read, write, link,* and *unlink*
files. Commands such as *cd* (to change from one directory to another directory), *cp*
(copy files), and *mv* (move files) are built from the basic system calls.

3.6.1 File System Definitions

A physical disk unit can consist of several logical sections or partitions. Each section
of the disk may contain a logical file system consisting of a boot block, a superblock,
inode list, and data blocks. Each section of the disk has a device file name. The disk
driver is designed to handle multiple partitions.

   The UNIX system has the following types of files:

1. Ordinary files.
2. Directory files.
3. Special files (devices).
4. FIFO files for pipes.

   Ordinary files are files that contain information entered into them by a user, an
application program, or a system utility program. The UNIX system treats ordinary
files as a sequence of bytes, called byte-streams. An ordinary file can contain *text*
information as a string of characters (bytes) or *binary* information as a sequence of
words. The UNIX kernel imposes no format or structure to the internal sequencing of
the bytes or words in a file.

   Directory files manage the cataloging of the file system. Directories associate
names with groups of files that typically reflect the structure of the user's application.

Directories may be created for each user, or for each project. A user's directory may be created as a *sub-directory* under a project directory. Further levels of sub-directories may be created, e.g. for source files, data files, and program files. Directory files are ordinary files with special write protection privileges such that only the system can write into them, while read access is available to users under normal access control.

    Special files are used to access peripheral devices. Each I/O device is associated with a special file. Please refer to Section 3.7 for a detailed description of how special files are used for Input/Output Management.

    Files used by *pipes* are also special due to the first-in-first-out (FIFO) nature of these files. Please refer to Section 3.5.1 for a detailed description of how these files are used.

3.6.2 Directory Structure

The UNIX system features a multi-level hierarchical directory structure set up as an inverted tree with a single root node. Called *root,* this node is referred to as "/". The */usr* directory is the primary directory for user programs and data. Users can create further levels of directories under it to catalog their groups of files.

    On system initialization, only the *root device,* the device that contains the root directory "/", is known to the system. This name is built into the system. Other storage devices or file systems are attached by *mounting* them under the *root,* or under the *current* directory, or under any directory that is currently known to the system. The *mount* operation causes access to always take the new branch that is attached. The original branch is not accessible for the duration of the mount.

    A directory cannot be split across two file systems. All disk drives that are a part

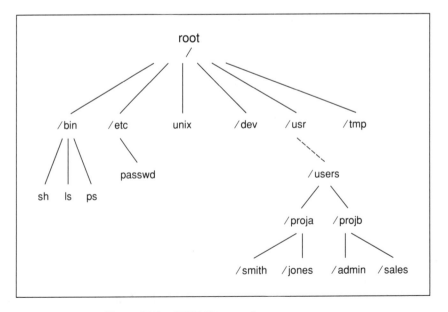

Figure 3-56. UNIX Directory Structure

of a file system must be on-line while that file system is in use. As such, all files associated with any directory that is accessible are available on-line.

Every directory is created with two file entries. One entry, called "..", refers to the directory one level above, commonly called the *parent* directory. The other entry, called "." refers to itself. A parent directory has an entry pointing to the sub-directory thereby maintaining the integrity of the tree structure. There are no other references to sub-directories. This ensures that there are no breaks in the tree traversal (i.e., there are no loose links that are inaccessible), and that the file access paths are always predictable through the directory hierarchy.

3.6.2.1 File Links

While directories are restricted to single references, files are not. The same file can appear in several directories and may be referred to by the same or different names. A directory entry for a file consists of the filename and a pointer to a data structure called an *inode* that describes the disk addresses for the file data segments. Since the file itself does not 'reside' in a directory, or 'belong' to a directory, the association between a directory and a file is generally called a *link*. A file may be linked to a number of directories. An important feature of the UNIX system is that all links have equal status. Access control and write privileges are a function of the file itself and have no direct connection with the directory. But a directory has its own access control and the user has to satisfy the directory access control first, and then the file access control to read, write into, or execute a file.

The concept of 'deleting' a file is called *unlinking* in the UNIX system. 'Deletion' from a directory results in the removal of the entry (*unlinking*) for that file in the directory. The file is inaccessible after the last link is removed and its inode is added to the free list. The disk space used by the file is reclaimed for use.

3.6.2.2 File Access Controls and Permissions

Access to all files and directories in the UNIX system is controlled by *permissions*. Permissions are checked, whether file access is called through a command entered at the shell level, or through a program. Permissions are defined for *read, write,* and *execute* access. Permissions are granted at three levels, *owner, group,* and *other.* Permissions are checked internally in the system on the basis of the *effective user id.* The routines *geteuid* and *setuid* are used for finding the effective user id and also for setting it to another number.

3.6.3 Inodes and File Identification

Each file has an *inode* structure that is identified by an *i-number*. The inode contains the information required to access the file. This information includes the following:

1. File type and mode (ordinary, directory, special, etc.).
2. Number of links to the file.
3. Owner's user ID.

4. Owner's group ID.

5. File access permissions.

6. File size in bytes.

7. 3-byte address of up to 13 disk blocks.

8. Time and date of last access (as time offsets).

9. Time and date of last creation (as time offsets).

10. Creation time and date (as time offsets).

Depending on the implementation, there may be 8 or 16 inode structures per disk block. The disk block addressing scheme is also implementation dependent and is described in the following section under physical file organization in greater detail. The disk block addresses provide an index to all disk blocks used for the file data.

The disk inode described above contains information about a file and may change if this information changes, even if the file itself is not modified. For example, changing owner's ID, access permissions, or the number of links. Any change to the file also requires changing the inode due to the file size and access time parameters. These are changed in the inode when the file is written back.

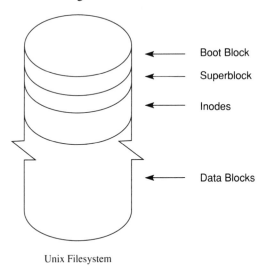

Boot Block

Superblock

Inodes

Data Blocks

Unix Filesystem

Figure 3-57. UNIX File System Organization

Figure 3-58 provides an overview of the data structures used for file system management. Let us now look at the manipulation of these structures by the kernel.

Every file in use has two other structures associated with it. These are the *file structure* and the *in-core inode*. A *file structure*, an entry in the *file table*, is set up for every open or create of a file. A file may have more than one file structure associated with it. The *in-core inode* contains all information located in the *disk inode*. In addition, it includes the following:

1. Inode access status flags
   a. Inode is locked (modification in progress)
   b. A process is waiting for inode to become unlocked

    c. The *file information* in the in-core inode is modified, i.e., it may differ from the disk inode

    d. *File contents* changed, in-core inode modified, i.e., both may differ from the disk inode

    e. The file is a *mount*'ble device.

2. Reference count acquired from file table entries.

3. Device ID where disk inode resides.

4. Disk address for file pointer.

5. Last logical block read (file position).

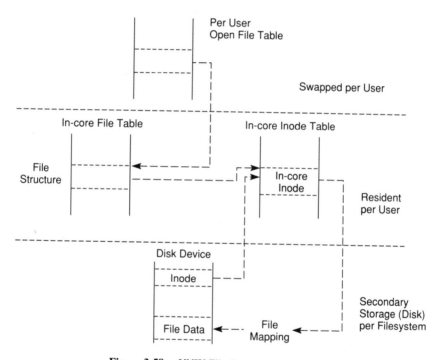

Figure 3-58.   UNIX File System Data Structures

    The inode *lock* is used to prevent two processes from attempting to modify a file or its inode at the same time. The *process waiting* flag is the equivalent of a 'call back' so that when the inode is unlocked, the process waiting is informed.

    The *in-core inode* entry is created by reading the disk inode into memory and entering it into the *in-core inode* table. The maximum number of entries into this table is a system configuration parameter and defines the maximum number of unique files that can be open at one time. There is only one in-code inode per file regardless of the number of references to that file. The reference count variable is used to keep track of file references. The inode remains active until the reference count winds down to zero.

    When the reference count winds down to zero, the in-core inode is returned to the *free inode list*. The disk inode is updated whenever file information changes or the file is modified and is written back. If only file information changes take place, the in-core inode modification flags are used to determine if the disk inode should be updated.

3.6.3.1 Inode Free List

Depending on the implementation, disk blocks are 512 bytes or 1K bytes (AT&T UNIX System V), or 4K bytes (Berkeley UNIX 4.2bsd). The number of inodes per block varies from one implementation to another. The total number of inodes is a configuration parameter determined at the time the file system is created. An inode is of the order of 64 bytes in length for UNIX System V. The total number of blocks required to hold all inodes is calculated and the disk blocks are allocated as contiguous blocks. The inodes can, therefore, be accessed as fixed length records in a sequential data space. The relative position of the inode in this data space is its *inode number*. The list of free inodes, as well as the size of the inodes, is maintained in the *superblock*. The superblock also has the index number of the next free inode in the free inode list.

There is no list maintained for active inodes. The system assumes that any inode not on the free list is in use. The active inodes are accessed through the directory structure which associates a filename with an inode number.

3.6.3.2 File Identification

The initial access to a file is by its pathname, usually by system calls like *open* and *link*. The start of the pathname is either the current directory, the root, or any other specified directory, as follows:

```
/usr/projectA/filename
../projectB/filename
filename
./filename
```

The kernel does a linear search of the directory file and locates the inode of the sub-directory. It then searches the directory file of the sub-directory and locates the inode of the filename or of the next level of sub-directory as the case may be. Section 3.6.6 describes the details of the algorithms and the use of the inodes.

3.6.4 File System Integrity and Security

File system integrity is a crucial issue in a system where a number of users may access the same file and may potentially update the same record (a string of bytes at a given offset) at the same time. Only one of the updates may actually take place. File system security is equally important in a shared file system to ensure that only authorized users can access data in the file system. The UNIX system has a number of tools and facilities for providing users the means to build a system with a high level of integrity, and a system that is reasonably secure for most applications. Security of file system data is an important component of an overall security plan.

3.6.4.1 File System Record and File Locking

File system record locking and file locking features existed in Berkeley implementations before they were added as an enhancement with file system hardening in AT&T UNIX System V.2 release. In UNIX System V.2 and up, the following four types of locks are available:

1. Advisory Cooperative—Informs user process of lock status but does not deny access to locked data.
2. Mandatory—Access is denied to non-cooperative processes if data record is locked.
3. Exclusive Write—Record is locked for exclusive writes (no reads are permitted).
4. Shared Reads—Only shared reads are permitted (no writes are permitted).

Other schemes have been used for other implementations of UNIX. The key features of the AT&T UNIX scheme are described here since it appears to be the most comprehensive and the most flexible.

3.6.4.2 File and Directory Security

The UNIX system file system security is built around a file permission scheme that provides access at the *user, group,* and *other* (any logged-in user commonly called **world**) classes with *read, write,* and *execute* permissions for each class. Typically, the *user* is the owner, and has all three types of permissions; while group and other have *read* and *execute* permissions. Group and other can also have write permission. Read permission is required for displaying or copying the contents of the file.

Access to a directory requires permissions to the directory. Access to read or execute a file requires appropriate read or execute permissions for that file. The file access permissions are checked on every file open, read, write, or execute operation (checked by the *namei* routine). Write permission is generally retained by the owner. The permissions are specified in a permissions parameter in the disk inode. This parameter is copied into the in-core inode for that file when the file is opened. The algorithms for file and directory access described later in this section provide some insight at the levels in the kernel where permissions are checked.

The *umask* variable can be set as the default level of permissions for all files created on the system. By setting the *umask* value at a preferred secure level that restricts global read or execute access to files and provides only for group access to read or execute files, a level of security adequate for most applications can be achieved.

3.6.4.3 File Data Encryption

Most UNIX implementations provide the capability to encrypt data stored in files for security. While not adequate for most secure defense system requirements, encryption provides good security for most business uses.

3.6.5 Physical Organization of the File System

The physical organization of the file system has changed with every major release of the UNIX system. These changes include disk block sizes, disk block addressing algorithms, and inode organization. While Berkeley UNIX 4.2bsd uses 4K byte blocks, AT&T UNIX System V uses 1K byte blocks. Earlier implementations used 512 byte blocks. The following discussion is based generally on the AT&T UNIX System V implementation and key differences for other implementations are pointed out.

3.6.5.1 Logical Addressing

The file system in UNIX is built as a logical disk. A physical disk unit may consist of several logical disk sections where each is set up as a file system. These may be brought under a common hierarchy, as shown in Figure 3-59, by executing the *mount* system call. A logical disk may be viewed as a one dimensional array of blocks. However, only the key parts of the logical disk allocated at the time of creation of the file system are set up as contiguous blocks on the physical disk. The rest of the logical disk blocks are allocated as needed. The physical disk does not provide a physically contiguous file system. The logical disk file size is essentially used to define the upper limit of the size of the logical disk. The physical disk may be used up before this logical upper limit is reached and restrict the actual size of the logical disk.

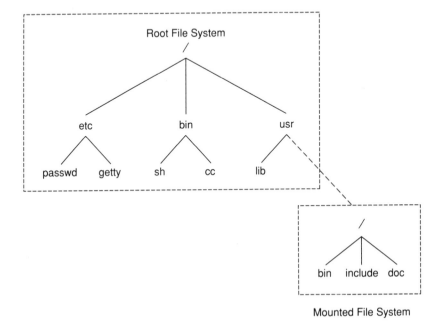

Figure 3-59. UNIX Mounted File System Organization

A logical disk is divided into the following four sections (Figure 3-57):

- Block 0   —Boot block.
- Block 1   —Superblock.
- Block 2 − m   —Inodes.
- Block (m + 1) to n —File space.

The boot block generally contains a program that loads the UNIX kernel from the file system, and transfers control to the start address of the kernel. If the system is already running, and the disk is being accessed for a *mount,* the boot block is ignored.

The superblock contains all of the information that defines the current state of the file system. This information is listed in Figure 3-60.

- Size in blocks of i-list (inode list)
- Size in blocks of the file system
- Number of free blocks in the file system
- A list of the free blocks available on the file system
- The free inodes list
- Inode lock flags
- Flag to indicate that the superblock has been modified
- Flag to indicate that the file system has been mounted for *read-only*
- Time and date of the last superblock update (time offset)
- Total free blocks in the file system
- Total free inodes in the file system
- File system name
- File system disk name

Figure 3-60.   Partial List of Contents in the Superblock Structure

As we noted earlier, the total number of inodes in the file system is a configurable parameter. The inodes are set up to start at block 2 and the required number of contiguous blocks are assigned, up to block *m* as described above. For example, if there are 16 inodes per disk block, and the file system is defined to have 64,000 files, the inodes use up 4,000 disk blocks. This size changes with different implementations of UNIX. The implementation of Berkeley UNIX 4.2 bsd is very different and the inodes in that implementation are distributed across cylinders of the disk for access optimization.

Figure 3-61 shows the evolution of disk block addressing as the UNIX system adapted to larger disk files and larger file systems. The concept of indirect addresses is the mechanism adopted to deal with large files.

AT&T Level 6 UNIX:
   Small Files: 8 direct blocks
   Large Files: 7 Indirect Blocks,
      8Th. Block is double indirect block

AT&T Level 7 UNIX: 512 byte blocks
   13 disk block addresses:
      10 Direct Blocks
      1 Indirect Block
      1 Double Indirect Block
      1 Triple Indirect Block

AT&T UNIX System V: 1K byte blocks
   Same addressing scheme as AT&T Level 7 UNIX

Berkeley UNIX 4.1bsd: 1K byte blocks
   Same addressing scheme as AT&T Level 7 UNIX

Berkeley UNIX 4.2bsd: 4K byte blocks
   Inodes are distributed on cylinders for faster seeks.

Figure 3-61. UNIX Implementation Differences

3.6.5.2 Disk Block Address Translation

As we just noted, the concept of indirect block addresses was developed to address the need for accessing large files while retaining fast access for small files. Figure 3-62 describes the concept as applied to AT&T System V (i.e., use of 13 disk address blocks).

File access for small files is very rapid due to a lower number of disk accesses to read the direct address blocks only. As the file increases in size, the number of disk accesses increase disproportionately due to the indirect blocks. This increase is much more noticeable in very large files that get in the range of double and triple indirect addressing. The following chart describes the addressing capability of this scheme for an implementation that provides 128 addresses in each indirect block.

Direct Blocks	10	=	10
Indirect Blocks	n	=	128
Double Indirect Blocks	n**2	=	16,384
Triple Indirect Blocks	n**3	=	2,097,152
TOTAL BLOCKS		=	2,113,674

A significant advantage of this scheme is that very large files can be created. For example, if the number of addresses per block (n) is 128, the files can have over 2 million blocks. For AT&T UNIX System V, the value of n is 256 and over 16 million

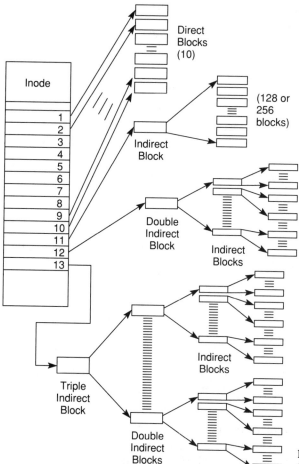

Figure 3-62. UNIX Block Addressing Scheme

blocks become addressable. However, the use of 32-bit byte addresses limits the maximum file size to 4 million blocks, or to 4 gigabytes.

3.6.5.3 Logical to Physical Address Translation

The logical byte or word address in the file is first converted to a logical block number in the file. Since UNIX files are constructed as a sequential array of bytes or words, the logical block address number is equal to *byte address/block size + an offset* (or *word address/block size in words + word aligned byte address*) in the next block. The inode provides the logical block address in the file system as the *logical block address + an offset*. This may require the use of levels of indirect blocks as described above. The logical block number on the logical disk of the file system is then mapped to the physical disk address. The *bmap* routine provides the mapping to the physical disk. Figure 3-63 illustrates the address translation process.

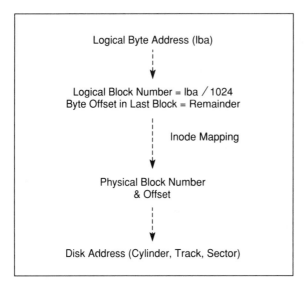

Figure 3-63. Logical to Physical Address Translation

3.6.6 File Access and Control Routines

A number of routines are used to create files, allocate inodes and disk space, and to control access to files. The key routines are listed below.

1. NAMEI —Translate filenames to inodes.
2. IGET   —Allocate and access inode table entries.
3. ALLOC —Allocate and free disk blocks and inodes.
4. FIO   —Routines to manipulate file table structures.
5. SYS2   —System call interface routines.

3.6.6.1 The *Namei* Routine

The *namei* routine is called via the kernel routine for a system call whenever a file is accessed by system calls like *mkdir, open, creat, rm, exec,* etc. Each of these calls requires the creation or unlinking of a file or directory, or requires the creation of an in-core inode. The *namei* routine parses the pathname specification and locates the inode of the target directory.

The *user structure* has elements that specify the root directory as well as the current directory for the process. The pathname may start at the root or at the current directory, and may include a number of intermediate directory specifiers. For example,

/usr/projectA/source/fortran/filename
../projectB/filename
/usr/projectB/filename

```
namei:
input: pathname specifier

    Call iget for first pathname segment
        Get inode as current inode

Loop:
    If pathname has more directories
        Read next pathname segment
            If inode does not exist
            else if it is not a directory
            else if user does not have access permissions
                Return error
            else
                Locate inode as current inode
            Read directory
            If match found
                Get new inode number
                Release current inode
                Make new inode current inode
                If mount flag set in inode
                    Get mount structure pointer to mount table
                    Get inode number of new root directory
                    Release current inode (iput)
                    Make mounted system inode current inode
                    Lock inode
                    Increment reference count on it
                Goto loop

    else
            Return—no match
    else
            Return inode
```

Figure 3-64.   Algorithm for *namei* Routine

The *namei* routine executes a loop for each directory specifier segment in the pathname. The main loop of the namei routine consists of the following operations:

1. Check to see if the inode exists.
2. Confirm that the inode is for a directory.
3. Check permissions to see if search access is available to the user.
4. Store directory entry in pathname field in user structure.

This process is carried out as long as *namei* succeeds in finding a match. The *namei* routine calls the *iget* routine to locate inodes. Every time an inode is located, it is locked only for the duration of the matching process. The final inode for the last directory is locked and returned as the current inode. Figure 3-64 on the previous page describes the algorithm for the *namei* routine.

3.6.6.2 The *Iget* and *Iput* Routines

The routine *iget*, described in Figure 3-65, reads in a disk inode and sets up an in-core inode. Since a file can have only one in-core inode at any time, the routine first checks to see if the inode is already in memory. If the inode does exist and it is locked, *iget*

```
iget:
input: Name of disk where inode resides
       Inode number

Loop:
            Is inode in in-core inode pool
                If yes, is it locked
                    If yes, sleep (until it unlocks—event)
                    Goto loop
                else
                    Increment reference count
                    Return inode
            else
                Look for free inode
                    If none free
                    return error (exceeded limit)
                Remove from free inode list
                Set inode number
                Move inode to new hash queue
                Copy disk inode
                Set reference count to 1
                Return inode
```

Figure 3-65. Algorithm for *iget* Routine

sleeps on the event of the inode becoming unlocked. If the inode exists and is unlocked, or unlocks due to an event, the inode is locked, the reference count in the inode is incremented, and a locked inode is returned. If there is no inode in the in-core inode pool, a new inode is removed from the free list and the inode number is reset to the new number. The inode is removed from the old hash queue and placed on the new one, and the disk inode is copied into it. The reference count of the in-core inode is set to *1* and a locked inode is returned.

The kernel maintains a free list for inodes which have been released (i.e., the reference count is zero), on an expectation that there may be a reference to the same inode soon if there are any links to the file. The *iget* routine always checks the free list to see if the inode is already in the in-core inode pool. If it finds the inode, the routine locks the inode, increments the reference count in it, and attaches it to the new hash queue.

The *iput* routine, described in Figure 3-66, is the counterpart to *iget* and releases inodes when a file is unlinked (i.e. closed). It requires a pointer to the in-core inode. The inode is locked before entry to this routine, and remains locked until the procedure of releasing the inode is completed. The reference count is decremented. If the reference count drops to zero then the routine checks if there are any links left. If there are no more links left, then the disk space is set free, the file type is set to null, and the inode is set free (equivalent of a file being deleted). If the link count is positive, the disk inode is updated, and since there are no more references and therefore no process is using the file any more, the inode is placed on the free list. The inode is then unlocked and is available for reuse.

```
iput:
input: Pointer to in-core inode

    If reference count == 1 (last reference being removed)
        Lock inode
        If inode link count <= 0
            Free disk blocks
            Set file mode to 0
            Set flag to update/change
            Free inode (ifree)
        If accessed, updated, or changed
            Update disk inode (iupdat)
        Release inode
        Move inode to free list and reset pointers
        Re-initialize flag, number, and count
        Return
    Else, Decrement reference count
    Release inode
```

Figure 3-66.   Algorithm for *iput* Routine

3.6.6.3 The Alloc and Free Routines

The *alloc* routine, described in Figure 3-67, is used to get the next available free disk block from the free list for the specified file system. The superblock maintains a partially chained list of free blocks available in the file system. It keeps track of one small pool of these free blocks. The last free block of this pool points to another batch of free blocks. When the superblock runs out of free blocks in its available list in the pool, it goes out and gets the addresses of another full batch and refills its pool. This approach optimizes free disk block search time.

```
alloc:
input:
    Call getfs
        Map device # into pointer to in-core superblock
            (performs linear search through mount table)
        Check consistency of in-core free blocks and inode counts

    While superblock locked,
        Sleep (wakeup on unlock)

    If no more blocks
        Return error to user

    If this is the last block on free list
        Lock superblock
        Call bread to read the last block
        Copy batch of new free block addresses to superblock
        Call brelse to release block buffer
        Unlock superblock
        Call wakeup on superblock unlocked event

    If block count is in error
        Return error to user

    else: (Free block found)
        Call getblk, get buffer for block removed from superblock free list
        Clear buffer
        Decrement superblock free list count
        Mark superblock modified
        Return buffer
```

Figure 3-67.   Algorithm for *alloc* Routine

The *free* routine is a counterpart to the *alloc* routine, in that it places specified disk blocks back on the free list pool of the specified disk or file system. It also starts by calling *getfs* to map the device number into a pointer to the in-core superblock. The routine sleeps if the superblock is locked. If the block number is entered as the last entry in the free list pool, then the pool is reset for future use. The addresses of this batch of disk blocks in the pool are entered as a list in the last block pointed to by the pool to form the address chain, and the free list pool is reinitialized. If it is not the last entry, it just marks the block number in the pool and returns.

3.6.6.4 Organization of Free Lists

Each mounted file system has a free list, as depicted in Figure 3-68, in its superblock. The superblock is read into memory during execution of the *mount* system call. The free list contains up to 50 (this number is implementation dependent) block numbers of free blocks (NCFREE). The remaining free blocks are chained together as groups.

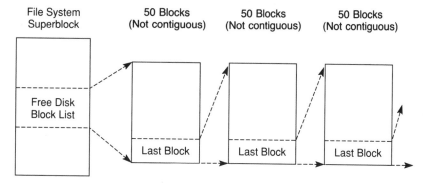

Figure 3-68.   Structure of Free Lists

3.6.6.5 The *Ialloc, Ifree,* and *Update* Routines

The *ialloc* routine, described in Figure 3-69, allocates an unused inode on the specified disk or device. Creating a new file requires allocation of an inode. The superblock keeps a list of free inodes. A free inode is allocated from this list. If this list is exhausted, the routine does an inventory of the inodes if it determines that there should still be free inodes. The total number of free inodes is a file system parameter and is maintained as a variable in the superblock.

A loop is used to go through and locate a free list. If an inode is found, it returns without going around the loop. If not, it sets up the loop to find unused inodes to fill up the superblock free list. This approach has some interesting performance implications. By batching up general searches through the inode blocks on disk, the system attempts to optimize performance.

The *ifree* routine is used to free the specified inode on a specified device or disk. Inputs to this routine are the file system disk name and the inode number to be released. The inode number is stored in the superblock free inode chain. If the superblock is locked, it increments the file system free inode count and returns. Otherwise, it checks to see if the inode list is full. If not, it stores the inode number in the inode free list and returns. If full, it checks to see if the inode number being released is less than the first inode number in the free list. If so, it sets the first inode number in the list to the inode

```
ialloc:
inputs: file system
        mode
        number of links

        Call getfs to map device number in a pointer to in-core superblock

    Loop:
        While superblock is locked
            Sleep (until unlocked—event)
        If inode free list in superblock is not empty
            Call iget to get inode
                If none found, return null (no inode)
            If inode found is really empty
                Set it up
                Write inode to disk
                Decrement free inode count in superblock
                Return
            else:
                call iput to release inode
                Goto loop
        else:
            Lock superblock
            Get inode number from superblock inode list
            Call bread and brelse to fill up superblock inode free list
            Unlock superblock
            Wakeup processes (superblock unlocked)
            If inode found
                Goto loop
            else:
                return null (no inode)
```

Figure 3-69. Algorithm for *ialloc* Routine

number being released. If, on the other hand, that number is higher than the first inode number, it does not change the free list.

The *update* routine is called whenever a *sync* is issued, that is, when the disk is updated. The sync is issued periodically to flush (i.e. write to disk) all tables and buffers that have been modified since the last sync. All superblocks that have been modified and that have the disk block free list and the inode free list unlocked, are written back provided they were not mounted for *read only*. It also writes out all inodes to disk that have been accessed, modified, or created, provided they are unlocked at that time. Periodic syncs reduce the likelihood of system corruption in case of power failure, and also keep the disk and memory versions consistent for normal operations.

3.6.6.6 FIO Routines for File I/O

The key routines in this module are *closef, suser, ufalloc, getf, access, owner,* and *falloc.* The following functions are performed by these routines:

- *getf*   —Convert user supplied file descriptor into a pointer to a file structure and check if it is in range.
- *closef*   —Closes files (decrements reference counts).
- *access*   —Checks access permissions.
- *owner*   —Check if inode is owned by current user.
- *suser*   —Check if current user is superuser.
- *ufalloc* —Allocate user file descriptor.
- *falloc*   —Allocate user file descriptor and file structure.

The *closef* routine takes the pointer to the file structure (the file table entry) as a parameter. If the reference count on the file structure is greater than *1,* it decrements it and returns (the equivalent of closing a file for that user or process). If the reference count was *1,* decrementing it means that there are no more processes using that file anymore. The system needs to clean up and reclaim the file structure and the in-core inode space. The routine first locks the inode. It then sets the reference count to *0,* and moves the file structure to the free list. For files that are not special files, the *iput* routine is called to release the inode. The appropriate device close routine is called for character, block, and FIFO files. Further processing is done to flush the buffers, and to *umount* the device if appropriate. The *iput* routine is then called to release the inode.

The *access* routine is called with a pointer to the in-core inode (from *namei* routine) and the type of access requested (*read, write,* or *execute*). It calls *getfs* to get a pointer to the superblock for the file system. The access is denied if write access permission is requested for a file system *mounted* for *read only.* A superuser is always granted all permissions including write permissions, overriding the read-only restrictions of a mounted file system. For all other requests, the requested mode is checked against the available modes for that file. A user error is returned in the user structure if access is denied.

The *owner* routine calls *namei* to look up the pathname and to locate the inode. It returns an inode pointer if the current user is either the owner or a superuser. Otherwise, it releases the inode and returns null.

The *falloc* routine is called with the inode pointer and a flag as parameters. It scans the *open file table* in the user structure for a free user file descriptor. If there are no empty slots (i.e., the user has exceeded the limit on open files), an error is returned in the user structure. If successful, the file descriptor is allocated and it scans the file table for an available file structure. If none is found, it sets a flag for *system open file overflow* and returns an error in the user structure. If successful at both of these steps, the address of the file structure is stored in the file descriptor, and the reference count in the file structure is incremented. It returns the address of the file structure.

```
copen:
argument: none
input:    filename
          mode
          permissions

    If mode is neither FREAD nor FWRITE return user error
    If mode is CREAT
        Call namei to get inode for target directory
            If directory does not exist
                Set error in user structure
                Return
            else
            Set to end of directory
                Set it for truncation
            If O_EXCL mode set
                If file exists
                    Set error in user structure
                    Release inode
                    Return
                else
                Set for create
    else (mode must be OPEN)
        Call namei to get inode of directory
        If mode is for OPEN
            If mode is not for CREAT (is OPEN for FREAD)
                Check access permissions
            If mode is for FWRITE
                Check write access permissions
                Set user error if write is to directory
            If no error (open successful)
                Release inode
                Return
    If mode is for TRUNCate
        Call itrunc
        Release all file blocks
        Release inode
    If a half open
        Close file
    else
        Call openi to handle special files
        If open successful
        Allocate user file descriptor
        Allocate file structure
        Call iput to release inode
```

Figure 3-70.   Algorithm for *copen* Routine

3.6.6.7 System Call Interface Routines

The *open, creat, read, write,* and *close* system calls are serviced by routines in this module. It includes other routines to manage disk access. The *open* system call of the UNIX system creates as well as opens files. The *creat* system call maps to the equivalent of an open call with O_CREAT and O_TRUNC flags set, i.e. if the file does not exist, it is created, and if it exists it is truncated to zero length but the mode and owner are not changed. Even though there are two system calls for *creat* and *open* and there is a service routine for each, a common routine called *copen* is called by the two service routines and it handles file creation as well as file opens.

3.6.6.8 The *Copen* Routine

A file can be opened for read only (O_RDONLY), write only (O_WRONLY), read/write (O_RDWR), append (O_APPEND), and exclusive open (O_EXCL). The *copen* routine handles the conditions based on these flags. Figure 3-70 describes the algorithm of the *copen* routine.

The *copen* routine, described in Figure 3-70, is called with the filename as a parameter and mode and permissions as arguments. The routine first checks to ensure that the mode is set to either read or write. If the mode is CREAT, it calls *namei* with the filename as input to get an inode. If the directory does not exist for the CREAT mode, an error is returned in the user structure. If the directory exists and a file also exists in the specified name, the file is truncated to zero length. If the call is to CREAT with an O_EXCL flag, and the file exists, an error is returned in the user structure. If the open is for FREAD or FWRITE (i.e. not for CREAT), the access permissions are checked. The routine is also capable of cleaning up incomplete opens (*setjmp* call). If successful, it calls the *openi* routine to set up the file, allocate a user file descriptor, a file structure, and unlock the inode before returning.

Figure 3-71 shows an example of opening and closing a file.

```
/*   This program converts all text in a file to lower case and writes it out to an output
file. */

#include        <stdio.h>
#include        <ctype.h>
#include        <fcntl.h>

#define    USAGE     "usage: lc <filename>\n"

main(argc,agrv)
        int        argc;
        char       *argv[];
{
        int                fi;
        int                fo;
        char               *pattern;
```

```
        char              *tempname;
/* Make sure user supplied correct number of arguments. */
        if (argc != 2) {
                write(2, USAGE, sizeof USAGE-1);
                exit(1);
        }

/* Open input file. */
        fi = open(argv[1], )_RDONLY, 0);
        if (fi < 0) {
                perror(tempname);
                exit(1);
        }

/* Create temporary filename and open file to lowercase text. */
        pattern = "lcxxxxx";
        tempname = tmpnam(pattern);
        fo = open(tmpname, O_CREAT |O_WRONLY, 0);
        if (fo < 0) {
                perror(tmpname);
                exit(1);
        }

/* Read in each character from the file. */
/* If character is upper case, convert it to lower case. */
/* Write converted character to output file. */

        while (read(fi,&c, 1) > 0) {
                if (isupper(c)) c = tolower(c);
                write(fo,&c, 1);
        }

/* Close files on completion. */
        close(fi);
        close(fo);

/* Unlink (delete) original file and rename temporary file. */
        unlink(argv[1]);
        link(tempname,arg[v]);
        unlink(tempname);
}
```

Figure 3-71.   Example of File Open and Close

3.6.6.9 The *Link* Routine

This routine services the *link* system call. There is potential in this routine for a file being deleted while a link is in progress, and there is potential for deadly embraces since most of the work done is on an unlocked inode. The inode is modified first to reduce this impact. Another approach to reducing this impact is to allow only a superuser to *link* directories. There is an implied assumption that a superuser will be careful and would not set the system up for deadly embraces. The *mkdir* call was set up in later releases of UNIX to allow users to create directories without risk of deadly embraces.

The algorithm for the link routine is described in Figure 3-72. The *namei* routine is called to get the inode of the existing file. If the link limit is exceeded, an error is set in the user structure and the routine returns an error. Otherwise, the link count and access time parameters in the inode are updated. The *namei* routine is called again to get the inode of the directory under which the file is being created. If the filename is already in use, the inode is released and a user error is returned in the user structure. If not in use, a new entry including the filename and the inode of the existing file is created in the directory file for the linked filename. The inodes of the directory as well as the file are released. Whenever a user error is returned after the inode link count is incremented, the routine goes back to correct it before returning.

```
link:
arguments: none
input: existing filename pointer
        Link filename pointer

    Call namei to get inode of existing file
        If too many links
            Set error in user structure
            Release inode
            Return
    Update inode—link count, flags, time
    Check if new filename exists
        If yes
            Release inode of this file
            Set error in user structure
            Rewind link count on existing file
            Return
    Check if existing and link file are on different logical devices
        If yes
            Set error in user structure
            Decrement link count on existing file
            Return
        else
            Write directory entry
            Release inode
            Return
```

Figure 3-72.   Algorithm for *link* Routine

3.6.6.10 The *Close* Routine

The *close* routine services the close system call and calls the *closef* routine to decrement the reference count in the file descriptor and the file structure. The file is unlinked for that user (or process). Special processing is required for special files (devices) on the last close.

```
rdwr:
arguments:
inputs: mode
    pointer to file descriptor
    pointer to inode
    address of buffer in user process
    number of bytes to be read

    Call getf to locate file structure from file descriptor
        If none found,
            Return
        If flags and modes incorrect for this read or write
            Set error in user structure
            Return
    Set count, segment flag, and base address in user structure
    Get inode
    If it is a regular (ordinary) or directory file
        Lock inode
        If mode is APPEND or FWRITE
            Set offset equal to size of file
        else
        If FIFO file
            Lock inode
            Set offset to 0
        else
            Offset is set to current file offset (default)
    If mode is FREAD call readi
    If mode is FWRITE call write
    For regular (ordinary), directory and FIFO files
        Unlock inode
        Update file table offset for next read
    Update user structure for byte offset in file
    Release buffer
    Return
```

Figure 3-73. Algorithm for *rdwr* Routine

3.6.6.11 The *Rdwr* Routine

The *rdwr* routine, described in Figure 3-73, services file *reads* and file *writes*. The mode flag set to FREAD or FWRITE is used for conditional execution of code. Most of the processing is essentially the same for a read or a write operation.

The routine first calls *getf* to get the file structure from the pointer in the file descriptor. It then checks the permissions to see if it is a valid file descriptor for a read or write operation. If it is not, a user error is returned. If valid, the user structure is set up for user address, byte count, segment flags, and file mode flags. The inode number is obtained from the file structure and the inode is locked if the file is a regular (ordinary) or a directory file. If the mode is to *write* or *append*, then the file offset is set to file size, that is, it points to end of file. Otherwise, if a FIFO file, the inode is locked and the file offset is set to *0*. The *readi* or *writei* routine is called depending on the system call.

```
readi:
argument: Pointer to Inode

    Check that the byte count is > 0
        If not, return error
    Check that byte offset is not negative
        If so, return error
    Switch on Type of file
    If character device
        Use major and minor device numbers
        If TTY device
            Read lines
        Else
            Read it as a special file
        break
    If FIFO file
        If file size is 0, return
        If file mode is no delay read, return
        Else
            Set offset in user structure to file read pointer in inode
    If block device, regular file, or directory
        Call bmap and bread to read file
        Move data to user process
    Default
        Set error in user structure
        Return
```

Figure 3-74. Algorithm for *readi* Routine

3.6.6.12 The *Readi* and *Writei* Routines

The *readi* and *writei* routines perform the actual read and write operation that is set up by the *rdwr* routine. The type of file—block device, character device, directory, regular (ordinary), or FIFO is used as the switch for the case statement. The read or write processing varies with the type of the file. These routines are described in Figures 3-74 and 3-75.

```
writei:
argument: Pointer to Inode

    Check that byte offset is not negative
        If so, return error
    Switch on Type of file
      Case: character device
        Use major and minor device numbers
        If TTY device
            Use line write routine
        else, Use character device write routine
      else, break;
      Case: FIFO file
       FIFOloop:
        While File Size+ #of bytes to write > PIPSIZ
            If pipe closed, break;
            If # of bytes > PIPSIZ
                write in space available
            If mode is NO DELAY, return;
        If pipe is closed
            signal all processes sleeping on write to pipe, break;
      Case block device, regular file, or directory
        While no user error and byte count positive
                Call bmap to translate byte offset to disk blocks
                Call getblk to allocate buffers from buffer pool
            If error set in user structure
                Release buffers (brelse)
            else, call bawrite (block ahead) or bdwrite (block delayed)
            If regular or directory file
                set size in inode to current offset
            If FIFO (pipe)
                increment size by # of bytes written, rewind to start at end
        If FIFO (pipe) & user error or byte count = 0
            wakeup all processes waiting for a write to pipe
            goto FIFOloop;
      Default
        Set error in user structure
        Return
```

Figure 3-75. Algorithm for *writei* Routine

As we noted in Section 3.5 only one process can access a FIFO file at any given time for reading or writing. A *read* function always succeeds on a FIFO file. It returns the actual number of bytes read if the file has less bytes than what the user specified for the read call. However, if the FIFO file is empty on a *read* call, the process *sleeps* until the pipe is written into by another process, unless the read call is set for NO DELAY, in which case the read fails. Similarly, if there is insufficient space to write into a FIFO file on a *write* call, the process *sleeps* until the FIFO file is read from by another process and sufficient space is created, unless the write call is set for NO DELAY. The kernel keeps track of the reads and writes and ensures that a *read* does not *wait* on an empty pipe, nor a *write* on a full pipe. If a pipe is closed by all writers without satisfying processes *sleeping* on read requests, the pipe is closed and the sleeping processes wakeup and return with *0* bytes read. Conversely, if there are processes *sleeping* on write requests, and the last reader closes the pipe, the sleeping processes are sent an error signal with a *wakeup*.

The switch-case statement is very interesting. The first case statement is for a character device. The second case statement is for a FIFO file. The third case statement is for block device, regular, and directory files. The third case statement is, however, within the FIFOloop and is executed for FIFO files also.

Let us now look at an example of file access. Figure 3-76 shows the C code for opening and reading a file.

```
/* This program reads a file and writes it to the block special tape device. */

#include <fcntl.h>
#include <stdio.h>

static unsigned char buf [4096];

main(argc, argv)
int argc;
char *argv[];
{
        register int fi;
        register int fo;
        register int n;

        if (argc < 2) {
        fprintf(stderr, "Usage: %s file\n", argv[0]);
        exit(1);
        }
```

```
/* Open specified file. */

    fi = open(argv[1], O_RDONLY);
    if (fi < 0) {
        perror(argv[1]);
    exit(1);
    }

/* Open tape device for block I/O. */

    fo = open("/dev/mt0", O_WRONLY);
    if (fo < 0) {
        perror("/dev/mt0");
    exit(1);
    }

/* Read and write 4K blocks. */

    while ((n = read(fi, buf, 4096)) > 0) {
        write(fo, buf, n);
    }

    close(fi);
    close(fo);

}
```

Figure 3-76. Example of File Opened for a READ

3.6.6.13 File and Record Locking

The routine *fcntl* provides file and record locking control over open files. The main body of the routine is a switch-case statement that switches on the value of command arguments (*cmd*) set in the *fcntl* call. The file can be set to remain open or be set to close on the execution of an *exec* system call. It also provides for reading or setting status flags as provided in the argument of the system call. The *fcntl* system call is available in AT&T UNIX System V. Most other implementations use *ioctl* for ordinary files.

3.6.7 Mounted File Systems

As we saw earlier, the UNIX file system is a hierarchical inverted tree with files as leaves. There can be multiple branches between the root and the leaf. A formatted block device (a disk or a diskette) may be mounted at any branch directory level of the current hierarchy. The mounted file system is managed primarily through a *mount table* and the *superblock* of the mounted file system.

3.6.7.1 The *Mount* System Call

The *mount* system call is used to mount a new file system. The old branch levels below the mount level become unavailable. The mounted file system is treated as the root file system except for a restriction on *links*. Links are not allowed to span file systems (this is implementation dependent) and the *link* routine checks for this condition. Figure 3-77 describes the directory structure before and after a *mount*.

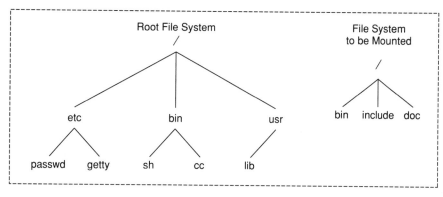

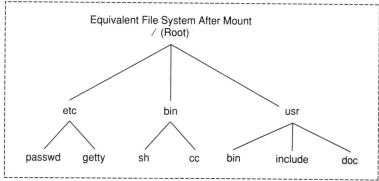

Figure 3-77.   A Mounted File system

The mount table consists of entries, called *mount structures,* for every mounted file system. A *mount structure* consists of the following information:

1. Device number (major and minor).
2. Pointer to buffer containing file system superblock.
3. Pointer to in-core inode of directory where file system is being mounted.
4. Pointer to in-core inode of root directory of new file system.
5. Mount flags.

The *smount* routine, described in Figure 3-78, services the *mount* system call. It

```
smount:
arguments: none
inputs: Filename for block special file
        Directory name where file system will be mounted

   If user not superuser
      Return user error
   Call namei to get inode of special file for file system being mounted
      If no inode
         Return
      If not block special
         Set error in user structure
         Return
   Extract device number
      If already mounted
         Set error in user structure
         Return
   Set directory pointer in user structure
   Call namei, get inode for directory where file system will be mounted
   If directory not found,
      Release inode
      Return error
   If not directory
      Set error in user structure
      Return
   If reference count not 1
      If reference count not 0
         Release inode
         Set error in user structure
         Return
   Allocate free slot in mount table
      Set up device number and flags
   Call getblk to get free buffer from buffer pool
   Set new superblock offset, byte count, base address, and segment flag
      (in user structure)
   Copy superblock into buffer
   Mark mount structure in use
   Enter inode number in mount structure
   Call iget to get root inode of mounted device
      Enter it in mount structure
   Mark inode of directory where file system mounted as mount node
   Call iput to release block special file
   Unlock inode of directory where file system mounted
```

Figure 3-78. Algorithm for *mount* Routine

first checks to see if the calling user is a superuser. Only a superuser can mount file systems. There is an implied assumption that a superuser would be more careful in handling the file systems. It then calls *namei* to get the inode of the special file that will identify the file system being mounted. This must be a block device file. The major (and minor) device numbers are extracted and it checks to ensure that the file system is not already mounted. The *namei* routine is called again to get the inode of the directory where the file system will be mounted. It ensures that the reference count on the inode is 1 (i.e., no other users are using it) and the inode number is not *0*. A free slot in the mount table is allocated and the device numbers and flags are set up in it. The routine then calls *getblk* to get a free buffer from the buffer pool for the superblock of the file system being mounted. The user structure is set up for the new superblock offset, byte count, base address, and segment flag. The superblock is then read in. The mount structure is marked in use and the inode number of the directory where the file system is mounted is entered in it. The root inode of the mounted file system is obtained by a call to *iget* and a pointer to it is entered in the mount structure.

The mount table provides the means for switching from the normal directory branch to the mounted file system branch. The routines *namei* and *iget* are designed to manage the switch from the normal branch to the mounted file system branch.

3.6.7.2 The *Umount* System Call

Just like the *mount* system call, only a superuser can unmount a file system. The *umount* system call handles unmounting of file systems. The routine *sumount* services the *umount* system call. Figure 3-79 describes the algorithm for the *sumount* routine.

The routine *sumount* calls *getmdev* to check if it is a valid device number. The *getmdev* routine calls *namei* to get the inode of the block special file and extracts the major (and minor) device number for the file system being unmounted. It confirms that it has the right device, and that the device is actually mounted. If a user error is set during this phase, the routine returns with a user error. Any unused 'sticky' files (files with sticky bit set) left in the shared text table are removed. It calls the *update* routine to update the superblock. The mount structure entry for the root inode of the mounted file system, if not null, is set to null after locking the mount structure and releasing the inode (iput). If files from that file system are still in use, a user error is returned. If not, the block special device is closed after invoking its close routine and a call to *binval* invalidates its buffers in the buffer pool. The inode pointer is obtained from the mount structure, the inode is locked and the mount node flag in the inode is cleared. The *iput* routine is called to release the inode. The *brelse* routine is called to free the buffer used for the superblock and the mount structure is released.

3.6.8 Disk Caching

Disk caching is performed in many computer systems in hardware using a look ahead feature such that disk blocks that may be required soon are copied into cache memory and temporarily stored until they are needed.

```
sumount:
arguments: none
inputs:      Filename for block special file

    If user not superuser
        Return user error
    Call getmdev which calls namei to get inode of block special file
        Get inode of block special file
        Extract and validate device numbers, device actually mounted
            Return error if not
        Release inode of block special file
    If error set in user structure
        Return
    Remove unused shared text entries of files from mounted file system
    Call update to update the superblock
    If inode pointer for mounted file system in mount structure is not 0
        Lock mount structure
        Release inode
        Set inode pointer to null
    If files from file system still in use
        Set error in user structure
        Return
    Close block special device by invoking device close routine
    Call binval to invalidate its buffers in buffer pool
    Obtain inode pointer of directory from mount structure
    Lock inode
    Clear mount flag in inode
    Call iput to release inode
    Call brelse to free buffer used for superblock
    Free mount structure entry in mount table
```

Figure 3-79. Algorithm for *sumount* Routine

   The UNIX system provides an implementation of the caching feature in software within the kernel. We have touched upon the topic of system buffers used for temporary storage of disk blocks. The kernel maintains a pool of internal data buffers that contain recently used disk blocks. The kernel checks this pool of buffers before scheduling a disk block to be read from the disk. The disk block is written back to disk from the buffer pool only if its contents are modified. The kernel employs this design to minimize disk transfers, and to retain in memory as much frequently used data as it can. The architecture of the buffer pool is described in detail in Section 3.7.2.

   The buffer pool helps improve performance by delaying disk writes. A user program may execute several *write* calls on the same disk block. Rather than write the block for every write call, the kernel makes the changes in the buffer and writes out the buffer on the periodic system *sync* or if the user program executes a *fflush* call to flush the buffers. A good example of this is the use of the buffer pool to copy the superblock and inodes. The superblock undergoes constant modifications. Maintaining a copy in the buffer pool reduces the overhead of keeping the disk copy in sync with the current state of the file system.

Other advantages of this scheme are that several users can be accessing data from the same file using current copies of the data since the disk block copy in the buffer pool is maintained current. The writing of the data to disk is an orderly process managed by the kernel thereby avoiding repeated and haphazard transfers of the same data blocks to disk. Other notable advantages are the ability of the kernel to perform data alignment so that the user programs always get properly aligned data in buffers. This allows user programs to be portable since the kernel deals with hardware data alignment differences.

3.6.9 Performance Issues

A number of different architectural features of the UNIX System affect its operational performance. Key architectural features of file system management that impact performance include the following:

1. Regular files and pipes.
2. Swap memory.
3. Disk partitioning.
4. Buffer pool size.

Chapter 5 on System Performance issues treats each of these architectural features in greater detail. The reader is encouraged to read that chapter carefully to get a clearer understanding of performance issues. The following briefly describes the performance related features of file system management.

3.6.9.1 Regular Files and Pipes

Files are used for storing user data as well as for communicating data between programs. Data can be communicated either via regular files or via pipes. A regular file consists of 10 direct blocks and 3 indirect blocks. A direct block requires less disk accesses than an indirect block. Small amounts of data that can be contained in direct blocks, and is required frequently by programs, can be maintained in regular files. Transitory data, however, should be communicated via named or unnamed pipes (or FIFO files).

3.6.9.2 Swap Memory

Swap memory, as we saw in Section 3.2 is used to temporarily store text, data, and stack on disk for a process that is blocked. Swap memory is set up to be contiguous. The size of swap memory is a configurable parameter. In a typical operating environment, swap memory is set at about 2 to 3 times the size of physical memory. Spreading swap memory on a number of disks speeds up access in a system with multiple disk drives and multiple disk controllers.

3.6.9.3 Disk Partitioning

The size of the disk partitions is a configurable parameter. The sizes of *root, swap,* and *usr* partitions are configurable. The partitioning of disk file systems should take into account performance impact of swap space.

3.6.9.4 Buffer Pool Size

A larger buffer pool allows more disk blocks to be retained in memory for longer periods of time. This reduces the potential of a process becoming blocked for a disk block I/O. In a system with multiple applications using a large number of files from a number of file systems, increasing buffer pool size significantly reduces file data access time.

3.6.10 Summary

This section described the detailed architecture of the UNIX file system. We learned about the physical as well as logical organization of the disk file system, and the role played by inodes in tracking file information. We then looked at the file creation and access routines. Other topics reviewed include mounted file systems, disk swap device, and file system performance issues.

3.6.11 Exercises

1. What routines check for file access permissions?
2. If a disk block is set for a delayed write, what happens if that block is needed by another process before the write is completed?
3. What is the difference between the in-core inode and the disk inode for a file? How could the architecture of the disk inodes be improved for faster file search?
4. How do two processes access the same file? How do they maintain file positions? Can they both be writing to the file at the same time?
5. If two or three processes start large disk file transfers (copies to same disk), what is the effect of it on the buffer pool? Is there a better algorithm than the least-recently used algorithm for freeing up buffers in the buffer pool? Develop the architecture for an alternative system and explain the benefits of that algorithm.
6. Describe the events in the kernel for a *write* system call.
7. How does the kernel prevent write operations to a file system *mounted* for *read-only*?
8. Explore the operations of the buffer pool.

9. Trace the operations of the *namei* and *iget* routines. What system calls use these two routines?

10. What is the maximum number of files that your system can accommodate? What is the maximum limit for UNIX System V? What is the maximum limit for Berkeley UNIX 4.3bsd?

3.7 INPUT/OUTPUT

The UNIX system architecture is unique in its handling of device input and output. Unlike most other operating systems where device I/O and file I/O are very different concepts, the UNIX architecture has been formulated to treat devices as special files. Every device has associated with it a special file that is linked to the directory */dev*. This architecture also allows the creation of special files that manage resources other than devices or, in effect, manage pseudo devices like memory.

While at the user level devices are manipulated as files, at the kernel level devices are managed by device drivers. Figure 3-80 describes the architectural path from a user

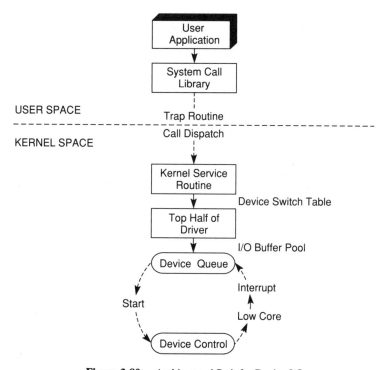

Figure 3-80.   Architectural Path for Device I/O

system call to a device. There is a device driver for each type of device, e.g. disks, tapes, ttys, etc. In the UNIX system, devices signal their need for attention through interrupts. Interrupt service routines, also known as device handlers, service interrupts and start or stop devices, and transfer data to or from devices. They also invoke kernel driver routines to convey the results of the device action to the appropriate process.

This section describes the architecture of the I/O subsystem, the processing of system calls through the I/O subsystem, and the device driver functions and interfaces.

3.7.1 I/O Definitions and Basic File I/O Concepts

The UNIX system manages devices under two categories—as *block* devices or as *character* devices. Character devices are also called *raw I/O* devices. Block devices are devices that are designed for high speed data transfer in fixed block lengths. Examples of such devices are disks and tapes. Almost all other devices are character devices, for example terminals, plotters, printers, and so on. Data transfers for character devices, though generally shorter in length than data transfers for block devices, vary in length from transfer to transfer. Block devices may also be accessed by character device drivers for low level or raw I/O transfers.

The UNIX system uses a special file for each device class. Special files for block devices are called *block special* files. Special files for character devices are called *character special* files. A block I/O device may have a *character special* file associated with it in addition to the block special file to allow users to perform raw I/O.

The principal system calls (e.g. *open, read,* and *write*) and their corresponding kernel routines used for the disk file system are also applicable to devices. They provide appropriate processing for special files and call device drivers as needed.

Two switch tables are used to identify device driver routines for devices. The *block device switch table* is a table of addresses of driver routines for block devices. The *character device switch table* likewise, has entries for addresses of driver routines of character devices. The entries provide addresses for kernel routines for each of the main operating system calls as they apply to each device.

3.7.2 I/O Architecture

The I/O architecture path is described in Figure 3-80. This figure describes the flow and the key components that form the I/O subsystem. Interrupt service is one of the major components of the I/O subsystem and provides the primary interface to the hardware.

3.7.2.1 Interrupt Handling

The kernel handles two types of interrupts. *Device interrupts* signal completion of some I/O function and indicate that the device needs attention. *Hardware traps* are usually a result of internal CPU error conditions. This section describes the processing of device interrupts.

Interrupts are asynchronous and may occur at any time. Some device interrupts may be temporarily masked out by the kernel. All interrupts are masked out during execution of critical code sections. An interrupt may be the result of a data transfer request from a device by a process other than the running process. If the running process is operating in user mode, the interrupt causes a switch to kernel mode by executing a *trap* instruction. Pre-defined vectors are set up that associate device numbers with interrupt handling routines. Interrupts are automatically vectored through fixed virtual addresses (called vectors) in kernel space. The vectors are two 16-bit words that consist of the interrupt service routine address, and the new processor status word (new PS).

On interrupt, the CPU switches to the kernel mode and the old PC (program counter) and the PS (processor status word) are stored on the kernel mode stack. The address of the device interrupt handler is loaded from the interrupt vector into the new PC, and the interrupt priority level mask is entered in the PS. The interrupt handler processes the interrupt and on completion, returns control to the interrupted process.

To provide an effective and orderly way of optimizing system response and performance, different devices are installed with priority levels that determine their relative importance in getting CPU attention. A class of devices generally shares a priority level (e.g., all disk drives share a priority level). Interrupts at a certain priority level can be locked out by calling the *spl* function, or alternatively, the CPU priority can be raised to lock out all lower priority interrupts. For example, priority levels may be set up as follows:

- 0—Clock.
- 1—Keyboard.
- 4—Serial I/O.
- 5—Disk Drive.
- 6—Magnetic Tape Drive.
- 7—Printer.

The clock is at the highest priority level (0 is highest and 7 is lowest). Typically, a device that has interrupted waits to be serviced. This wait is not always acceptable for real-time process control devices that require service within a fixed time period. The UNIX kernel may require some changes to adequately address specific real-time response requirements. At any given time, more than one device may be waiting for interrupt service. The highest priority device is serviced first. An interrupt may be serviced only in one of the following four instances:

1. A user mode process is scheduled (in control of the CPU).
2. A kernel mode process becomes blocked, or it voluntarily relinquishes control and sleeps for an event to take place.
3. The kernel mode process is not in a critical region and can be interrupted for a short duration if the interrupt is from a higher priority process.
4. The time quantum (usually 1 second for most implementations) is completed, i.e. a process has been running for the full time quantum and a clock interrupt causes rescheduling.

3.7.2.2 Timeouts

Timeouts are used largely by driver routines as time alarms and cause the process that they are running under to *sleep* for a certain number of *clock ticks* and, potentially, relinquish control of the CPU to other processes. This may be done to implement a transmission delay, e.g. *a break,* or to receive a signal after a given time duration has expired. A *wakeup* causes re-scheduling of the process.

Timeouts are implemented in the form of a *callout table* that consists of clock ticks, the address of the function to be called at expiration of the time period, and a function argument as the components of the table entries. The callout table is set up in an ascending order of the clock tick number, i.e. the earliest alarm first. The table entries for clock tick numbers are decremented on every clock interrupt. When the entry at the top of the table is decremented to *0* (i.e., timeout expired), the function specified is called with the particular argument, and the rest of the table entries are moved up. All interrupts are turned off during this part of the processing.

3.7.2.3 System and User Time

Operation in user mode takes place in *user time*. Operation in kernel mode takes place in *system time*. The third time variable is recent CPU usage (a *proc structure* field). Serving an interrupt causes some adjustments in process user time and system time parameters. Some adjustments take place for servicing clock interrupts also. For all interrupts other than a clock interrupt, if the interrupt occurs while a process is in user mode, the user time value in the user structure is incremented. The process suspends and the process system time and the system date (and time) are incremented. If the interrupt occurs in kernel mode, and it is serviced, a partial context switch takes place and the system time for the process is incremented. These adjustments set up the process to resume after the interrupt for its leftover time quantum only.

The clock handler produces two types of clock interrupts, the first type at every clock tick and the second type periodically after several clock ticks. Some operations are carried out at every clock tick, such as adjusting process and system time parameters. Other operations are performed after several clock ticks.

In case of the second type of clock interrupt, the pre-emption flag is set if a higher priority process becomes runnable or if the normal scheduling time quantum (1 second for UNIX System V) for the running process has expired and there are other runnable processes; process residency times for all processes resident (fully or partially) in memory are incremented; all processes that have expired timeout alarms are signalled; process priorities are adjusted on the basis of their compute-bound nature; and finally the *runin* flag is checked to see if the scheduler can swap a process in, and if so, make process *0* runnable.

It should be noted that the discussion above points out the *interrupt driven* nature of the UNIX Operating system.

3.7.2.4 User Interface

The concept of special files in the UNIX filesystem present a mechanism for a user to access devices. Devices are treated like files and system calls used for disk file access are also used for device access.

The file system calls *open* (or *mount* for mountable devices, e.g. magnetic tapes and disks), *close* (or *umount* for mountable devices), *read,* and *write* are used to access block I/O devices. The calls *open, close, read, write,* and *ioctl* are used to access and control character I/O devices.

Figure 3-81 describes the user to device driver interface. The device drivers for UNIX reside within the kernel of the operating system. They are activated either by a system call, or by a device interrupt. System calls are serviced by lower level kernel routines. Device interrupts are handled by device interrupt handling routines. Device handling routines may also call upon kernel routines to perform required functions.

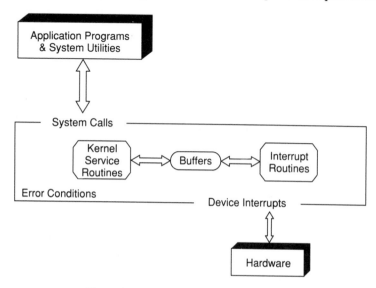

Figure 3-81.   User to Device Driver Interface

Kernel routines perform the following functions on devices:

1. Initiate an I/O operation on the device.
2. Perform device specific functions.
3. Handle interrupts from the device.
4. Perform retries.
5. Handle device access errors.

3.7.2.5 Special File I/O

Each I/O device is associated with a special file. I/O operations on the special file initiate a transfer on the device associated with that special file. Special files, however, do not use file system space, and like directories, they are marked as being *block* or *character* devices. The following describes the interpretation of some fields from the entries that may be found in the */dev* directory. The first column specifies a block *(b)* or a character *(c)* device. The numbers after the read/write permissions are the major and minor device numbers. The reader is encouraged to list the contents of the */dev* directory on their system to compare the contents with the system configuration. The contents of the *dev* directory appear as follows:

cr--r-----	1	root	sys	2,	1	Dec	1	1987	kmem
brw-r-----	1	root	sys	0,	2	Dec	1	1987	swap
brw-r--r--	1	root	sys	0,	0	Feb	10	09:18	root
crw-rw-rw-	1	root	sys	23,	5	Jun	13	1987	ptype5
crw-rw-rw-	1	root	sys	16,	0	Apr	21	10:15	tty
crw-rw-rw-	1	root	sys	22,	7	Jun	13	1987	ttyp7
crw-rw-rw-	1	bin	sys	35	0	Oct	28	1987	generic

3.7.2.6 I/O Device Addressing

Devices are addressed by *major* and *minor numbers*. There is one device driver for each distinct device type (e.g., disk drives, magnetic tape drives, terminals, etc.). Similar device types share drivers. Multiple controllers for similar device types can also be handled by the same driver. Similar device types, for example, disk drives, from different manufacturers, are often attached to different controllers. Separate drivers may be used for different controllers to adjust for variations in manufacturer-specific hardware interfaces. *Major device numbers* are indexed to the *block device switch* table or the *character device switch* table. The *minor device number* identifies the device unit number.

For disk drives, the *minor* number refers to the device number and the partition number. The lower three bits of the minor number identify the partition number. Examples of disk partitions are *swap device, tmp, root, usr*, or even the whole disk. For magnetic tape drives, the major number refers to the controller slot number and the minor number refers to the drive number, the rewind bit, and the tape density.

3.7.2.7 The I/O Buffer Pool

The UNIX kernel uses disk data blocks such as superblock very frequently, and user processes need frequent access to other disk blocks. Disk access is optimized by retaining some disk blocks in memory and writing them back only if they are modified. The kernel sets aside some memory for this purpose. This memory is structured as a buffer pool. Each buffer can hold data the size of a disk block. In addition, a buffer includes a buffer header that identifies the usage and contents of the buffer.

The buffer pool is used for block device read and write operations. Data transmission from the device to the *read* and *write* I/O routines and vice versa is performed via a system buffer selected from a buffer pool. Buffers are linked to a *driver associated list* and may also be linked to a *free list*. Buffers are organized in queues hashed as a function of the device number and the disk block number. These hash queues form the *driver associated list*. This organization helps in performing fast searches for disk blocks. The number of hash queues is a configurable parameter. This buffer pool is manipulated as an I/O cache, and a buffer is allocated from the free list each time a *read/write* to a new disk block is issued. For each *read/write* call, the kernel passes a buffer header address to the *driver strategy* procedure. The driver strategy procedure queues the I/O for a device on its associated work list.

The kernel attaches all buffers to the free list on system initialization. When a buffer is required, it is removed from the head of the free list unless the disk block had been loaded in a buffer previously. A released buffer is returned to the tail of the free list, except in some error situations where it is left with unusable information and is available for reuse immediately. In such situations, it is placed at the head of the queue so that it may be reused before other buffers.

A buffer, once associated with a device, remains associated with the device even if it is on the free list, until it is actually reused and becomes associated with another device. Each block device has a device table that describes the state of the device. It also has two pointers that point to a doubly linked list of all buffers associated with that device. These link pointers are maintained in the buffer header. One set of links in the buffer header are the forward pointers, and the other set are the backward pointers. The buffer pointers are retained even after the buffer is returned to the free list. The kernel attempts to match existing buffers to the device block number to be read. If it finds it on the free list, even somewhere in the middle, it removes it from the free list and the buffer is ready for use. The kernel also ensures that two buffers are not assigned the same disk block to avoid potential data revision conflicts. In all cases, the kernel has to search through the entire buffer set. As we noted earlier in this section, the kernel sets up the buffers in queues hashed by the major device number to achieve good performance. A buffer can be on the hash queue and the free list at the same time. Once used, a buffer remains associated with a device and is linked on a hash queue. Figure 3-82 shows the relationship among the buffer header, the hash queue, and the free list.

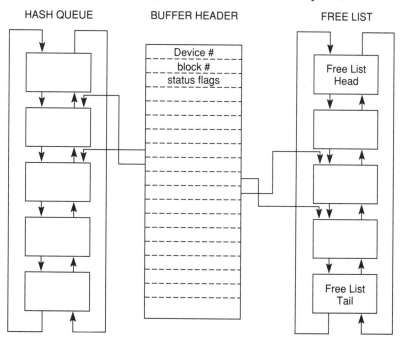

Figure 3-82. The I/O Buffer Pool

The buffer header consists of the following information:

- Status flags (current state of the buffer).
- Device queue pointer (device table).
- Forward and backward pointers on free list.
- Forward and backward pointers on hash queue.
- Available queue pointer (position on free list).
- Device number—major/minor (device to which buffer is currently attached).
- Transfer size (data size).
- Low order core address.
- Words for clearing.
- Superblocks.
- Inode list.
- Block number on disk.
- High order core address.
- Error information (words not transferred).
- Request start time.

The status flags maintain the status of the following key parameters:

1. Read when I/O occurs.
2. Transaction completed.
3. Error—transfer aborted.
4. Busy (not on the forward/backward linked list).
5. Process is waiting—issue *wakeup* when busy flag clears.
6. Do not wait for I/O completion.
7. Do not write until block leaves free list.

A buffer remains on the free list but is marked busy for the duration between being allocated and being removed from the free list. This procedure is particularly important for a process scheduling and interrupt driven system. This procedure avoids system conflicts that may be caused when a second process, scheduled after allocation of the buffer by the first process, attempts to allocate the same buffer before it is removed from the free list. The *getblk* routine is called to assign a buffer from the free list if the buffer is not already on the hash queue.

3.7.2.8 The *Getblk* Routine

This routine is a part of the buffered I/O routines. It is called with device number and disk block number as the arguments to the call. If the block is already associated with a buffer, it returns the buffer pointer. Otherwise it looks for the oldest non-busy buffer and reassigns it.

Its loop first enables all interrupts and calls *bhash* to locate the hash queue for that device. If the buffer is not found on the hash queue, it checks to see if the device block is in the queue (i.e., if it has been read into a buffer previously, then its buffer may still be in the free chain). If the disk block is found, it looks for the buffer on the free chain.

```
getblk:
arguments: Device number
           Device block number

  Loop:
     Enable all interrupts
     Call bhash to hash device number and block number
     For buffer not in queue
       If block number is in queue & block is stale
             (buffer found, was used but is free now)
         continue; (jump out to the else)
         Disable clock interrupts
         If buffer is BUSY
             Sleep (until event—buffer freed)
             Goto loop
         else, continue
        else (buffer not BUSY)
           Call notavail to remove buffer from free list
           Mark it busy
           Return buffer pointer
     else (buffer not in queue)

     If there are no buffers on free list
           Sleep (until event—free list has free buffer)
           Goto loop

     else (Buffer found)
     Call notavail and remove buffer from free list,
     If buffer set for DELAYED WRITE
           Set up for asynchronous write and call bwrite
           Goto loop

     else (Buffer found is really free)
     Set up buffer
           BUSY flag
           Backward and Forward pointers
           New device hash queue pointer
           Disk block number
           Transfer size
     Return buffer pointer
```

Figure 3-83. Algorithm for *getblk* Routine

If it finds it, the routine disables clock interrupts, and checks if the buffer has the BUSY flag on. If the BUSY is on, it sleeps on an event that the BUSY will go off and the buffer will be freed. The routine executes a *goto* to the start of the loop. If the BUSY flag is not on, all interrupts are enabled and it calls *notavail* and returns. The *notavail* routine marks the buffer BUSY and removes it from the free list. The buffer pointer is returned.

If the buffer is not on the hash queue, a new buffer has to be acquired. It disables the clock interrupt again and checks the forward free list. If there are no free buffers, it sleeps on the event of a buffer becoming free and goes back to the start of the loop. The routine goes back to the start because another process may have assigned a buffer to that disk block in the meantime and, therefore, it must go through the entire sequence again to maintain the integrity of the system. However, if it does find a buffer, it calls the *notavail* routine and removes the buffer from the free list. If the buffer has a DELAYED WRITE set it is not really free. The delayed write has to be taken care of first. The routine then performs an asynchronous write and calls the *bwrite* routine. It returns to the start of the loop again because other processes and events could change the buffer status before this process is scheduled again. If, however, it does find a really free buffer, it sets up the buffer by marking it BUSY; sets up its forward and backward pointers; and sets up the new device queue pointer, the disk block number, and the transfer size. The buffer pointer is returned to the calling routine.

3.7.2.9 Device Drivers and Hardware Interfaces

Figure 3-84 shows the relationship between the device drivers and the associated devices and peripherals in the system.

Figure 3-85 describes the interface between a library routine for a system call and the appropriate kernel service and driver routines for that call.

The device hardware interfaces with the device driver through interrupts. The upper half of the driver, as shown in Figure 3-86, resides in the kernel service routines (also called kernel routines). The lower half of the device driver is called the interrupt service routine (or the interrupt handler). Device interrupts typically indicate completion of an I/O request. Interrupt service, therefore, very often results in process scheduling.

The drivers use I/O buffers that contain data specific to the controller for that device including the following:

1. Status flags.
2. Queue of work requests for that controller.
3. Device ID.
4. Controller busy flag.
5. Error status.
6. Device register data.
7. Temporary storage.

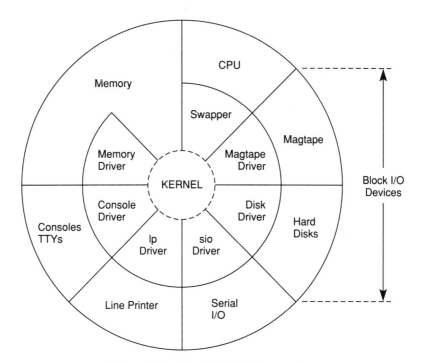

Figure 3-84.   Kernel Device Driver Interface

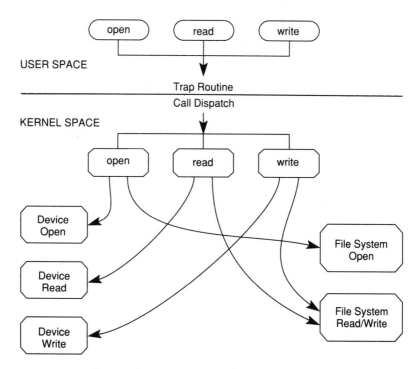

Figure 3-85.   System Call to Kernel Routine Interface

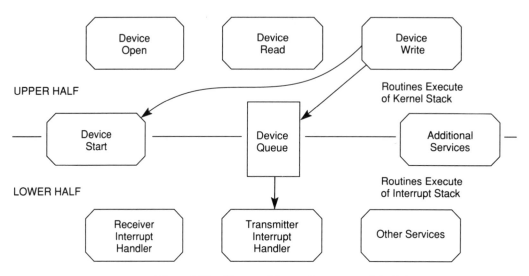

Figure 3-86.   Upper and Lower Components of the Driver

3.7.2.10 Device Switch Tables

I/O devices, for most implementations, are mapped through the top page of the kernel virtual address space. It should be noted that I/O devices are not mapped in user space. The *block* and *character device switch tables* provides the association between the kernel and the device drivers. The initialization and setup of the device switch tables is controlled by *C* language modules *(conf.c/c.c)* that contain no code, but include *bdevsw* and *cdevsw* structures that define the configuration. The configuration file is compiled with the kernel; and for each device defined in the configuration file, a set of fields are set up in a device switch table. The contents of *conf.c* include the following:

1. Device switch tables *(bdevsw* and *cdevsw).*
2. Device address table *(dev_addr).*
3. Device count structures.
4. Per-device structure declarations.
5. Device initialization table *(dev_init).*
6. Other system configuration and tuning parameters.

The *Block Device Switch Table* (see Figure 3-87) may be viewed as a two-dimensional table with the routine type *(open, close, strategy)* as the columns, and devices as rows. A row in this table is the only link between the UNIX kernel code and the driver for that device. This concept is very similar to the concept of the *System Call Dispatch Table*. Besides providing a very clean and well defined interface, a significant advantage of this architecture for system integrators is the ease of adding custom device drivers to the UNIX system.

Device	open	close	strategy	buffer
b0	nulldev	nulldev	rkstrategy	rktab
b1	gdopen	gdclose	gdstrategy	gdtab
b2	gtopen	gtclose	gtstrategy	gttab

Figure 3-87.   Block Device Switch Table

The *Character Device Switch Table* (see Figure 3-88) is also a two-dimensional table with the routines for *open, close, read, write,* and *ioctl.* This table is also initialized and setup by the same *C* language programs to reflect the actual configurations of peripheral devices on the system.

Device	open	close	read	write	ioctl
c0	conopen	conclose	conread	conwrite	conioctl
c1	syopen	syclose	syread	sywrite	syioctl
c2	nulldev	nulldev	mmread	mmwrite	nodev
c3	sioopen	sioclose	sioread	siowrite	sioioctl
c4	mtopen	mtclose	mtread	mtwrite	nodev
c5	lpopen	loclose	nodev	lpwrite	nodev

Figure 3-88.   Character Device Switch Table

The *conf.c* configuration file for the kernel also contains a third switch table used by the system, the *Line Control Switch Table*. This table lists the routines that describe the control parameters for terminal lines and modem control. Figure 3-89 describes

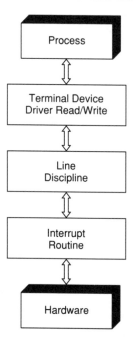

Figure 3-89.   Use of Line Discipline

how line discipline routines are used. The structure used for this table is set up for *open, close, read, write, ioctl, input, output,* and *modem control.* This table determines the line discipline that will be used for that terminal. The line discipline is selected using the *ioctl* system call. The line discipline routines act on the data contained in *c-lists.*

The *dev_addr* table is used to define the device bus addresses and assignment of interrupt handlers to vectors.

The per-device structure declarations are used to generate *tty structures* for terminal drivers.

A separate table in *conf.c* called *dev_init* includes pointers to driver initialization entry points. Calls to interrupt handlers appear in executable code generated in the hardware interface file *low.s.*

3.7.2.11 Block Device I/O

Block device I/O drivers usually support disk and tape drives. They typically have fixed length data transfers, e.g. 1K bytes for AT&T UNIX System V and 4K bytes for Berkeley UNIX 4.2bsd. The functions supported include device open and close, and a strategy routine that handles block transfers. Device drivers consist of two parts. The first part provides kernel service to system calls. The second part is the *device interrupt handler.*

The device interrupt handler (or routine) handles device interrupts, calls the driver strategy routine to start block transfers, manages and dispatches device errors, and resets devices and device statuses.

Block devices may also be set for for transfers of variable lengths. They are set up as *character devices* for this purpose. The same device may have two drivers that access it, one set up as a block device driver and the other as a character device driver. Data transfers through the character special file is in the form of large blocks of unbuffered data. In either case, the logical byte number is converted to a physical disk block address. The disk block is then read into memory. If the data is modified, for example, in a read and write call, the disk block is written back.

3.7.2.12 Character Device I/O

Character device I/O is set up for devices like terminals, printers, and plotters. A *character special* file is set up for each character device that will be accessed. The data transfers are small variable length blocks of unbuffered data. The logical byte number of is converted to a physical disk block address. In this case also, the block is read into memory and information is added to it before it is written back. If there is more data more blocks may be written out.

3.7.3 Block Device I/O Routines

The example in Figure 3-90 shows the use of block device read and write calls.

```c
/* This program reads a file and writes it to the block special tape device. */

#include <fcntl.h>
#include <stdio.h>

static unsigned char buf[4096];

main(argc, argv)
int argc;
char *argv[];
{
        register int fi;
        register int fo;
        register int n;

        if (argc < 2) {
                fprintf(stderr, "Usage: %s file\n", argv[0]);
        exit(1);
        }

/* Open specified file. */

        fi = open(argv[1], O_RDONLY);
        if (fi < 0) {
                perror(argv[1]);
        exit(1);
        }

/* Open tape device for block I/O. */

        fo = open("/dev/mt0", O_WRONLY);
        if (fo < 0) {
                perror("/dev/mt0");
        exit(1);
        }

/* Read and write 4K blocks. */

        while ((n = read(fi, buf, 4096)) > 0) {
                write(fo, buf, n);
        }
        close(fi);
        close(fo);

}
```

Figure 3-90.   Example of Block Device I/O

The *open* and *close* routines are called via the *block device switch* table when the device is opened or closed. The open routine sets up the controller I/O buffer, allocates hardware I/O channels if necessary, and initializes error logging information. The close routine is called on the last close on the device. It releases the I/O channel if appropriate and performs device specific cleanup if necessary.

3.7.3.1 The *Open* Routine

Since devices are treated as special files, the procedures and the routines used for opening a block device are the same as for ordinary files. Section 3.6 describes the procedures and Section 3.6.2 describes the *copen* routine that opens or creates files. The reader is encouraged to review that routine at this time. At the end of that routine, there is a call to the *openi* routine that handles device opens. Figure 3-91 describes the algorithm for the *openi* routine. The open modes specify the type of open. This parameter is used by the driver open routine. A printer, for example, is generally opened for O_EXCL (exclusive) use only. A terminal can be opened as the default terminal for the process or for serial I/O. Hence, *openi* checks the user structure entry for the default TTY.

```
openi:
Arguments: Inode pointer
            File mode for creation

    Get device number from inode
    Switch (on device type)
        if character device
            Use major device number as index to device switch table
            Return user error if device number exceeds table count
            If user structure has no entry, set it to this device
            Call driver open procedure with minor device number
            break

        if block device,
            Use major device number as index to device switch table
            Return user error if device number exceeds table count
            If user structure has no entry, set it to this device
            Call driver open procedure with minor device number
            break

        if FIFO
            Call openp to set up pipe.
            break
    Return
```

Figure 3-91.   Algorithm for the *openi* routine

3.7.3.2 The *Close* Routine

The *closef* routine is called by the *close* routine to service the *close* system call. Figure 3-92 describes the algorithm for the *closef* routine. It checks if the reference count in the file table entry is greater than 1. If so, it decrements it and returns. If the reference count is 1, then it locks the inode, sets the reference count to 0, and frees the file table entry as well as the in-core inode because the file is no longer in use. The inode for a file still in use by other processes is not freed.

```
closef:
Arguments: file descriptor (file table entry pointer)
Inputs:      inode pointer
             File mode
             device number

   If reference count is not 1
       Decrement file descriptor reference count
       Return
   Lock inode
   Set reference count to 0
   Release file descriptor
   switch (on file type)
       if character device
           Use major device number as index
           Call device close routine
           break
       if block device
           Use major device number as index
           Call device close routine
           break
       if FIFO
           Call closep to close pipe.
           break
   Return

   if block device
       if device is mounted
           Flush modified buffers
           Use major device number as index to block device switch table
           Call driver close routine
           Call binval to invalidate device blocks still in buffers
       Release inode
```

Figure 3-92. Algorithm for the *closef* routine

3.7.3.3 The *Read* and *Write* Routines

The routine used to service the *read* and *write* system calls is *rdwr*. It in turn calls the *readi* and the *writei* routines described in Section 3.6 to perform the actual read and write operations. These same routines are used for block and character device read and write. Figure 3-93 describes the sequence of routines for block reads and writes and illustrates a block read operation.

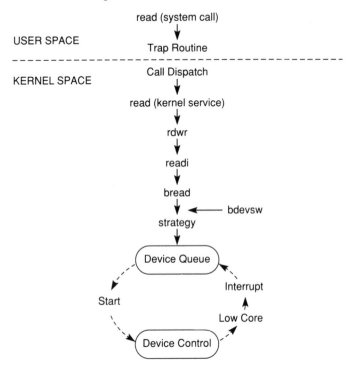

Figure 3-93.   Block *read* and *write* Control

3.7.3.4 I/O Strategy Interface

The *strategy* routine handles requests for transfer of disk blocks. It places the addresses of the disk blocks on a device queue. A device queue may be an ordered queue or a sequential queue. The *strategy* routine takes the address of the buffer headers as an argument and verifies if the block requested is on a disk or some other block device, and checks if it is already in a buffer. If a buffer already containing this block is found, the buffer is marked BUSY and removed from the free list. If not found, it converts the logical block number to a disk address or some other block device address; queues the request on the controller I/O work list queue (also called the request queue; and re-organizes the controller I/O work list queue if appropriate; and calls the device start routine if the controller is not busy.

The device start routine processes the first request from the controller request queue. It sets up controller registers for the device including *track and sector* addresses, transfer size and address, and transfer type. It then marks the controller busy, sets controller off, and then returns. The controller is released by the device interrupt routines.

3.7.3.5 Raw I/O on Block Devices

This is a method used for very fast access to block devices. This does not use the buffer pool and requires a second special file marked as a *character special file*. *Read* and *write* requests are transferred by the file management routines to the driver using the *character device switch* table.

3.7.4 Character I/O

Character I/O encompasses a wide range of devices and utilizes a different buffering mechanism than the block device I/O. Each character device is associated with a *character device special file*. Major and minor device numbers are used to identify the device driver and the device unit number.

The buffering mechanism used for character I/O is very different from that used for block I/O. The data for character I/O is not always in fixed lengths, and is usually not very large. The buffering of data for character device I/O is performed in buffers associated with the drivers that, for most UNIX implementations, are 24 bytes long or can be set by the CBSIZE parameter in the *param.h* file. Called *cblocks* or *c-structures*, these buffers are linked together in a structure called *c-list*. Another structure, called the *tty structure*, is used for character I/O. One *tty structure* is associated with each device used for terminal I/O.

Terminal I/O is a special case of character device I/O and is described in greater detail following this section.

3.7.4.1 The *Open* Routine

The *open* routine is called when a *character device special* file is opened. The device ID is a parameter for the open call. If it is the *first open*, the TTY structure is initialized for this port and the device/line characteristics are set up in the controller for the type of communications link used for that port. The *openi* routine described for block device opens is also used for character device opens.

If it is other than the first open, the appropriate *line open routine* indicated by the line discipline is called. The line open routine allows different ports to be operated with different characteristics.

3.7.4.2 The *Close* Routine

The *close* routine uses the *minor device number* to index to the appropriate TTY structure. The appropriate *line close routine* indicated by the line characteristics in the TTY structure is then called. If this is the *last close,* further interrupts from that port are disabled and the communications channel is disconnected. The *closef* routine used for file I/O and block device I/O is also used for character device I/O.

3.7.4.3 The Read and Write Routines

The *read/write* routines use the minor device number as a parameter to index to the appropriate TTY structure. The general read/write routines are then called with the line discipline information. These routines are described in Section 3.5 as the *readi* and the *writei* routines.

The device I/O control routine *ioctl* reads and writes device status. Also called the driver controller routine, it sets up the multiplexor controller registers according to the operation requested and adjusts information in the *TTY* structure on the state of the line, queues, and so on.

3.7.5 The Terminal Interface Subsystem

This is a special case of character I/O. A number of data structures are used to define *device characteristics* and the type of *processing of the data* required. Figure 3-94 describes the sequence of operations performed for terminal I/O.

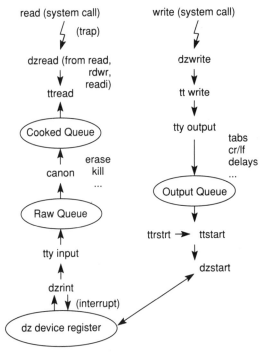

Figure 3-94. Architectural Path for Terminal I/O

3.7.5.1 The Use of C-lists

Figure 3-95 shows the organization of C-lists. A single device can use more than one c-list. For example, terminal drivers use the first *c-list* for output characters, the second for raw characters or partial lines and the third for *complete* input lines (canonical form).

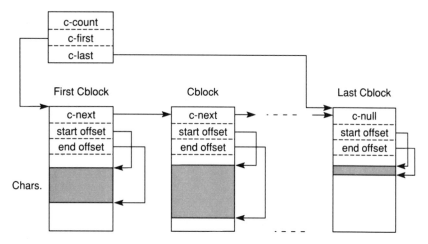

Figure 3-95.   Organization of C-lists

The head of the c-list consists of a structure consisting of a character count, pointer to the first *cblock,* and a pointer to the last *cblock.* The *cblock* structures consist of three pointers and the data bytes in that block.

The *start offset* (c-first) points to the current start character in the cblock. The *end offset* (c-last) points to the current last character in the cblock. Some implementations of UNIX also include a *data size value.* A cblock is, in effect, a dynamic buffer, i.e. characters are added to the tail of the cblock (end-offset) as they are read in from the terminal, and are taken off the head of the cblock (start-offset) as the kernel routines process them. The end offset increases as the characters are read in and the start offset also increases as the characters are taken off. When the start offset equals the end offset, i.e. there are no more characters in the cblock, the cblock is released. If the end offset attempts to go past the end of the c-list, a new cblock is added. The kernel maintains a list of free cblocks. All released cblocks are added to the free list.

3.7.5.2 TTY Structure

A TTY structure is needed for each UNIX character device that is used for normal terminal I/O. There is one structure for each TTY port. It consists of addresses of c-lists, addresses of input and output control flags, line discipline routines, and other parameters required for character I/O. The TTY structure includes the following:

- C-list structure for raw I/O.
- C-list structure for canonical queue.
- Input buffer structure.
- C-list structure for output queue.
- Pointer to routine to start output.
- Pointer to routine to start input.
- Destination channel for a multiplexor.

- Device address.
- Device number.
- Mode flags settable by *ioctl* call.
- Internal state (timeout, device open, busy, etc.).
- Process group name.
- Number of delimitters in raw queue.
- Line discipline.
- Printing column of device.
- Erase character.
- Kill character.
- Input speed (receive).
- Output speed (transmit).
- Character input since a *ttwrite* for TTYs.
- Local mode word.
- Local state bits.
- C-list structure for control queue.

The internal state flags include, the following.

1. TIMEOUT —Delay timeout in progress.
2. WOPEN   —Waiting for open to complete.
3. ISOPEN   —Device is open.
4. FLUSH   —Output queue has been flushed during DMA.
5. CARR_ON —Software copy of carrier present.
6. BUSY   —Output is in progress.
7. ASLEEP   —Wakeup when output done.
8. XCLUDE   —Exclusive use flag against open.
9. TTSTOP   —Output stopped by Ctrl-S.
10. HUPCLS   —Hang up on last close.
11. TBLOCK   —Tandem queue blocked.
12. SPEEDS   —Used by driver.

3.7.5.3 Line Discipline

Line discipline routines perform the required conversion of data in the c-list structures for the raw queue and set up the converted data in the c-list structure for the canonical queue. For example, backspace characters are sent to the raw queue, but are interpreted and acted on before the data enters the canonical queue. The canonical queue, in effect, has processed lines, i.e. on entry of a carriage return, the characters like backspace, kill (i.e. erase line), etc. Line discipline also checks the mode flag to perform operations like character *echo* on terminals, terminal hangup signals, etc. The line discipline can also be set up to perform no conversion.

3.7.5.4 General Terminal I/O Routines

The general terminal I/O routines include *open, close, read, write, receiver interrupt, transmitter interrupt,* and *control.* We have already looked at these routines under the character device switch table descriptions. The following description briefly describes the terminal specific functions of these routines.

The *open* routine, called by the driver *open* routine, calls the *control* (ioctl) routine to initialize the *TTY* structure; defines the terminal characteristics; and marks the port open.

The *close* routine, called by the driver *close* routine, marks the port closed and flushes all input and output buffers before releasing them.

The *read* routine, called from the driver *read* routine, reads characters from the processed input queue and writes them into the user's data area. If the processed input queue becomes empty before the request is satisfied, the raw queue is checked; the line discipline routine is called to process the data; and the data is transferred to the processed queue. If the raw queue falls below its *low-water-mark,* the process is unblocked to allow the driver controller routine to initiate a device read.

The *write* routine, called from the driver *write* routine, transfers data from the user data area to the input queue and processes it on the fly. If the output queue passes its *high-water-mark,* the routine calls the driver controller routine to initiate a device write. It *sleeps* if the write is not completed.

The *receiver interrupt* routine adds received characters to the raw queue. It calls the *driver controller* routine to transmit an *XOFF* if the raw queue *high-water-mark* is reached. It also handles data over-run situations, delimiters, erase and kill characters, as well as received *quit* and *break* characters.

The *transmitter interrupt* routine is called from the *driver interrupt* routine if the output queue becomes empty. It issues a *wakeup* to the user process if the output queue drops below the *low-water-mark* or becomes empty, or it writes characters out of the queue to the port.

3.7.6 Summary

In this section we looked at the Input/Output subsystem and the architecture for some of the important routines that make up the I/O subsystem. We also looked at the use of the device switch tables for character I/O and block I/O. Other important architectural components we looked at are the device interrupt handlers and device drivers. The general terminal I/O routines and the manipulation of the c-lists is another noteworthy component of the I/O subsystem.

3.7.7 Exercises

1. What are the entry points into the UNIX kernel?
2. Can the same device be opened for block I/O and raw I/O at the same time? Explain.
3. Typically, a message written from another terminal is displayed on your screen

irrespective of what you may be doing. Can you prevent that if it starts interfering with your work? How?

4. Write a device driver for a diskette device used as a) a tape device and, b) a disk device. What are the key differences in these drivers?

5. Write a line discipline routine for a DEC VT300 series terminal. How do you handle the function keys in your line discipline routine?

6. How would you set up a driver for dynamic multi-application window terminal? What would its interaction with multiple processes be like?

3.8 NETWORKING

The first integrated network communications capability in UNIX was developed for Berkeley UNIX 4.2bsd as the *sockets* implementation. Sockets provide a programming interface for networking. The 4.2bsd kernel implements the equivalent of the data link through the session layers (i.e., layers 2 through 5) of the ISO model. The Ethernet 802.3 standard was selected for the physical link and the data link layers. The Transmission Control Protocol *(TCP)* and Internet Protocol *(IP)* are used at the Network and Transport layers. TCP/IP protocol was developed under the DARPA Internet program and is intended for use as a highly reliable host-to-host protocol in a packet switched network, and in interconnected systems of such networks. Figure 3-96 describes the ISO model mapping of network software.

ISO Layer	AT&T UNIX System V.3	Berkeley UNIX 4.2bsd	SUN Microsystems 4.2bsd
Application	RFS Application Using Streams	Application Using Sockets FTP, TELNET, rlogin	NFS, Application Using Sockets FTP, TELNET, rlogin
Presentation	Stream Modules (Transport Library)	Library Routines	XDR (External Data Representation)
Session	New System Calls for Streams	New System Calls to Implement Sockets	Remote Procedure Calls and Sockets
Transport & Network	Protocol Modules for TCP/IP, XNS, SNA, OSI, etc.	TCP IP	TCP or Network Disk Protocol IP
Data Link & Physical	Ethernet (IEEE 802.3) Token Ring,SNA, etc.	Ethernet (IEEE 802.3) Address Resolution Protocol	Ethernet (IEEE 802.3) Address Resolution Protocol

Figure 3-96.   ISO Model Mapping of Network Systems

Networking in the AT&T UNIX System V first appeared as the *streams* implementation in Release 3. System V Release 2 introduced the Remote File System *(RFS)* implementation.

3.8.1 Berkeley UNIX 4.2bsd Networking

Berkeley adopted the architecture based on *sockets*. Additional system calls and kernel service routines were developed to provide comprehensive socket management. The File Transfer Protocol *(FTP)*, User Datagram Protocol *(UDP)* for datagram service in the Internet domain, and the TELNET protocol for terminal emulation were also provided.

3.8.1.1 Sockets

A socket is defined as the concatenation of the node address on the network and the port address of the process within the node, where the node is a UNIX host. A socket is the equivalent of a network address for a process. A connection may be established between the sockets to start a session.

3.8.1.2 TCP/IP

The Transmission Control Protocol *(TCP)*, described in Figure 3-97, is an integral part of Berkeley UNIX 4.2bsd and 4.3bsd kernel implementations. Berkeley also implemented an Address Resolution Protocol *(ARP)* that maps TCP/IP addresses to Ethernet 802.3 addresses, providing a convenient local area network interface. TCP corre-

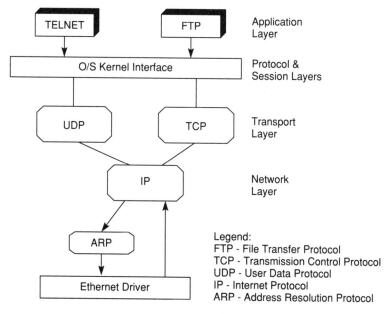

Figure 3-97.   The TCP/IP Networking Model

sponds to OSI layer four and controls data transfer for end-to-end service. TCP establishes a connection when two processes need to communicate. *Binding* establishes the link between a process and a socket. TCP maintains information about each connection, including sockets at both ends, data segment sequence numbers, window sizes, etc.

TCP connections are full duplex. Transmission reliability is achieved through the use of sequence numbers for data segments. If a particular segment is not received, that segment is re-transmitted.

The Internet Protocol *(IP)* roughly corresponds to OSI Layer three and has responsibility for datagram service across a network or an internetwork. It provides addressing and data fragmentation, that is, it breaks up data into smaller chunks called datagrams and adds the internet address of the destination for the datagram in the *internet header*. IP provides for type of service, time to live (time limit for delivery), options (time stamps, security, routing), and header checksum.

3.8.1.3 System Calls and Utilities

Berkeley implemented 17 system calls for implementing the socket interface. It brought over FTP for reliable file transfer and the TELNET protocol for remote terminal emulation from *ARPA*s previous network. Berkeley further implemented *rpc* (remote procedure call) and *rlogin* (remote login) as replacements for trusted hosts, and further provided *rsh* (remote shell) for the UNIX system.

3.8.2 AT&T UNIX System V Streams and RFS

Figure 3-98 illustrates the AT&T UNIX System V Streams-based networking model. The AT&T Streams architecture is a layered architecture where the streams are the interfaces between the protocol layers and the UNIX kernel. This provides the capabil-

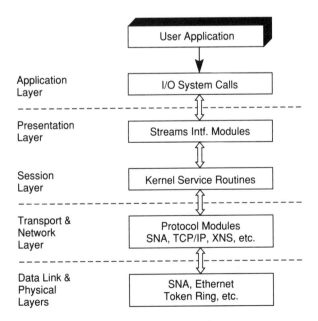

Figure 3-98. The AT&T UNIX Networking Model

ity to implement different protocols to operate with the same Streams interface. The interfaces are implemented as a set of new system calls that reside at the level of the sessions layer of the OSI model, and as a set of Streams interface modules that form the presentation layer between the user's application and the system calls. The RFS implementation also supports a Transport Layer Interface *(TLI)* for low level access to networking for system applications. The underlying architecture of a stream in the UNIX kernel is described in Figure 3-99. The Streams Interface is called in the same manner any other communications interface is called using a set of system calls that are serviced by kernel service modules.

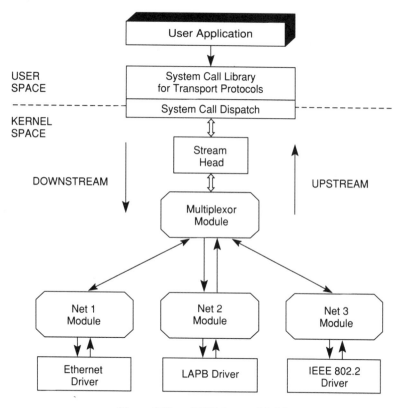

Figure 3-99.   AT&T Streams Model

A stream has three parts: a Stream head, optional processing modules, and a driver (also called a Stream end). The Stream head provides the interface between the Stream and user processes. One or more modules (optional) process data travel between the Stream head and the driver, for example, canonical conversions in a TTY driver. The driver may be a device driver, providing communications or other I/O services from an external device, or an internal software driver, commonly called a pseudo-device driver.

Figure 3-100 describes the AT&T streams architecture. Using a combination of system calls, kernel routines, and kernel utilities, the *streams* interface passes data between the driver and the Stream head in the form of messages. Messages that are

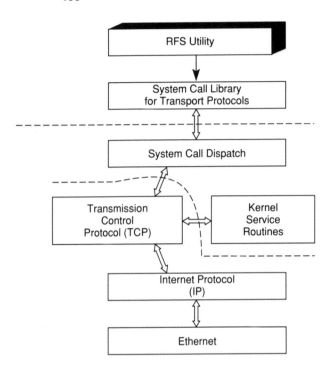

Figure 3-100.   AT&T Streams Architecture

passed from the Stream head toward the driver are said to travel downstream, and messages passed in the opposite direction are said to travel upstream. These messages contain data being passed between the user space and the Streams data space in the driver.

3.8.2.1 System Calls and Utilities

Streams provide a simple interface through system calls. The system calls include:

1. *open*   —Create a Stream to the specified driver.
2. *close*   —Dismantle specified Stream.
3. *read*   —Receive data from a Stream.
4. *write*   —Send data to a Stream.
5. *ioctl*   —Push protocol control modules for a particular device in Streams stack.
6. *getmsg*   —Receive Data and Control message from Stream.
7. *putmsg*   —Send Data and Control message to Stream.
8. *poll*   —Notify application program when selected event occurs on a Stream.

The Remote File System *(RFS)* is a utility provided with AT&T UNIX System V.3 that uses the Streams interface. This allows plugging in any of several different network protocols and makes RFS independent of any one kind of network hardware or software.

Figure 3-101 describes the RFS architecture. RFS provides transparency be-

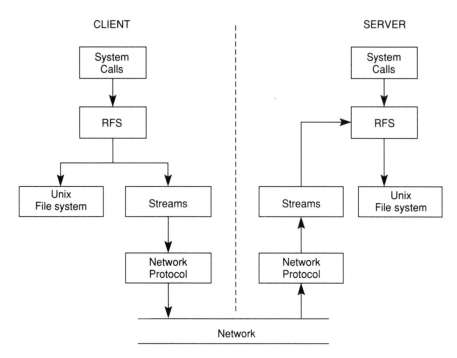

Figure 3-101.   AT&T RFS Architecture

tween remote and local file systems and maintains security and integrity of the system for concurrent file access. This capability is provided retaining the normal UNIX file system semantics. The *adv* command sends a message to the *name service* node that it is making files available as a server. The *mount* command allows administrators on the *client* system to make a remote file system available for use locally in a transparent manner. A network connection is set up between the client and the server consequent to a mount command. The server keeps track of how many remote users have a file open at a given time and it also maintains security by distinguishing between local opens and remote opens. Remote access can be restricted to the privileges of selected local accounts. The user is encouraged to read Chapter 4 for more detailed architectural analysis of RFS.

3.8.3 Network File System (NFS)

The SUN Micro-systems Network File System *(NFS)*, described in Figure 3-102, has been supported on a number of UNIX implementations. NFS supports transparent network wide read and write access to files and directories. Workstations or disk file servers *export* selected file systems to the network to make them sharable resources. Workstations *import* file systems to access files.

The base protocol for the Sun Micro-systems UNIX implementation is TCP/IP. The divergence from the Berkeley implementation of TCP/IP occurs at the Session layer where Sun has implemented Remote Procedure Calls (RPC). The RPC are layered on top of the TCP/IP socket interface defined for TCP/IP. The RPC allow

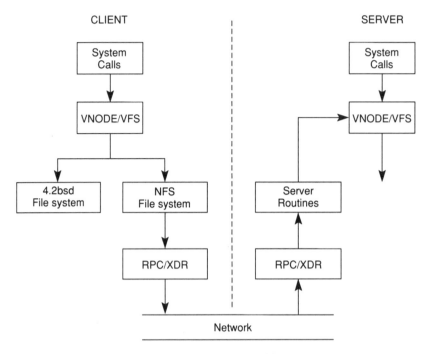

Figure 3-102.   SUN NFS Architecture

communications with remote services in a manner similar to procedure calling mechanisms of procedural programming languages.

At the Presentation layer, the Sun implementation has defined the External Data Representation *(XDR)*. The XDR definition allows different machines to communicate, despite variations in their data representations, by standardizing network data representation. The data is translated to the standard representation before it is sent to the network.

The NFS implementation also includes the implementation of a virtual file system *(VFS)* that uses *vnodes* to separate file system operations from the semantics of the implementation.

The standard *mount* command of UNIX 4.2bsd has been extended to allow network users to mount files for shared access. The *exportfs* command exports file systems to the network. The NFS architecture is called a *client/server* architecture where the file system being exported is called the server and the user importing the file system is called the client.

3.8.4 Comparison of RFS and NFS

While the major design goals of the two implementations, transparent sharing of disk file system resources across a network, were very similar; the driving design philosophies and the actual implementations have some significant and interesting differences. Consequently, their uses may tend to be very different. Let us look at the key differences between the two.

3.8.4.1 Philosophy

RFS is designed to support identical UNIX nodes on a reliable network and operates in a mode that closely ties the server and the client. NFS, on the other hand, is designed around a philosophy that any workstation should not be dependent on, or be controlled by, another node; and therefore, supports a *stateless* design that can function in a less-than-fully-reliable network.

3.8.4.2 Implementation Differences

The following specific implementation differences are worth noting:

RFS	NFS
State sensitive design	Stateless design
Requires reliable protocols e.g. TCP/IP	Tolerates other protocols e.g. UDP
Recovery complicated after failure	Automatic recovery after failure
Does not support diskless workstations	Supports diskless workstations
Requests for remote file I/O depend on previous operations	Each request is independent and can be handled as a datagram.
Supports UNIX only	Supports other operating systems
Supports standard UNIX semantics, i.e. full file sharing and all local operations can be performed on remote files.	Implements special calls to manage remote file sharing. Semantic differences prevent some remote operations.
Provides full file system sharing	File sharing, not file system sharing

It is also worth noting that some of the node independence provided by the stateless design of NFS has been compromised with the implementation of record locking. The lock manager maintains the locking state of each file in the server. However, on a server crash, all locks are removed from proper recovery.

3.8.5 Summary

This section introduced us to the two most prominent networking architectures available for UNIX systems. We looked at the ISO layer equivalents and the features available in each protocol. We also compared the merits and limitations of the two architectures.

We have now reached the end of Chapter 3. Let us also review here what we have learned in this chapter.

This chapter is clearly the most important chapter of the book. It starts out by describing the most prominent tables and structures used by the kernel. It provided us a detailed description of the information contained in these structures that the kernel uses for managing processes, the CPU, and other system resources. We looked at the sub-systems including memory management, process management, interprocess communication, file system management, input/output management, and networking. For each sub-system, we first looked at the overall architecture and then looked at the algorithms of the key routines in the kernel for these sub-systems.

3.8.6 Exercises

1. What are the differences between sockets and Streams?
2. What are the differences between AT&T's RFS and SUN Micro-systems's NFS?

4

Distributed and

Multiprocessor Systems

Evolving hardware technologies have provided a number of different configuration options for sharing the processor load of an application, and distributing access to databases among a number of processors. The introduction of minicomputers started a movement toward decentralization of data processing systems that has continued with the paradigm of desktop workstations. The concept of distributed processing spans a number of functions including the use of co-processors as accelerators, process migration for networked systems, parallel processing for more processing power, and parallel or slave processing for fault tolerant systems.

As packing densities of ICs increase, and magnetic and laser recording technologies advance, significant new migration paths emerge for total information processing systems. Upwardly mobile 32-bit microprocessor families, with large memories and disk storage systems, are changing the manner in which computer systems are configured. Desktop workstations have added a third layer to the mainframe and minicomputer data processing hierarchy. The initial implementations of distributed file systems in this hierarchical environment have provided efficient *movement* of data but not *sharing* of data. The data redundancy across the network and ensuing loss of revision controls have made data management on these systems a very difficult task indeed. As disk storage capacities on workstations increase to over 100 Mbytes range, the task of data sharing will become even more complicated. An evolution to the information processing system from its hierarchical nature to a shared distributed nature is in progress.

Role of New Technologies in the Office

Computer-generated graphics summarize weeks of work in a simple, easy-to-comprehend image. They present material that the eye can capture and the brain can assimilate rapidly. They present trends visually, measure corporate performance graphically, and motivate managers to act. By letting the manager grasp the significance of a wide array of numbers, computer generated graphics have become a powerful tool for the manager. Pie-charts, bar-graphs, and dynamic line graphs condense a lot of information into a powerful presentation that is capable of transferring the gist of the information very rapidly to the executives or potential customers. Similarly, window management techniques are making systems easier to use.

Decision Support systems are emerging as a major new application area for the benefit of managers and executives. The technology changes noted above have provided a major boost to decision support systems. Voice-Mail and Voice-Data Systems further add to the needs of storage requirements and communications capabilities.

Artificial Intelligence (AI) is a technological advance that can be used in all development areas. For effective use of AI techniques, the basic tools—databases, languages, etc.—will be specialized. To fully exploit the capabilities of AI techniques, a system needs to be able to spread the database around on different nodes of the network, and be able to access large amounts of data that are then compacted into a decision point for the user. One of the most important developments for AI is the capability to share resources across a local area network (LAN).

The powerful capabilities of computer-generated graphics, the mushrooming use of graphics in all aspects of computing, and high resolution displays make storage requirements very intense and require large computing capacities for efficient operation. As complex systems become easier to use, the micro-computer is quietly, but significantly, changing the manner in which businesses use computers. Whereas a departmental system served as the hub of communications, the desktop has individualized the process. The increasingly powerful super micro is beginning to play the role of a *group computer* aimed at increasing productivity of tightly knit workgroups. Groups within a department are loosely knit via a LAN and the departments, in turn, are linked by a corporate-wide LAN. This facilitates different departments, e.g. Finance, Sales, Marketing, etc., to share common data and process it according to their own requirements. Two important trends to note here are 1) Data is being shared at various stages of processing, and 2) Processing of data is becoming more and more user specific. As we move into the information age, the dichotomy of independence of processing and sharing of data will become more pronounced. The effective use of LANs will be the driving force for the next generation of office systems.

Evolution of Networked Systems

Networking was made a household word by Xerox's announcement of Ethernet in 1980. However, local area networks continued to be long on promises and short on performance. The promises—simple and powerful medium for transfer of data, and all systems on the network can share all resources completely and effortlessly—have not yet materialized. The reality is that LANs require the users to become communications experts overnight, and in typical applications they replace the system bus, and do it very inefficiently. However, improvements in technology, a better understanding of the nature and usefulness of LANs, reductions of cost of installation, and a more knowledgeable user base, have combined to make LANs a very important component of the modern office. The greatest expectation from a LAN today is the ability to share data.

The most common cabling schemes are based on twisted pair, coaxial cable, multiple core cable, and fiber optics. The twisted pair is generally not used above 1M bits/sec. Fiber optics, on the other hand, is typically used for speeds over 10M bits/sec while the coaxial cable fills the middle range. For this reason, network load and consequently the required cabling scheme become a very significant issue in the selection of the network systems and software.

4.1 DISTRIBUTED SYSTEMS CONCEPTS AND ISSUES

Distributed systems is a term that applies to any system where the different tasks of an application are performed by different CPUs, or where the CPU resources are pooled to collectively perform a task, an application, or a departmental function. The CPUs share the computing load and are used in a manner such that they present an appearance of a single large system. The CPUs, memory, file systems, and peripheral resources may be shared on a system-wide basis, and there is a common mode of accessing these resources for all users or applications on the system. This section describes the types of distributed systems and the nature and effects of the types of coupling among the components of the distributed system. Sections 4.2 and 4.3 further analyze distributed processing and distributed file systems.

4.1.1 Distributed Systems Concepts

There are essentially three types of configurations that render distributed processing. Let us take a look at these configurations.

4.1.1.1 Co-processors and Accelerators

Co-processors have been used for a number of computation-intensive functions, including array processing for multi-dimensional matrix evaluation, accelerators for vector analysis of screen display elements for CAD/CAM applications, floating point arithmetic, communications links, and the like. A co-processor is typically system resident and is attached to the same system bus as the main CPU. The co-processor may run a scaled down version of the same operating system running on the main CPU, or it may run a different executive program. Co-processors typically share some part of the main memory of the main CPU. Very clearly defined protocols are used between the CPUs. These protocols provide for the passing of addresses of data, that the co-processor is required to process, from the main CPU to the co-processor. The appropriate code to process this data is also downloaded to the co-processor.

4.1.1.2 Networked Load Sharing Systems for Distributed Processing

The concept of network based load sharing is illustrated in Figure 4-1. A high speed LAN is used to connect the different systems. The CPU resources are used as a pool of resources and the load across the network is balanced by migrating processes to underutilized CPUs.

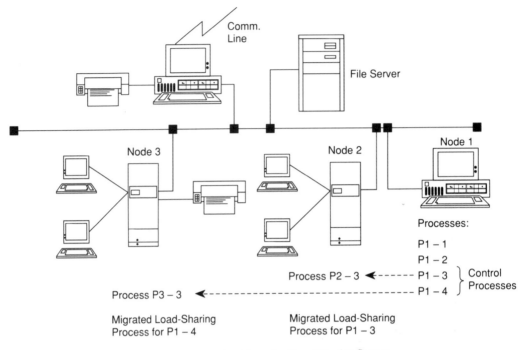

Figure 4-1. Networked Load Sharing System

Distributed processing is a term that is often used for parallel processing systems but more aptly applies to distributed processing across LANs. The effective LAN data transfer rates are a magnitude lower than the transfer rates on a system bus. However, for less demanding applications, networked load sharing is a very flexible and cost effective solution for increased processing requirements. A number of different schemes and solutions have been proposed and implemented for commercial systems.

4.1.1.3 Multiprocessing and Parallel Processing Systems

Multiprocessing is defined as the execution of multiple processing elements CPUs performing a number of concurrent tasks in a system with the intent of maximizing overall throughput from the system. The multiple CPUs pool resources and are used on an as-needed basis to share the load.

Parallel processing is the concurrent execution of multiple tasks of the same application. There is no architectural difference between multiprocessing systems and parallel processing systems, and the two are used interchangeably throughout this chapter. The architectures for multiprocessing and parallel processing have been developed in a number of flavors. The common theme in these architectures is that most applications perform a number of parallel tasks and the performance of the overall system can be improved either by a more powerful CPU or by distributing these tasks across a number of processors. A highly effective performance is achieved by

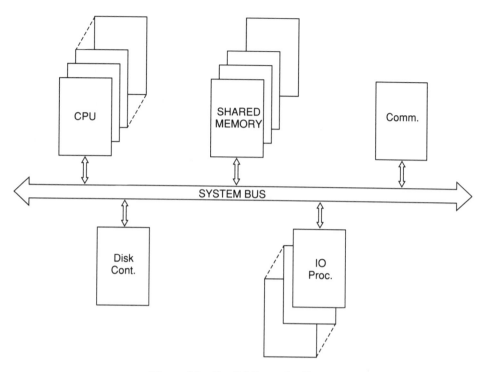

Figure 4-2.   Parallel Processing System

distributing tasks across a number of processors. Figure 4-2 describes the typical architecture of a parallel processing system. The major impetus to the development of this technique is the cost advantage gained by using lower speed components that pool the resources of the CPUs for a much greater overall throughput.

It is important to differentiate between load sharing across LANs and load sharing among CPUs of a multiprocessing system. For this chapter, the term *load sharing* will be used to describe load sharing across LANs. The terms *multiprocessing* and *parallel processing* will be used for a host computer that contains a number of CPUs sharing a system bus.

4.1.1.4 Fault-Tolerant Systems

Fault-tolerant systems use many of the same concepts as parallel processing systems. Whereas fault-tolerant systems typically manage only two or four CPUs, parallel processing systems manage much larger numbers of CPUs.

4.1.2 Distributed Systems Issues

This section introduces the concepts of *coupling* between processors, migration of processes from one CPU to another in a load sharing network, and adapting applications for parallel processing.

4.1.2.1 Coupling of Distributed Systems

The nature of the coupling has a significant impact on the extent to which the processors interact with one another and consequently, the extent of changes that are made to the kernel, the reliability of the system, the transparency of distributed operations, and the capability to recover from CPU or system failure.

Co-processors and parallel processors usually have the tightest coupling while networked processors are loosely coupled. Another aspect of coupling is the relationship set up for the CPUs—master/slave relationship versus peer relationship. Due to the inherent tighter coupling of the master/slave relationship, failure of either the master or the slave impacts the other. A peer relationship provides a better chance of recovery due to a less rigorous dependence of one CPU on another. A third aspect of coupling is performance. Generally, tighter coupling implies better performance because the operations are performed within pre-set guidelines and pre-set arbitration rules. In a peer relationship, resource contention has a negative impact on performance. However, high performance is achieved in multiprocessing systems by performing arbitration to resolve resource contention, especially, shared memory access.

4.1.2.2 Load Sharing Through Process Migration

Process migration is a term used to describe the concept of copying the image of a process already running on one CPU from that CPU to another CPU, the *server,* in a load sharing network. This is done if the original CPU, the *client,* is overutilized and is likely to bog down. Depending on the nature of the implementation, the original process (the *client* process) is terminated, or else it is reduced to a skeletal process that tracks the operations of migrated process.

Migration of a process from an overutilized CPU to an underutilized CPU helps achieve load balancing and uniform performance across the overall system configuration. Process migration is dynamic and does not require any changes to the application program or the compiler. It is managed completely by the operating system and the extensions to the operating system. These extensions to the UNIX kernel track the CPU load and process requirements, and then manage the processes that have migrated to ensure that their operating environment (files accessed, interprocess communications, etc.) remains the same.

4.1.2.3 Adapting Applications for Parallel Processing

A parallel processing system, unlike a load sharing network, treats all CPUs as a part of one system, and the application is constructed to take advantage of the different CPUs by spreading tasks across them. Most parallel processing systems require substantial enhancements to the UNIX kernel such that it can disperse processes across multiple CPUs on the bus and provide high speed communications to keep them synchronized. Resource contention, especially shared memory access, requires special attention in such systems. Some implementations have a specially developed *C* compiler or a post processing utility that determines the multi-tasking or multiprocessing requirements of an application and builds an executable file that pre-defines distribution of processes across some selected CPUs on the bus. Alternately, the distribution is done on a dynamic basis using the multiprocessing information set up in the executable file.

4.2 DISTRIBUTED AND PARALLEL PROCESSING

Parallel processing is a very specific implementation of distributed processing. Whereas distributed processing refers to a corporate wide system view to processing, parallel processing is a more system specific view to processing. This section describes the high level architectures of various types of distributed processing systems along with the advantages and disadvantages of these systems.

4.2.1 Co-processing Systems

Co-processing systems have been used for a number of applications, including array processing, graphics and communications front-ends, fault tolerant systems, and so on. In almost all implementations, there is a strong, tightly coupled, master-slave relationship. In fault tolerant systems, the slave processor functions as an understudy of the master to take over should the master fail.

Typically, the slave processor runs its own operating system kernel and exchanges data with the master via shared or mapped memory. In some implementations, interprocess communications is used as an alternative means of exchanging information.

In a fault tolerant system, the master processor is very sensitive to failure of the slave processors. Fault tolerant systems are designed through hardware extensions or through augmentations of the operating system kernel. They are designed to respond very rapidly to processor failures and to recover very quickly from such failures. Where recovery is not possible or is not designed in, the operating system traps and fails. Most parallel processing systems avoid this problem and maintain a simpler design by using peer level relationships.

4.2.2 Networked Load Sharing Systems

Load sharing across systems attached to a LAN is a very effective way of extending the overall performance of the system. Not every CPU in the network is operating at its peak load at any given time. Load sharing attempts to migrate processes from over-utilized CPUs to underutilized CPUs.

4.2.2.1 Master-Slave vs. Peer-to-Peer Relationships

In a load-sharing network, the user is connected to one node of the network while the process runs on another node of the network. In a well designed system, the user should not be aware that the process migrated from the local system to a remote system. The remote system is called the *server,* and the local system is called the *client.* Obviously, the client continues to play a role in interfacing with the user and passing on user keystrokes to the server. The client also needs to keep track of the files opened and current file positions in all open files in case the process migrates to another server or if the server fails.

The relationship between the client and the server is important. This relationship may be formulated as a tightly coupled master-slave relationship, or as a loosely coupled peer-to-peer relationship. In a tightly coupled master-slave relationship, the client closely monitors the server, directs all actions of the server, maintains a sizable amount of parallel information, and frequently checkpoints the server. In a peer-to-peer relationship, on the other hand, the client hands off the task to the server and retains only enough information to restart the process on another node should the server node fail. The client acts as a conduit for all information between the server and the user program. Due to the loose coupling, the client does not need to checkpoint the server very frequently.

In a tightly coupled system, recovery from a client or a server failure is more difficult than recovery in a loosely coupled system. In a peer relationship system, the processes do not depend on each other very greatly and recovery from failure is much easier.

4.2.2.2 Kernel Changes

Kernel changes are required, both in the kernel of the client and in the kernel of the server. The client kernel needs to be modified to support an automatic node migration capability. The client kernel tracks its loading factors and on reaching a pre-defined high-water mark, broadcasts a process migration request to nodes on the network. Any node that has spare capacity and the required resources to continue processing as a server responds. Consequently a client/server connection is established.

In addition to the kernel changes, the concept of a client process has to be developed along with a communications front-end that watches network traffic from servers and directs it to the corresponding client process in the node. After starting a server process, the client process becomes a skeletal process that needs scheduling only when the user or the server need attention. The kernel scheduling algorithms may need some change to give a client process the capability to preempt any process on the system should there be a server failure so that it has enough time to recover and start another server process.

The kernel of a server node needs changes to develop the concept of a server process and to design a communications front-end that maintains constant interface with the client front-ends. In addition to the communications front-ends, the kernels of the client and the server need to maintain information on available resources.

The communications front-ends maintain lists of client and server processes in the local node. The front-ends also maintain a virtual circuit with remote servers serving clients on the local node. The UNIX kernel design makes such enhancements feasible without significant redesign. The Remote Procedure Call (RPC) and the Client/Server Relational Database models are important steps towards commercial realization of such systems.

4.2.3 Parallel Processing Systems

Multiprocessing offers a number of advantages over uniprocessing. In a multi-user environment, the level of CPU availability and throughput are greater because processes can remain scheduled for longer periods and a number of processes can operate concurrently.

There are two basic approaches to multiprocessing in commercial systems— *distributed memory multiprocessors* and *shared memory multiprocessors*. These two approaches are based on different custom hardware designs and provide different levels of programming complexity.

Distributed Memory Multiprocessor systems are configured such that each CPU has its own memory. The architectural concepts for load-sharing networks resemble the basic concepts for distributed memory multiprocessor systems. Within a distributed memory system, the processors are loosely coupled and each processor is essentially self-sufficient. The processors do not need constant communications during execution of an application. Distributed memory multiprocessors are most useful for applications that can be broken down into several unrelated parts. Performance can degrade noticeably if the parts are not really unrelated and require plenty of interprocessor communications. In general, distributed memory multiprocessor systems have complex connection schemes and are not easily adaptable to general purpose applications.

Shared Memory Multiprocessor systems are configured with a common shared memory pool and are tightly coupled via a high-speed system bus. The processors must coordinate access to shared memory and, typically, require a lock-and-test mechanism. A high-speed system bus and local on-board cache memory are usually employed to achieve good performance.

Shared memory multiprocessor systems are designed with a symmetric layout of CPUs. All CPUs in a *symmetric shared memory multiprocessor* system are identical and any CPU can execute both user code and kernel code. This makes the system transparent to applications and any process can run on any CPU. Programs written for a uniprocessor system can also run on a symmetric shared memory system without change because a CPU is a resource that is shared just as any other resource. A process waiting to be scheduled runs on the first CPU freed up. The responsibilities for executing processes, handling interrupts, and performing system housekeeping functions are shared by all CPUs in a dynamically load balanced system.

Shared memory multiprocessor systems provide an efficient means of interprocess communications via shared access to memory and can adapt to a wide range of application requirements.

Both parallel processing architectures just described share some common characteristics. The key issues that characterize the architecture of parallel processing systems are the following:

1. A multiple processor system has multiple streams of activities.
2. There are multiple system and interrupt streams that can interact.
3. Normal data storage and access protection schemes are inadequate.
4. Interprocess and interprocessor communications are required.
5. Processors perform different functions of same application in parallel.

The UNIX architecture in its current form was not designed for parallel processing, but its inherent design flexibility makes it a good candidate for extensions to the kernel. The UNIX architecture has only two external points of entry for the kernel—the *trap* instruction for the processing of system calls (and errors), and hardware interrupts that are serviced by interrupt service routines. UNIX processes operate in a fairly protected environment. A process can be either in *user mode* or *kernel mode*. Processes are protected in the kernel mode through restrictions on preemption. Processes can further protect themselves from being interrupted by raising the processor priority level during critical sections of code. This architecture, though adequate for a single processor system, is not adequate for multiprocessor systems. Preemption works well on a single processor system. On a multiple processor system where processes operating on different processors may have system level conflicts, the local preemption restriction or the priority control are not adequate. The architecture has to be evolved and a scheme is required that addresses system-wide conflicts. These conflicts may include priority conflicts due to interrupt levels on different processors, conflicts between processes on different processors, or conflicts between a process on one processor and priority interrupts on another.

The system-wide conflicts may be for shared memory, disk storage, or for a peripheral. Unless a scheme is developed to resolve conflicts and to sequence access in an orderly manner, data corruption can result from improper update sequences. Ideally, the architecture is extended for multiprocessor systems in a manner compatible with the architecture for that function in a single processor system. This provides consistency with single processor systems such that an application does not change at the source level when moved from one environment to another.

The key architectural issues that require special design attention, and that result in extensions to the UNIX kernel are the following:

1. Process creation and scheduling across multiple processors.
2. Memory management across multiple processors.
3. Prevention or arbitration of resource allocation conflicts.
4. Interprocess communications across processors in the system.
5. Shared I/O management.

4.2.3.1 Process Creation and Scheduling

The *fork* system call creates a child process as a duplicate of the parent process. In a multiprocessor system there is some additional information that needs to be maintained because the child may operate on a processor different from the one the parent process is operating from. In effect, a process group may be spread over a number of processors.

Process scheduling is managed by the routine *sched* and the routine *swtch* performs the actual CPU scheduling. In a multiprocessor system, the scheduling has to take into account all processors and all processes across the system. Scheduling in such a case requires checking for a process that is unblocked, the availability of the processor that it will be scheduled on, and availability of memory to load it. When all of these conditions are satisfied, the process can be scheduled to run if no higher priority process is waiting to be scheduled for that processor.

The scheduling of the processor, performed by the *swtch* routine, is also more complex in the case of multiple processors. The *swtch* routine has to take into account the memory usage of other processors. This information is either maintained in a system-wide page table or by the use of resource locks. It has to also differentiate between the processors and set up the environment according to the resources available to that processor. These routines, in effect, operate essentially as before but with additional checks mandated by the muliple processors.

4.2.3.2 Memory Management

Parallel processor systems have been designed with a combination of some on-board cache memory per processor and shared memory banks. The distribution of process groups often results in processes running on different processors attempting to access the same memory. There are at least three schemes that have been used to address this. They consist of the use of systemwide memory page tables, memory resource locks, and local processor cache memory that is periodically updated and synchronized with the current contents of the shared memory or disk data. The local cache memory on two or more processors may contain the same memory segments. The segments are kept in synchronization by constantly watching for changes to that memory. If a processor is using its cache, the same segments located in the cache at other processors are marked *in use* and have to be updated before they can be used.

4.2.3.3 Arbitration of Resource Allocation

There are three potential schemes for arbitration of resource allocation conflicts. These include the following:

1. Systemwide allocation tables.
2. Resource locks.
3. Resource spoolers.

Both systemwide allocation tables and resource locks require modification of all routines that perform I/O access. Resource spoolers are handled at the driver level where the driver accesses a spooler and the arbitration for resource allocation is performed by the spooler.

4.2.3.4 Interprocess Communication Across Processors

Most implementations provide high speed interprocessor communications via the main system bus. Interprocess communications among processes on different processors is achieved as an extension to local interprocess communications by maintaining system-wide parameters and utilizing high speed interprocessor communications.

4.2.3.5 Distributed I/O Management

In a system with multiple processors, where some processors may be dedicated for I/O operation, the peripherals are attached to their local hosts, but are available as system-wide resources. Areas of conflict include device numbers, bus addresses, and access parameters. The modifications to the UNIX kernel result from an enhanced device number which also includes a processor identification. The bus address may also be extended. For peripheral devices, a systemwide table is required.

4.2.3.6 System-wide Tables

For performance reasons, parts of system-wide tables are maintained at each processor and complete tables are maintained either in shared memory or in a shared disk resource.

4.2.3.7 Other Key Kernel Changes

Other important changes to the kernel include functions like forced writes to disk to maintain a constantly updated shared disk storage, contiguous disk files for system data and system-wide tables, file and record locking for multiple processor updates, and system-wide shared memory tables; system-wide semaphores and signals; and so on.

4.2.4 Examples of Multi-processor Architectures

The following sub-sections describe briefly three architectures that are representative of the multiprocessor implementations.

4.2.4.1 The TI Multiprocessor System

Figure 4-3 illustrates the architecture of the TI Multiprocessor System. The TI System consists of five Motorola 68020 processors assisted by 68010 processors for I/O and mass storage control. Each 68020 processor runs an enhanced UNIX kernel. Each 68020 processor has a 256 byte instruction cache for high speed operation of program loops. An additional 8K byte cache is used for storing frequently used memory pages locally, and another 8K byte cache is used for storing frequently used pages of the application.

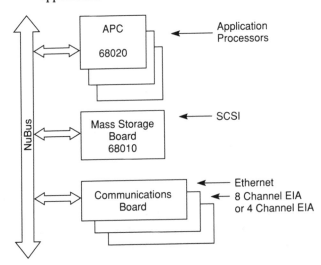

Figure 4-3. Architecture of TI Multiprocessor System

The architecture uses load sharing to optimize performance across the 68020 processors. It also uses record locking to properly sequence concurrent update requests from multiple processors. A forced write to disk is used to ensure that the disk data as well as in-core status remain in synchronization constantly.

4.2.4.2 Sequent Symmetry System

The Sequent Symmetry system is a tightly coupled symmetrical arrangement of processors. Figure 4-4 describes the architecture of this system.

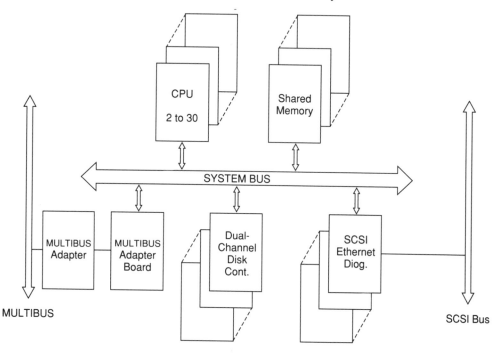

Figure 4-4.   Architecture of Sequent Symmetry System

The Sequent Symmetry system features a high-speed system bus. Each CPU board includes its own 64K byte cache memory with logic to maintain consistency between copies of data in CPU caches without requiring CPUs to write to system memory when shared data is modified.

The dual channel disk controllers are designed to provide two independent data channels to the system bus, with up to four disk drives on each channel. The two channels can transfer data simultaneously. The dual channel controller also manages overlapped seeks.

4.2.4.3 Encore Multi-MAX System

The Encore Multi-MAX is a tightly coupled symmetrical arrangement of up to 20 processors. Figure 4-5 describes the architecture of the system.

The Encore system, originally based on AT&T UNIX System V, also supports

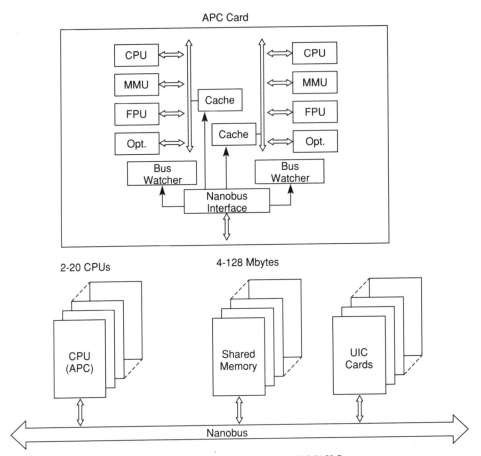

Figure 4-5.   Architecture of Encore Multi-MAX System

Berkeley UNIX 4.2bsd. The Encore system uses local cache on each CPU card for fast
local access. Since the same block of memory can be cached in several places, the
concept of bus-watching is used to achieve cache consistency. All caches listen to the
main bus and invalidate any entry that has been modified by some other processor.
This concept uses a dual-cache tag scheme, where *C tags* are used for actual cache
memory, and *B tags* are used to keep a copy of the *C tag* caches for bus watching.

The Encore implementation of AT&T UNIX System V uses a 4K byte page size.
As a peer level architecture, the base architecture is expandable and is being expanded
to support a much larger number of processors. The UNIX kernel has been modified
to support a multiprocessor environment.

4.2.5 Future Directions

While most current multiprocessor implementations limit the number of processors to
64, the future potential and direction is for much larger systems; with potentially no
theoretical limit on the number of processors. Neural nets are gaining a rapidly
increasing following. UNIX presents an opportunity for extensibility to support Neural

net systems. The evolution of UNIX has just begun. It should be noted that most standardization efforts remain limited to programming interfaces or user interfaces. The UNIX kernel has not undergone substantial change thus far, but future directions hold the potential for considerable evolution of the kernel architecture.

4.3 DISTRIBUTED FILE SYSTEMS ARCHITECTURES

Distributed file systems are a prerequisite for distributed processing systems. However, distributed data management can be used even by systems that do not provide for distributed processing. The concept of distributed file systems is useful for centralization of data storage, sharing of data, and using distributed resources as a collective system resource.

The following three architectural concepts cover a wide range of distributed file system implementations. Some of them are embedded in overall system products and are not observed independently in commercial products. They are presented here for completeness of discussion.

The *Network File Access Systems,* akin to public networks and generally provided by LAN vendors, are the simplest and provide remote login capabilities for file transfer and electronic mail. The transferred copy is modified, and is transferred back on completion of the task.

The *Distributed Network File Server* is the next stage in the evolution of data sharing and network file access. This technique provides for a user to have dynamic access to files from remote machines as if they were logged-on to a local file system. A central file server is key to the use of this system. In practice, users may still copy files to local disks due to the distinction maintained between local disks and central file servers.

The *Shared Transparent Distributed File System* is a major step toward a fully distributed and transparent file system. With facilities to spread files across nodes on the network, as well as share files and directories across the network, this environment provides a consistent and convenient interface to the database across the network. The user does not need to know the exact node location of a file, and has no reason to search or copy a file. The Shared Distributed File System can be further enhanced to spread a single file across the network for a truly distributed Data Base Management System. It can also be enhanced to provide low-cost fault tolerance for files.

4.3.1 File Access Methods and Networks

The file access method depends very directly on the operating system and the network scheme for its effectiveness and performance. Key issues for the selection of file access methods and networks are the following:

1. Effective data rate.
2. Consistency of interfacing and networking schemes.
3. Internet (Gateway) access to other LANs.
4. Network reliability and integrity.

Where the file access method couples the nodes tightly, the reliability of the end-to-end connection becomes a very important consideration. In a loosely coupled access method, consistency of interfaces is a more important consideration.

4.3.1.1 Independence from Networks

For a file access method to be really successful, it needs to be flexible enough to adjust to the different predominant networking schemes. If and when a standard emerges, the capabilities and performance of the file access method can be significantly enhanced. Until then, they have to cater to a multitude of connecting schemes, protocols, and networking requirements.

4.3.2 Network File Access Systems

The *Network File Access Systems* are the simplest and provide remote log-in capabilities for File Transfer and Electronic Mail. The user, however, has the responsibility for knowing where the data is stored and the path routing to reach that data. There are no capabilities to use the files in place where they are stored. A number of LAN vendors provide the capability as a part of their network software.

4.3.2.1 Architectural Considerations for Network File Access Systems

The architectural considerations for most such systems tend to be rather straightforward. The network may be single level LAN, or it may be multi-level LAN; or a network system consisting of a number of distinct LANs connected via gateways. There are two kinds of file transfers, transfer initiated by the host (source) system, and transfer initiated by the requesting system.

Electronic mail is an extension of the capability of a transfer initiated by a host system. The *UUCP* or the *rcp* utilities are excellent examples of this capability and are often used, both for file transfer and electronic mail. Both the host (source), and the destination system, need to be set up for the file transfer. For electronic mail, a *mail* program delivers the message to the appropriate mailbox.

For a transfer initiated by a requesting system, the requesting system may be the source or the destination for the transfer. The host (the system on the network being accessed) must be set up for the transfer to take place with a UUCP or equivalent program compatible with the program making the request.

4.3.2.2 Networking Issues

The major networking issues are addressing, especially for the multi-level network, and recovery from network/node failures. The addressing consists primarily of the node name for single level networks and includes the routing gateways for multi-level networks.

4.3.2.3 File Migration Concepts

Over a period of time, the typical usage of a network can be determined and the performance enhanced by routinely adjusting the location of data files for efficient transfers. The file migration technique is used to place the files most commonly accessed on the fastest medium available on the file server. Though very useful in practice, this technique requires very frequent and careful management of the network.

4.3.2.4 Advantages of Network File Access Systems

Network File Access Systems are generally easy to implement and manage. This method allows linking systems as network nodes that may have unlike operating systems and unlike CPUs. Only the file transfer protocol needs to be compatible. And, there is generally no additional system management after the file transfer software is set up.

4.3.2.5 Disadvantages of Network File Access Systems

There are a number of disadvantages compared to other methods of distributing data across networks. This method uses a LAN in a manner not much more effective than a leased telephone line. The issues of network loading due to constant transferring of files, especially at start of the workday, can put a heavy burden on the LAN requiring very high data rates for the network to be adequate.

4.3.3 Distributed Network File Server Systems

The *Distributed Network File Server System* is the next stage in the evolution of data sharing and network file access. This technique provides for dynamic access to file systems from remote machines while the system remembers user defaults. It allows the remote user to use files as if they were logged on to a local file system.

A number of Network File Servers (commonly referred to as distributed file systems) are commercially available. Examples of these are AT&T's RFS (Remote File System), Sun NFS (Network File System), The Newcastle Connection, LOCUS, etc.

4.3.3.1 Architecture of Distributed Network File Server Systems

The physical configuration described in Figure 4-6 is a typical network configuration and consists of CPUs connected via a LAN. The disk file systems, spooled peripheral devices, and communications links are available for access as a network resource.

Distributed Network File Server Systems are an extension of the hierarchical file systems, e.g., in the UNIX operating system. Figure 4-7 depicts the hierarchy of mounted file systems in a single UNIX system.

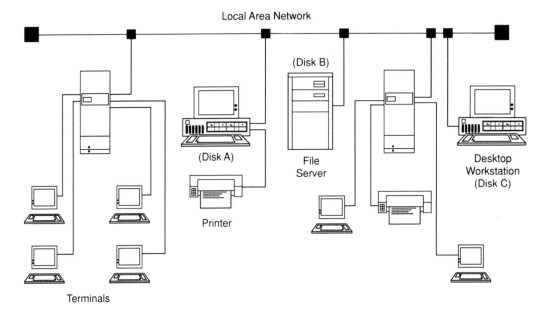

Figure 4-6.   Sample Network Configuration

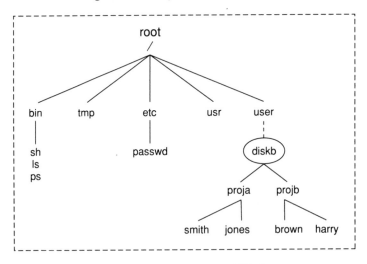

Figure 4-7.   Hierarchical Mounted File Systems

This model is extended to a network environment by providing a *network mount* as in Figure 4-8. Files on *dskb* are now available on *dska* and *dskc*.

The advantage of this model is that it is very consistent with the hierarchical arrangement of the UNIX file system. Once a file system is *mounted*, all files on that file system or directory are available to authorized users.

The main disadvantages of hierarchical models are that another level of hierarchy is required, thus making the overall hierarchy of the file system harder to remember and the same file is referred by different names on different systems due to hierarchy

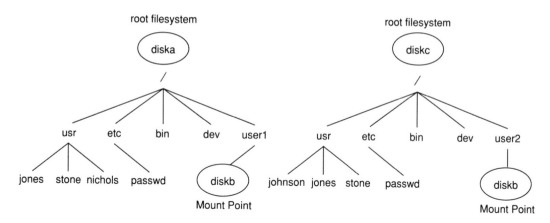

Figure 4-8. Network File System Example

extensions. Another disadvantage is that either a *super-root* directory must be created or the file name syntax must change to avoid naming conflicts. In a multiprocessing environment, processes on system *A* have to refer to the same files in a manner different from the manner in which processes on system *B* refer to them. Additionally, each node requires a *mount* of all other file systems. The addition of a file system results in a network wide activity to mount the new file system and there are "n*n" repetitions of the *mount* procedure to get the network set up. On a very large network, this can be a very tedious process.

4.3.3.2 Capabilities Provided by Network File Server Systems

The Network File Server Systems typically provide two levels of capabilities. *File Transfer Protocol* (FTP) across networks provides explicit transfer of data files from the disk storage of one node on a network to that of another node through the use of pre-defined commands and protocols. *Network Remote Login* allows a user at a workstation attached to one node of the network to login to another remote node and use it in the same manner as the local node. This allows sharing of data in a common file system across the network. The extended *mount* and *umount* commands of NFS provide access to file systems on other nodes. The required directory is, typically, made the default directory.

The primary application of this capability is in the use of Network File Servers, i.e. a node that has a large amount of storage and serves the primary function of providing disk access to remote users. Unlike the older concept of downloading information to the local node for use during the day and updating the master copy at the end of the day, in this concept files can be used as they are, and where they are, and there are no revision problems for files shared by a number of users. Depending on the implementation of the network, the fileservers may be systems different from the workstations and other nodes on the network, i.e. unlike systems can function in a network configuration.

4.3.3.3 Advantages of Distributed Network File Server Systems

The following describe the key advantages of these systems as compared to the other methods of sharing data.

1. Files on one node (generally the central file server) may be accessed and shared by many other users on other nodes. This advantage is more noticeable on networked workstations that do not have large local disk storage.
2. All users have access to the original data files and the problem of revision maintenance goes away.
3. Security is provided in addition to normal UNIX password protection by various schemes of authenticating user privileges.
4. Maintenance and administration of the system is easier since there are no copies of data files on the system.
5. Multiple copies of files require large volumes of data. A lot of disk storage is saved since there is no need for storage of multiple copies.

4.3.3.4 Disadvantages of Distributed Network File Server Systems

While there are many advantages, there are some significant disadvantages in the use of these systems, and these issues have to be kept in mind and planned for before setting up the network. These disadvantages include the following:

1. In a hierarchically *mounted* environment, failures of mounted nodes can cause substantial problems, indeed they can bring the network down. A number of schemes are being developed to counteract the effects of this tight coupling.
2. The set-up and administration of a network like this is complicated and requires a lot of work to ensure security and trouble-free access.
3. The user has to know precisely which node and directory contain the files they need to access.
4. The failure of the central file server can be catastrophic for a large organization. Not only does it put a lot of users out of work, but rebuilding a large system is time consuming and causes a lot of manhours of loss.
5. Almost all implementations require changes to user programs due to modifications to the UNIX kernel and altered or additional system calls. While the UNIX Operating System becomes non-standard, a prohibitively expensive penalty is paid in re-programming applications programs.
6. Applications with hard-coded pathname extensions have to be re-programmed for transfer to another node.

4.3.3.5 Examples of Distributed Network Fileservers

A number of distributed network fileservers are in use in UNIX based networks. Let us now look at the architectures of some of these systems.

The Newcastle Connection

The first of the prominent network fileserver schemes, the Newcastle Connection, was also the first to use the concept of a remote procedure call (*RPC*). The architecture of the Newcastle Connection is very simple. It consists of a Newcastle Connection layer located on *top* of the kernel, so that it can intercept all commands and system calls before they are passed on to the kernel. Any system call that is directed to another node on the network is intercepted and addressed through the RPC mechanism. A major advantage of this approach is that there is no change to the UNIX kernel. Conversely, this also placed a number of restrictions on the capabilities of the system. The Newcastle Connection is illustrated in Figure 4-9.

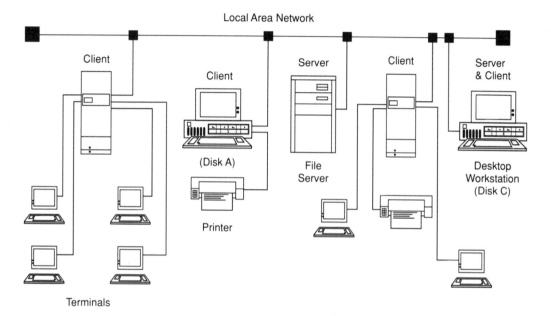

Figure 4-9.   The Newcastle Connection

A file is identified as being on a remote node if its *pathname* starts with the construct "/..". The problem of conflicts due to different nodes having identical user identifiers is solved by maintaining a table of recognized remote user identifiers and their permissions. They are recognized by the server system as being remote users and they are, therefore, tracked with their node name. Any user attempting to access a remote directory where that user is not listed in the table as being an authorized remote user is provided *guest* status with limited privileges, such as *other*.

Any files *opened* on a remote system are entered in a user level library structure, in the local system, that is checked for all read and write calls. Any remote node access calls are re-directed to the remote node.

The disadvantages of this approach are both function related and performance related. In terms of function, it requires setting up permissions for each user on each system accessible remotely. The user has to know the node and the directory where the file resides for file opens and follow-on transparent access. Performance is lower due to the additional processing for the screening of all I/O calls in the Newcastle Connection layer.

The Sun Network File System (NFS)

The Sun NFS, described in Figure 4-10, provides transparent remote access to file systems. An important design goal was portability to other operating systems and machine architectures. Other design goals include crash recovery from server file system crashes, transparent access such that access to local files or remote files is identical, reasonable performance, and maintaining UNIX system semantics.

NFS uses the Sun Remote Procedure Call (RPC) definition described in Chapter 3 (Section 3.8) for protocol definition and remote system access. It also uses the External Data Representation (XDR) to define data in a machine independent manner. The concept of implementation independence is carried further by defining a Virtual File System (VFS) that defines the operations that can be performed on a file system. In addition, a *vnode* interface defines the operations that can be done on a file and is an implementation similar to UNIX inodes, but for the VFS.

NFS does not allow shared root file systems. In its concept, common directories like */dev, /bin,* and */etc* should reside on a common fileserver. While this concept simplifies the design, potential failure of a fileserver impacts all nodes using that fileserver.

The *exportfs* command provides information on the components of the file system that a server will set up to be accessible by clients. The UNIX *mount* command (and system call) is extended to provide a network-wide *mount table*. The *cd* command is used with the pathname to make a directory on a remote file system, the default directory or a branch of the user's directory tree.

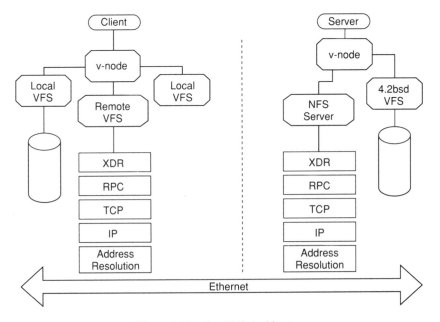

Figure 4-10.   Sun NFS Architecture

The NFS fileservers are stateless machines and do not track the state of files or provide any standard UNIX locking capabilities. Conflicts in the use of the same files from different nodes can arise. A locking scheme provided by Sun builds on the *stateless* server concept by maintaining client requested locks in memory only. The client, in that implementation, also maintains locked information on files locked by the client. By keeping lock information in two places, the network can recover from the failure of a server of a client.

Other advantages not quite apparent in the description above include the hierarchical operation that is very similar to the normal UNIX *mount*. Since files are shared in place on the fileserver, there are no revision conflicts. The stateless nature (compromised only by the locking scheme) ensures consistency of the system after recovery.

A disadvantage of this architecture is that the user or the system administrator do have to know which directories should be mounted at each node. The number of mounts required can take a fair amount of time on system reboot. Even though the servers operate as stateless machines, the tight coupling between the client and the server may cause data consistency problems on failure of a server.

The AT&T RFS (Remote File System)

The Remote File System (RFS) is a utility provided with AT&T UNIX System V.3. It uses the Streams interface, which allows embedding any of several different network protocols. This makes RFS independent of any one kind of network hardware or software.

The AT&T Remote File System is designed for transparent sharing of disk storage and peripherals. It provides remote file access across a network for sharing data, or sharing or accessing a special peripheral, e.g. a printer or plotter. Figure 4-11 describes the architecture of RFS.

The RFS uses the AT&T Streams networking interface to *mount* a directory structure under the user's current directory, or a specified directory that the user has access to, such that the files on the remote file system are accessible as though they are a part of the local file system directory structure. The AT&T Streams architecture is a layered architecture where the streams are the interfaces between the protocol layers and the UNIX kernel. This provides the capability to implement different protocols to operate with the same Streams interface. The interfaces are implemented as a set of new system calls that reside at the level of the sessions layer of the OSI model, and as a set of Streams interface modules that form the presentation layer between the user's application and the system calls. The RFS implementation also supports a Transport Layer Interface (*TLI*) for low level access to networking for system applications. The Streams Interface is called in the same manner any other communications interface is called using a set of system calls that are serviced by kernel service modules. Figure 4-12 describes an example of such a *mount*.

The AT&T RFS also supports *special files* for access to remote devices, and *named pipes* for communications. Another important feature of the RFS is the extensive support for network administration. RFS provides transparency between remote and local file systems and maintains security and integrity of the system for concurrent file access. This capability is provided retaining the normal UNIX file system semantics. The *adv* command sends a message to the *name service* node that it is making files

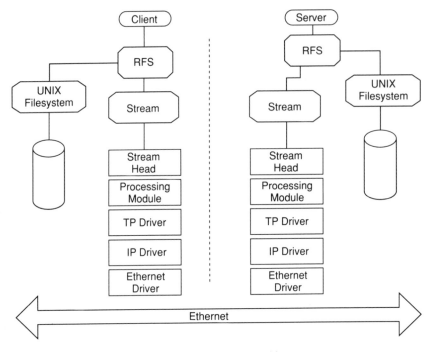

Figure 4-11. AT&T RFS Architecture

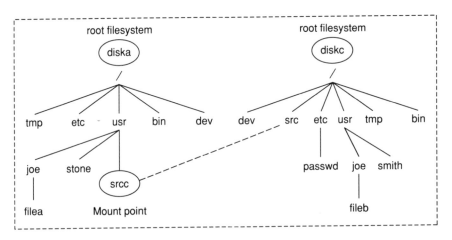

Figure 4-12. AT&T RFS Example

available as a server. The *mount* command allows administrators on the *client* system to make a remote file system available for use locally in a transparent manner. A network connection is set up between the *client* and the server consequent to a mount command. The server keeps track of how many remote users have a file open at a given time and it also maintains security by distinguishing between local opens and remote opens. Remote access can be restricted to the privileges of selected local accounts. The user is encouraged to read Section 3.8.2 for more detailed architectural analysis of RFS.

4.3.4 Shared Transparent Distributed File System Model

The *Shared Transparent Distributed Network File System Model,* called *Shared File System Model* or *Peer Model* for short in the following, is the first major step toward a fully distributed and transparent file system model. This model provides the UNIX user an option for multiple disk configurations that provide a consistent and flexible file access. It facilitates all programs to access all files in the same manner, so that the location of the node where the program is being run becomes inconsequential. With facilities to spread files across nodes on the network, as well as share files and directories across the network, this environment provides a consistent and easy to use interface for a distributed database across the network. The user does not need to know, or care for the exact node location of a file, and has no reason to copy a file for using it, nor has a reason to search for a file.

The Shared File System Model can be further enhanced to provide the capability to spread a single file across the network for a truly distributed Data Base Management System. Additionally, it can be enhanced to provide a low cost transparent fault tolerance for files by creating a back-up copy on a different disk and automatically updating it.

4.3.4.1 Capabilities of a Shared Distributed File System

The primary capability is convenience and natural access, and sharing of files across a network. Users may share files with ease and do not have to be aware of disk or network configurations. System programs are accessed locally to enhance network performance. The peer model provides a flexible environment for distributed applications. It is consistent with the UNIX file system architecture and, at the same time, can be enhanced to provide file redundancy such that two copies of the same file are maintained by the system and it ensures that the two copies remain in sync so that failure of a node will not even be noticed by users as long as their CPU has not failed. It can be further enhanced to provide Network Space Files (files can span homogeneous file systems across disks and across the local area networks, a capability highly in demand for shared database systems). Adding a new node to the network does not require full system re-configuration, nor does it require the network to be made inaccessible to the users for that duration. Disk file systems may be included or excluded without disturbing the network.

4.3.4.2 Logical View of the Shared Network

The Shared Distributed File Systems operate with the same physical configurations as the Distributed Network File Server systems, except that there is no need for a file server. By treating the union of file systems across the network as the network file server, Shared Network File systems eliminate the need of centralizing file server functions. Figure 4-13 shows the physical configuration of a shared network.

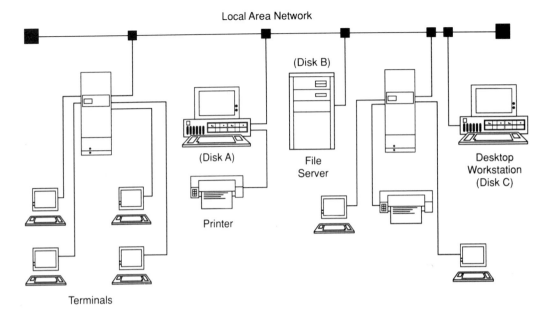

Figure 4-13. Physical Configuration of Shared Network

The logical view of the network may consist of CPUs, disks, printers, terminals, and communication lines where all of the devices are logically connected to the LAN. Disk file systems, spooled peripheral devices, and communications links are available for access as a shared network resource, except where specifically excluded from the network access due to a user decision that removes disk-sharing capability temporarily. Figure 4-14 shows the logical configuration of the shared network of Figure 4-13.

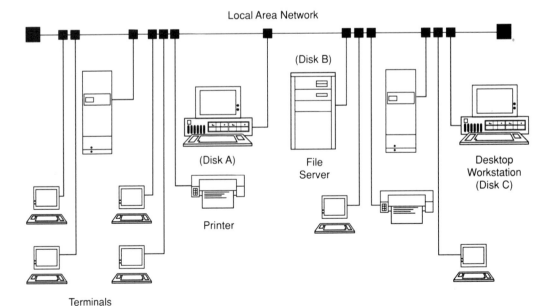

Figure 4-14. Logical Configuration of Shared Network

Ideally, access to network files should be convenient and should miminize user retraining. The Shared Distributed File System provides access to all sharable files (i.e., files not explicitly excluded from sharing) across the network just as in a single UNIX system. No new file naming syntax is needed to describe the files.

4.3.4.3 Shared File System Model

The Shared Distributed File System uses a peer model for coordinating file systems over the network. Instead of adding additional levels of hierarchy, the file systems are *overlaid* on each other, as shown in Figure 4-15. This provides the UNIX user an option for installing multiple disk configurations that provide a consistent and flexible file access. It allows all programs to access the files in the same manner, such that location of the node where the program is run becomes inconsequential.

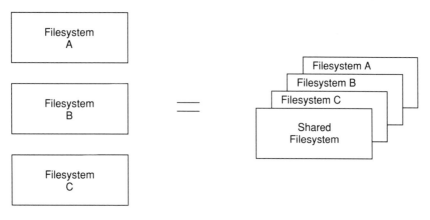

Figure 4-15.   Overlaying of File Systems

The Shared File System model lends itself to some interesting architectural concepts. Let us use Figure 4-16 to elaborate on these concepts. A node may identify itself as a *non-cooperating* node, that is, it can send out for disk service from other shared nodes but does not share its file system with other nodes. This is useful to ensure privacy or performance for priority work. Each node may have several file systems, but can make only some of its file systems available for sharing to the cluster. A *diskless node* is a node that has no local disk and is associated with some other CPU for disk access only. A diskless node may change its host fileserver. It must, however, elect to attach itself to one file system at all times.

A *network domain* consists of all nodes on the network that have identified themselves as *cooperating* file systems. Any user on any workstation can, under normal permissions, gain access to files on any of these file systems. A *user domain* is a subset of the network domain and consists of the set of file systems that the user requires the Shared Distributed File System to search on a non-specific file access. A user can change the user domain at any time through the use of *mount/umount* commands. This facilitates the user to enhance performance by limiting search operations to specific combinations of file systems. A *gateway* may be used for linking to other networks and clusters.

The *local* file system is the file system of the node to which the user terminal or workstation is physically attached. The *current* file system is the file system that the user has defined as the default file system by using a modified *cd* command. This may be the local file system or it may be another file system on the network that the user wants searched before all other remote file systems. A *remote* file system is any file system in the user domain that is not the local or the current file system. Normal global search routing is in the order—current, local, and then remote file systems in the user domain.

The *directory range* is defined as *current* or *global*. Setting the global range switches directory access from the *local disk* to shared access of all disks in the user domain that have an applicable directory. In other words, the range can be set to the local disk only, or it can be opened up to all disks specified in the user domain.

Implicit access is the natural mode of operation and for all such access the user lets the Shared Distributed File System decide which is the first available file meeting the pre-defined criteria, that is, within the user domain, specified directory, and local/global access.

Explicit access may be used where the location of a file is known and is important to the user for performance, or, to ensure that a file is always on a particular file system. The node name is required in the file pathname for explicit access.

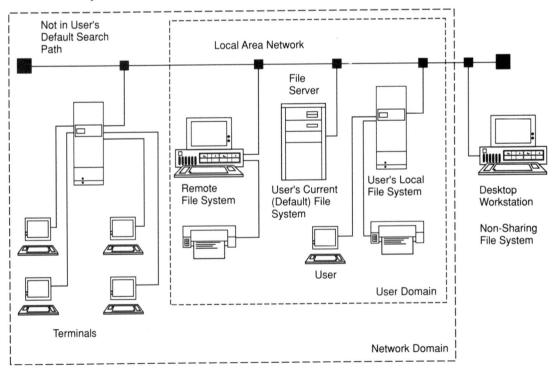

Figure 4-16.   Shared File System Model

The *shared file system* is distributed across several nodes in the network. Parts of the file system may reside on different nodes. The unique feature of the Shared Distributed File System is that it automatically routes file access to the correct node without user intervention.

One of the most notable features of this approach is that the individual file systems of the nodes are coordinated into one large file system, called the network file system. For example, the file */usr/joe/filea* is actually on *nodeA* and the file */usr/bob/ fileb* is on *nodeB*, yet the group of file systems appear as a single file system. Note that the specification of the node is not required when accessing the file. The Shared Distributed File System resolves the actual location of the file since it treats the union of file systems as a fileserver. Figure 4-17 shows the union of the file systems on *diska* and *diskc* of Figure 4-12.

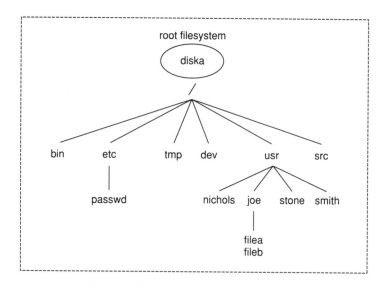

Figure 4-17.   Reconfiguration of Figure 4-12

An important point to note here that in a typical office environment, directories are set up as */usr/project/person*. A person may have directories under */usr* that have identical project names. Rather than treat it as a problem, this approach takes advantage of this fact. The union of all */usr* directories is treated as one directory, and the union of all identical project directories, e.g. */usr/projvenus*, is treated as one directory. Similarly, the union of all directories for *joe* related to one project is also treated as one network directory. By selecting the directory level at which a user operates, the scope of the access can be changed very rapidly and easily, and done in a manner very natural to project or group oriented activities. While other network file systems take the following approach: take several nodes and provide access to their file systems, the Shared Distributed File System approach is to provide one network wide file system whose data is distributed across several nodes. This approach is a truly distributed network file system.

4.3.4.4 Design Issues

An important design issue is whether the Shared File System is implemented in a user library or within the kernel. The implementation at the user library level involves translation of implicit network names to explicit files in system calls like *open, link, unlink*. There is no kernel change required for this. The disadvantages of this approach are poorer performance and, a change in the open file semantics across *exec* and *fork* system calls since some of the open file information is maintained in the user process.

The kernel level implementation involves changes to the *namei* and *iget* algorithms to accommodate translation of file names to inodes so that the node where the file is located is resolved at the same time. The advantages of this design are faster performance than a library level implementation, and open file semantics are maintained since the kernel is able to handle *fork* and *exec* calls for open files.

Another key issue is that this design supports the concept of a *network name space*. A data base system can be designed using the architecture of Shared File systems such that data files can be spread across the network. The union of files on different network nodes with the same filename and under identical directory structures is treated as one database file. Data base records and index files can, in this architecture, be located where they are used most frequently for optimum performance; while they remain available to the rest of the network in a transparent manner.

4.3.4.5 Advantages of the Shared Transparent File System

The following describe the key advantages of the Shared Transparent File System model for sharing file systems:

1. Files on any node can be accessed by any user on another node. All file systems in the network can be fileservers.
2. File systems are overlaid so that duplicate file names are taken into account.
3. The naming syntax for the directory hierarchy does not change and files can be accessed exactly as they are accessed in the local file system.
4. Application code with built-in file directory hierarchy references can run without any change.

4.3.4.6 Disadvantages of the Shared Transparent File System

While there are many advantages to this approach to a shared file system design, there are some disadvantages also. The disadvantages are as follows:

1. Handling of node failures may leave two copies of the same file on two file systems that may have a difference in contents. Revision management requires special attention.
2. Performance may suffer due to extensive file listing across the network as users tend to use more files distributed across the network.

3. The system administrator has to be more conscious of security issues as access is provided to file systems globally across a network.

4.4 SUMMARY

We looked at a number of ways in which UNIX has been extended beyond its basic capabilities for distributed file sharing, distributed load sharing, and distributed processing architectures. In this chapter, we looked at some real implementations as well as some conceptual ideas for potential implementations. We also looked at some key issues in evolving UNIX in these directions, and we also gained some insight about the adaptability of the UNIX architecture.

4.5 EXERCISES

1. What are the key issues in a Networked Load Sharing System? How do they compare with the key issues of a parallel processing system?
2. Compare the different schemes for distributed file systems. What are the pros and cons of each?
3. How would you determine if the network is capable of providing adequate response for a load sharing system? Also for distributed file system?

5

System Performance Issues

System performance is the ability to accomplish tasks with a minimum consumption of resources and the fastest response time. The key measures of system performance are the following:

1. System response.
2. System throughput.
3. Resource consumption.

System response is measured as the time it takes for the operating system to respond to user requests at the terminal. The time duration for the response depends on the function requested. While a user expects the system to respond almost instantaneously when entering or editing commands, the expectation changes when the user has entered the command and is expecting the system to open a file or to start a program.

System throughput is measured as the total of all application functions performed during a given time period. This is generally measured as the system response for a number of users performing a number of tasks simultaneously.

Resource consumption is a measure of the CPU usage, disk accesses, other input/output accesses, and terminal activity to determine how efficiently the operating system is using and scheduling its resources.

Performance Components of an Operating System

There are a number of components of the operating system and processes used in its operation that impact its performance. While most of these components are inherent in the architecture of the system, a number of these depend on code optimization. The following lists the major components that typically impact performance in operating systems. The discussion in this chapter will center around these components.

1. Hardware and microcode.
2. Coding algorithms and table searches.
3. Process scheduling and context switching.
4. File system access.
5. System call operation.
6. Operating system object code optimization.
7. User interface/shells.
8. Application design.

System performance in an operating system may be viewed as a chain. The weak link in the chain has the most noticeable impact on performance. In other words, the best throughput and performance is obtained when the overall system is balanced, such that all components are operating at their most efficient and are not holding up the operation of other components.

The components that get exercised the most frequently need greater attention even though their impact in any given cycle of operations may be low due to overall percentage of time spent in that component. The *process scheduling* component is a good example of this. The component itself is fairly small, but it is exercised so frequently that it has historically been the most important.

There are three important methods for determining what components of the operating system are impacting performance. The key measures of impact on performance are the frequency of use of that component and the identification of bottlenecks in the system. A bottleneck is defined as the link in a chain of operations that holds up other operations from operating at their most efficient performance level. Disk drives and communications channels, for example, are the most common bottleneck areas. The three methods used are the following:

1. Desk study of the architecture.
2. Code profiling and timing measurements.
3. Queueing theory and related measurements.

Desk study attempts to architecturally determine potential problem areas. An entire operational sequence is broken down into its logical components based on system activities. For example, a system call consists of the following activities:

1. Call set-up.
2. Process switching to kernel mode.
3. Rescheduling.
4. Execution of system call.
5. Process returning to user mode.

Each activity and the time to move from one activity to the next are studied independently. This study helps in assessing both sequencing problems and bottlenecks. An architectural desk-study can also concentrate on individual subsystems to determine the activities of the subsystem and potential conflicts and bottlenecks in the subsystem. Based on this study, a model of the subsystem is created. This model is combined with models of other subsystems into a complete operating model.

Code profiling is used to determine the operation of specific sections of code. It helps check out these areas and develop an operating map of the system that describes the paths used and the time durations for each path along with the frequency of use of each path. The models and the activity maps developed in the desk study are used as a guide to determine which sections of code need to undergo greater scrutiny with code profiling and timing measurements. Sections of code that are exercised very frequently become candidates for code optimization, and not too infrequently, logic enhancements.

Queuing theory is used to mathematically determine the system loading factors. Based on the loading factors, one tries to predict performance as well as determine more efficient algorithms for performing different functions. Good candidates for the queueing theory are process scheduling, I/O requests, and interrupts. In the ideal operating environment, a few processes are always waiting in the *ready-to-run in memory* state. If there are too many processes waiting in this state, the system response becomes poor. Similarly, if the system is interrupted too frequently, both response and throughput suffer.

The following sections describe the different components of the system that impact performance.

5.1 HARDWARE AND MICROCODE

A number of architectural design issues impact the performance of a system. Notable among these are the following:

1. Separate high speed buses for CPU, disk drives, and peripherals.
2. Backplane design.
3. Memory management, memory sharing, and memory speed.
4. Use of memory cache for shared memory and disk I/O.
5. Error detection and correction logic.
6. CPU architecture, CPU clock cycle, and support chips.
7. Floating point hardware/firmware.
8. Disk controller architecture.
9. Use of high-speed microcode.

In most high performance mini-computers, a mass-storage databus is used for high-speed access to block devices, especially disk drives, and a separate bus is used for terminals, plotters, printers, and other character I/O devices. There is often a separate bus linking the processor directly with memory. Multiprocessor systems also use a primary system bus that connects all CPUs and memory for shared operation.

Figure 5-1 describes an example of a multiprocessor bus architecture. The multiple bus architecture is designed so that each bus is optimized for the function it

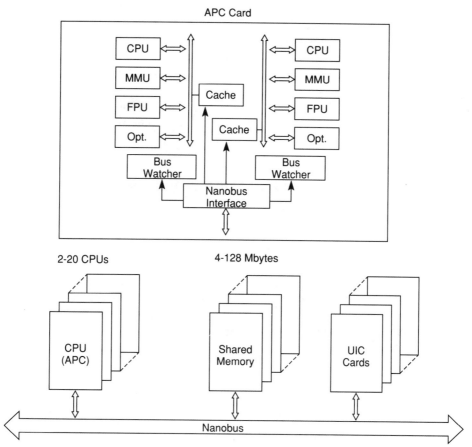

Figure 5-1.   Multiprocessor System Bus Architecture

performs. Factors that impact performance are the bit-width of the bus; arrangements like master-slave, multiple master, or periodic polling of arbitration unit; data transfer rates; and bus switching speeds (i.e. the number of access opportunities a device has in a given time).

The memory management unit is another very critical component for system performance. Factors that affect performance are whether memory is single-ported or multi-ported, can it be shared, type and size of available cache memory, memory interleaving, and memory transfer rates.

Cache memory is part of the overall concept of storage hierarchies where faster, but generally more expensive and less dense, memories are placed close to the processor, while less expensive and larger memories are used to fill cache as needed. Typically, most programs reference memory within a very small range over short periods of time. This *working set* of memory changes after some time as the program moves to another operation. For example, an array sort may use two small contiguous blocks of memory—one to read from and one to write into. While the primary memory holds the entire program and data area, the faster cache memory holds the program (text) segment being executed, as well as the data areas in use. The cache memory, if modified, updates main memory when a new block of primary memory requires the cache memory space.

The disk file system is important for operating system performance due to the frequency with which it is accessed for system data, user data, and process swapping. Use of multiple disk controllers improves overall performance and throughput by reducing file system bottlenecks.

Effective use of high speed micro-code for repetitive functions is another important performance consideration. Functions like process scheduling are good potential candidates for this.

5.2 CODING ALGORITHMS AND TABLE SEARCHES

A major part of the UNIX operating system is written in the *C* language. The level of optimization of the *C* compiler, availability of fast assembly language routines to perform searches of frequently accessed tables, optimization of hashing algorithms used to access *hash queues,* and tradeoff between storage and performance are issues that must be considered for any port effort undertaken. These issues may play a role in the development of system applications that optimize the use of sub-processes and interprocess communications either for flexibility or for better performance. The following lists some of the most frequently accessed tables and structures in the UNIX system:

1. Page frame tables.
2. Buffer pool and free list.
3. Process table entries.
4. File table entries.
5. Mount table.
6. In-core inode table.
7. Semaphore structures.
8. Shared memory table.
9. Message queues.

The algorithms used for searching through such tables impact file access and process context switching times. These algorithms merit special attention. Significant performance improvements can be achieved by configuration management. Changing the operating system kernel design should always be the last resort.

5.3 PROCESS SCHEDULING

Processes are created, scheduled, and terminated at least once every second (for System V) or at the clock tick (interrupt) if the process is blocked, preempted or interrupted. The policies employed for scheduling processes and the associated mechanics of re-scheduling play a very important role in the real and perceived (as seen at the user's terminal) system performance. Traditionally, the UNIX system has used a round robin scheduler that strives for fairness to all users while maintaining acceptable terminal response time. As we noted in Chapter 3 (Section 3.4), the kernel dynamically adjusts process priorities and favors interactive processes at the expense of compute bound processes. The *nice* system call allows some control but there is no way of guaranteeing higher priority for a specific process.

Short of redesigning the kernel, the only other means of improving performance on the basis of priority is to understand the workload on the system, to use the *nice* call to balance priorities to the extent feasible, and to recommend users schedule their tasks to achieve a better balance in the system load.

Some UNIX implementations have used a *fair share scheduler*. A fair share scheduler divides users into groups; each group gets an equal share of processor time. For example, a system may be set up with five scheduling groups, with a total of 10 processes. Each group gets 20 percent of processor time. The distribution may be such that the first group may have only one process while the second group may have four processes. The process in the former group gets 20 percent of processor time while a process in the latter group gets only 5 percent of the time. This scheme provides one means of assigning a favored status to a process.

5.3.1 Process Creation

The creation of a process sets up a new process as an image of the parent process and requires the copying of the text, data, and stack segments. The *vfork* system call is used to provide faster performance for a process that will be overlaid with a new program immediately. The application design should also look closely at how processes are invoked within the application and determine that invoking a child process is really necessary.

5.3.2 Context Switching and Scheduling

Partial context switching is required any time a process is rescheduled. Full context switching is required in swapping systems for a process that is swapped out. The time spent in context switching is not a major issue for normal operation of the operating system. It becomes a major issue if there is insufficient memory and a lot of process swapping takes place.

The *ps* command allows system managers to look at the status of all processes. In a normally operating mini-computer system, a couple of processes are usually waiting in the *ready-to-run in memory* and *ready-to-run swapped* states. The number of *ready-to-run in memory* processes consistently remaining over five during the day implies the need for a faster CPU. On the other hand, too many processes in the *ready-to-run swapped* and none or very few in the *ready-to-run in memory* state indicates insufficient primary memory to run the system efficiently. This situation is typically experienced by swapping systems.

5.3.3 Process Pre-emption

Standard UNIX System implementations support pre-emption of user mode processes only. A kernel mode process cannot be pre-empted by a higher priority process until it is blocked or it finishes its time quantum. The higher priority process waits until then. The UNIX System, however, supports interrupt processing at certain safe places where data structures are consistent in the kernel mode operation. The UNIX kernel may be enhanced, if needed, to support a user defined priority that has greater significance and control, and kernel mode process pre-emption. This kind of change will provide better response to compute bound users.

5.4 FILE/DATA ACCESS

The UNIX file system consists of partitions as we saw in Section 6 of Chapter 3. Except for the boot block and the swap device, the data blocks of files in other partitions are scattered randomly throughout the disk, resulting in large seek times for sequential reads. The data block sizes have, over the last few releases, been increased from 512 bytes to 1K bytes in System V and 4K bytes in Berkeley 4.2bsd.

The Berkeley 4.2bsd file system is based on a design different from System V. It uses the concept of cylinder groups. A cylinder group consists of a superblock, contiguous inodes for that cylinder group, and data blocks (i.e., a small file system). The data block allocation policies attempt to allocate space for a given file in the same cylinder group while other unrelated files are placed in other cylinder groups. This design attempts to reduce the seek time. The Berkeley 4.2bsd implementation also uses two block sizes—1K bytes and 4K bytes—to optimize disk usage.

While the disk drive can be accessed in the *raw* mode for a specific application, the user needs to understand the disk hardware very well to avoid potential *raw* mode disk access design pitfalls.

5.4.1 Buffer Pool

We looked at the architecture of the buffer pool in Sections 3.6 and 3.7. The size of the buffer pool is important to allow a number of disk blocks to remain resident in memory. The larger the buffer pool, the greater the opportunity for needed disk blocks to remain in memory.

5.4.2 Disk Block Allocation and Fragmentation

As noted in the architectural discussion in Chapter 3, only the first 10 blocks of file data are written in directly addressable blocks. Any file larger than 10 blocks requires at least three disk accesses to get the required block. A disk that has undergone a large number of file data writes and deletes gets very fragmented and files get distributed all over the disk.

If very fast disk access is required, and if files are anticipated to be larger than 10 blocks of data, the kernel would need to be modified to provide the capability of building large contiguous files. Some proprietary implementations of the UNIX system allow pre-allocation of disk blocks, i.e., all disk blocks required for the specified size of the file are allocated at the time of creation. The blocks may be allocated contiguously for fast access. Pre-allocation helps in faster write operations and faster sequential reads. This concept is very useful for fixed length databases, or databases where the total size of the file is predictable.

5.4.3 Swap Device

The *swap device* is the partition on disk where process images are stored while they are blocked. The *swap device* size and location are user configurable parameters. As we noted in Chapter 3, each region of a process text, data, and stack is stored on the swap device in contiguous blocks and garbage collection is performed on the fly. A swap device too small for the user load on the system may prevent users from logging on. A swap device too small would also cause too many blocked processes to remain in memory while there are also too many *ready-to-run swapped* processes swapped out to the swap device. This happens if the kernel has to make a number of attempts to find large enough contiguous blocks of swap space for the regions of the process.

Typically, the swap device is set to be 2 to 3 times the size of the physical memory. In a system with multiple disk drives and disk controllers, the swap space may be spread on different disk drives for better performance.

5.4.4 RAM Disks

The concept of *RAM disks* is not relevant for UNIX systems due to its inherent addressability of large memory spaces. The *swap device* would be a good candidate for a RAM disk. However, if there is memory available, there would be no need for a swap device since all processes can be accommodated in memory anyway. The only item other than the swap device that requires frequent disk access is file data. It does not appear that a RAM disk would be very useful unless the file size is very small and the file is shared by a number of users.

5.5 SYSTEM CALLS

As we noted, a system call often results in re-scheduling of the system. The kernel process may be blocked, or it may execute a *sleep* call. A review of the code is useful to ensure that the placing of the system calls is acceptable from a performance perspective, that the system call is really required. There may be an alternative to performing the function performed by the system call that avoids the complete system call overhead.

Another point to be noted is that some system calls produce the same result but operate faster. We have already seen the example of *vfork* instead of *fork* under process creation (Section 5.4) where an *exec* call immediately follows the fork. The different variations of the *exec* call are also a good example of system calls customized in certain ways to achieve better performance.

5.6 INTERPROCESS COMMUNICATIONS

The UNIX system provides a number of means for interprocess communication. Please refer to Chapter 3 (Section 3.5) for a detailed review of *named* and *unnamed pipes, signals, message queues, shared memory,* and *semaphores*. Each of these mechanisms provides a different function. For achieving good performance, it is important to study the differences in the operation and use of these mechanisms.

5.7 TERMINAL HANDLING

Terminals and workstations come in a variety of configurations and speeds. The connect point to the system or the network; the nature, type, and use for the terminal; and the capability of the system and the network to support the required number of terminals and workstations; are all important considerations for achieving acceptable performance.

5.8 NETWORK PERFORMANCE

The lower level protocols are defined primarily in terms of *media* (coaxial, twisted pair, fiber optic), *speed, topology* (bus, star, ring, complex), *signaling method* (baseband, broadband), and *access method* (token passing, CSMA/CD). Performance should be a major consideration in the selection of the lower level protocols.

The upper level protocols are concerned with *routing, end-to-end control, session management,* and *presentation* to the user or application. A wide range of protocols have been used and are under development.

The biggest single issue in the selection of protocols is the area of standard protocols. The most common protocol used for UNIX Systems is Transmission Control Protocol/Internet Protocol (*TCP/IP*). Other common protocols include *XNS, DECnet,* and *X.25*. Typical performance numbers like 70 Kbps net end-to-end transfer of real data on a 10 Mbps Ethernet LAN are fairly common. Various attempts are in progress to get higher end-to-end bandwidths. Total Ethernet real bandwidth ranges from 250 Kbps to 300 Kbps.

The design of the system or application becomes very important for achieving the highest throughput using standard protocols. In the case of *NFS* or *RFS* based networks, issues of server bottleneck become important. The ability to distribute the file-server across different nodes goes a long way in solving network performance problems.

Use of multi-level networks (or backbone networks) is another mechanism used toward achieving network functionality and architectural flexibility without sacrificing local network performance.

5.9 CODE OPTIMIZATION

The UNIX operating system *C compiler* has been designed primarily for portability, and adequate attention has not been paid to its performance aspects. Code optimization is an important issue, both for the UNIX code as well as for the application code. Since the same compiler is used to compile the operating system as is used for application code, the task of optimization is a little bit easier.

Two types of code optimization have been used in most compilers. *Peephole* optimizers are used to operate on code atomically and they look at code within a routine to optimize at that level. *Global* optimizers look at the overall code and optimize at a global level. Some level of global optimization can be done in a single pass. Better optimization is achieved through the use of multiple passes to obtain increasing optimization of code at the global level. Some global optimizers also use code profilers to determine which parts of the code are likely to be exercised most frequently and attempt to make that code inline code instead of a function call. It should be noted that global optimization does not necessarily result in more compact code. Its goal is performance rather than size.

Most *C* compilers have not benefitted from either type of optimization. Some commercial compilers are now available that are designed specifically for a high level of optimization. Evaluation and implementation of code optimization is an important step in improving overall system and application code performance.

5.10 APPLICATION DESIGN

Good performance is not accidental or automatic. It has to be designed into the application, preferably right from the beginning. As we have just seen, a large number of factors impact performance. The design of an application should take into account all of these factors and should clearly define the impact on performance for the design approaches used.

5.11 SUMMARY

Performance of an operating system is always an important issue. In this chapter, we categorized performance and listed the performance components of the UNIX operating system. We further looked at a number of significant design issues that affect performance and evaluated their potential impact on improving performance.

5.12 EXERCISES

1. In your system, use the nice call to change your user priority. Determine the impact of this change in performance.
2. Determine the size and location of swap space on your system. What is the impact of reducing it? Would increasing it improve system performance?
3. How does a large program make (compile) impact process scheduling?
4. How does a large file mv (move) impact process scheduling?

6

UNIX System Porting Issues

The UNIX operating system is, by far, the most frequently ported operating system. Over the years, its portability has been enhanced as more and more of the operating system code has been converted to the *C* language. The multiprocess architecture lends itself to the concept of providing two or more different operating system environments on the same kernel, e.g., UNIX and MS-DOS, or VM/CMS and UNIX. This chapter provides a general description of the porting process and the work involved in performing a port.

6.1 PORTING ISSUES

A number of issues play an important role in determining the type of port that is to be performed. The source and target hardware, the application operation environment and interface to other systems, nature of local area network if the ported system is to be used in a network environment, and co-residency of other operating systems, affect the design of the port. This section notes some of the hardware and environment-related issues that are discussed further in the following sections for each type of port.

6.1.1 Hardware Dependency

The system hardware plays an important role in any kind of a port, all the way from the instruction set to byte size, byte ordering, and memory management. The extent to which the hardware impact is felt depends on the nature of the port and the level of differences between the porting source machine and the porting target machine.

6.1.1.1 Instruction Set

The instruction set issues include the range of instructions, addressing schemes and modes, use of registers and indexing methods, alignment and use of stacks, and memory addressability. The direct impact of instruction set differences is on the code generator of the *C* compiler (most likely the portable *C* compiler since it is usually the first compiler ported and used for porting the operating system kernel). The code generator templates may require modification.

6.1.1.2 Interrupt Management

Schemes for interrupt management, direct memory access (DMA), and device data buffering differ from one system hardware to another system hardware. The I/O sub-system as well as the file management sub-system of the UNIX operating system will require redesign to adjust to the new hardware. The memory management system is almost always affected due to the differences in the implementation of direct memory access features.

6.1.1.3 Other Hardware Issues

Other hardware issues include byte sizes and byte ordering, architecture of the system bus, cache memory schemes, instruction pipelining, etc. These issues need to be studied in detail for designing the port strategy.

6.1.2 Environmental Constraints

The environmental constraints for UNIX ports consist primarily of the following:

1. Porting *source* system and porting *target* system.
2. The operating environment.
3. Application and system organization issues.

6.1.2.1 Porting Source and Target Systems

The porting source system is the system used for the development of the port and contains the version of the source code that is being ported. A number of porting source versions exist, for example, versions for the VAX family, the Motorola 68000 processor, and Intel 80286 and 80386 processors. Using the host source base that is the closest to the target hardware makes the port considerably easier.

6.1.2.2 Operating Environment and System Configuration

The operating environment determines the nature of the port. It defines the other systems that will be interfaced, the need to operate in a local area network environment, the existence of file servers that may contain common user data, co-residency or host/guest operating system environments, the number of users sharing the system, and so on.

6.1.2.3 Other Issues

This is a catchall category that includes all miscellaneous issues not described in the groupings above. Issues included here include security, reliability, special devices or peripherals, and any other special requirements for the application environment.

6.2 APPLICATION REQUIREMENTS

The manner in which the ports are done depends substantially on the requirements of the application. The application may require simply running some programs designed originally for UNIX and that may be ported to the new environment with some changes; or it may require that they run in the new environment without any change; or it may require a full UNIX environment such that a user notices no differences from the normal UNIX system environment.

   The application may require the port of another operating system environment to run as a guest on a UNIX kernel. The use of MS-DOS as a guest operating environment is a good example of this requirement.

6.2.1 Full UNIX Environment on Hardware Base

This is, by far, the most common port strategy. This is partially due to the ease of building a proprietary hardware/software system due to ready availability of UNIX source code, and partially due to the ease of maintaining such a system. The availability of fairly powerful desktop computers and the distribution of computing resources from centralized mainframes to satellite processors accelerated the use of UNIX as the operating system of choice for workstations. The *portable C* compiler along with the portable linker/loader have made this kind of port significantly easier. Except for a very small directly hardware related portion, the operating system kernel is written in the *C* language. The hardware dependencies are concentrated in well defined sets of routines.

6.2.2 Full UNIX Environment on Another Host

A number of variations of this approach have been implemented. These vary from the implementation of a *C* compiler and a set of *C Libraries* that emulate the UNIX system calls to allow porting application programs, to the implementation of a shell that also provides a UNIX-like user interface, to more rigorous ports that attempt to emulate an authentic UNIX environment such that the user is not aware of a non-UNIX kernel.

6.2.3 Another System Environment as A UNIX Process

The most common example of this is an MS-DOS operating environment as a guest on a UNIX system host. Most operating systems emulated to run as a guest process with the UNIX kernel are inherently small operating systems that do not provide multi-user and multi-tasking capability provided by UNIX.

There are, however, instances where a process in a sophisticated multi-user, multi-tasking system is designed to emulate a UNIX process. This has been done in cases where creating the operating environment of another operating system is easier than porting a very large application operating on it. Ports of this nature are generally not offered as commercial standalone products. They are bundled in with the application for which they were developed.

6.3 PORT STRATEGIES

The most common port of the UNIX Operating System is called a *full port*. In a full port, the UNIX Operating System is ported directly to the hardware of a new Processing Unit. Examples of this are ports to the Intel 80386 processor based systems and the Motorola 68020 based systems.

Another kind of a port has been carried out to provide a UNIX Operating System environment on other 32-bit architecturally compatible host kernels. This type of a port allows processes of UNIX or the host system to coexist and operate as processes of the same system. However, the interface provided to the user emulates the UNIX system very closely.

The third kind of port provides the same operational interface as the previous one. However, in this port the UNIX kernel is retained and the environment of the guest operating system is built as a process running in the UNIX kernel. The system calls of the guest operating system are converted to the system calls of the host operating system using a system call interface layer.

Let us now take a close look at the key issues in the porting process for the different types of ports.

6.3.1 Full Ports

A full port is a port that is carried out directly to the hardware of the target machine. The UNIX operating system operates as the host or as the only operating system on the target hardware. This section describes the key areas of hardware dependency in the UNIX system, and the typical sequence of events leading to a successful port.

The machine dependent code exists primarily in two areas. The most significant area is the code that interfaces directly with the hardware for the functions of memory management, CPU scheduling, and error handling. The other significant area is the set of interrupt handling routines, and to some extent the kernel device driver service routines.

Very often the third area that needs significant re-design is the set of libraries that service hardware related system calls, e.g., calls for device management, interprocess communications, network management, etc.

6.3.1.1 Target System Instruction Set

The UNIX implementations, both AT&T System V (Release V.2 and V.3) and Berkeley UNIX 4.2bsd and 4.3bsd have been ported to a number of new CPU architectures including, among others, the Intel 80286 and 80386, Motorola 68010 and 68020, and Cray Research's Cray 1 and Cray 2. UNIX ports have also been made to RISC (Reduced Instruction Set Processor) machines. UNIX ports run on both 16 bit and 32 bit architectures, typically operating in the 0.5 MIPS to 20 MIPS range. Obviously, there are exceptions to this rule. Higher MIP architectures mostly fall in the class of multiprocessor systems described in Chapter 4.

Even though the UNIX System is highly portable, this wide range of target systems makes every port a unique and special experience. Some key issues that require special attention in the design stage for the port are the following:

1. Data path size—16 bit or 32 bit.
2. Byte ordering and byte alignment.
3. Address size—16 bit or 32-bit.
4. Use of microcode.
5. System Bus architecture.
6. Instruction set:
   a. Register operations
   b. Addressing modes
   c. Stack management.
7. Memory management.
8. I/O Architecture.
9. Interrupt levels.
10. Instruction pipelining.

The data sizes affect the definition of long and short integers and pointers. The bus address size affects the maximum size of data transfers, as well as direct memory addressability.

6.3.1.2 Machine Dependable Code

The *C* level routines that interface directly with the hardware are essentially contained in two modules in the UNIX system. These modules are called *machdep* and *macherr*. The assembly language code that interfaces with the hardware started out at under 1,000 lines of code in Version 7, and has been continuously reduced and is significantly smaller now. This code handles the functions of changing memory map, context switching, and interrupt handling. The development of the *portable C* compiler and the *portable linker/loader* bundled under the *software generation system* has made the porting effort considerably easier.

The *machdep* module contains *startup* code that identifies the operating system, displays real and available memory sizes, and sets up the map from the memory mapping register. This module also includes code to start the clock; send an interrupt to a process; copy a number of bytes from one physical memory location to another; clear sections of physical memory; create a duplicate of a process; change protection codes of text (code); check size of data, text, or stack of a process; manipulate page tables; and set up initial memory.

The second module, *macherr,* has routines to check the CPU state, and to process memory parity, CPU timeout, or bus errors.

These two modules along with the assembly language routines typically require to be re-written completely. The re-write becomes more involved if byte ordering and memory management of the target system are significantly different from that of the *porting source* machine.

6.3.1.3 Device Drivers

The device drivers, as we noted earlier, include two parts. The lower half is the device handler and the upper half is the kernel service routine. The following may require substantial re-writes of the device handler routines:

1. Device controller architectures:
   a. Intelligent or non-intelligent
   b. Direct memory access capability
   c. Co-processing capability.
2. Additional or different devices supported.
3. Overall system and bus architecture.

This is true whether the port is for AT&T UNIX System V or for Berkeley UNIX 4.2/4.3bsd. The key issue is the difference in the hardware of the source system from which the port is to be carried out and the hardware of the target system.

6.3.1.4 Kernel Port

The port of the kernel software is relatively straightforward. A code translator is required to port the operating system kernel after making the appropriate changes based on the instruction set differences, the system hardware, and the device level differences. The target code is created on the *source* system and transferred to the target system using either an existing loader, or a loader built specially for the port. The kernel requires debugging at the following levels after the port:

1. To get it operating at all.
2. To remove causes of system hangs and crashes.
3. For proper operation of:
   a. Process management
   b. Memory management
   c. File system management.

It continues to be re-compiled on the source system until some level of stability and reliability is achieved.

At this stage the *C* compiler can be ported and debugged. The kernel is now compiled on the target system using the new *C* compiler. The kernel requires debugging further to achieve acceptable reliability for the kernel as well as the *C* compiler.

6.3.1.5 *C Libraries*

The *C Libraries* may require some change for the port to the target system due to hardware and device differences. The port may be carried out using a translator that translates known and well defined code segments from the *source* system to the *target* system. Special devices or special memory management techniques may require rewrites of some system calls.

6.3.1.6 Utilities

Due to its wide-ranging popularity with developers at all levels, the UNIX system can boast of a wide array of utility programs. AT&T UNIX System V distribution has close to 100 utility programs and Berkeley UNIX 4.3bsd distribution has over 150 utility programs. The port of these is relatively straightforward and does not require too many changes. The changes are generally well defined and are achieved with relative ease.

6.3.2 Extended Ports

An extended port is a port that is carried out directly to the hardware of the target machine but that requires substantial enhancement of the UNIX kernel. Most extended ports are targeted to multiprocessor systems. The UNIX System was designed for a uniprocessor system; but many new computer systems, for example Encore Multi-MAX and Alliant FX/8, support multiple processors. While an extended port is similar in nature to a full port, the UNIX kernel requires significant modifications to run symmetrically in a multiprocessor computer system.

Let us take a look at the types of kernel changes that have to be implemented for an extended port.

6.3.2.1 Multiple Execution Streams

In a uniprocessor computer system, there is only one execution stream, whether it is a user or a kernel process, or a hardware interrupt. In a multiprocessor system, on the other hand, a number of processes operate in parallel on different processors. Each processor has its own execution stream, and these streams interact with each other. Context switching and CPU scheduling become considerably more complex. In a uniprocessor system, the system stream code sequence switches between user mode and kernel mode due to system calls and memory management exceptions. An interrupt trap starts an interrupt stream code sequence. An interrupt stream operates entirely in kernel mode. Conflicts are prevented by ensuring that processes in kernel mode are not preempted by higher priority processes. Interrupts are also locked out during critical code sections by raising process priority.

A multiprocessor system not only has to deal with context switching within the environment of a single processor, but also has to contend with synchronization and control across processors; especially where processes interact across processors. One solution to this problem is to tightly couple the processors in a multiprocessor system.

The key design issues that require substantial new code development include the following:

1. Data structure protection schemes.
2. Scheduler redesign.
3. Interprocessor communication.

The *data structure protection schemes* include attempts to design global memory locking architectures. The locking mechanism is, typically, built into the hardware. This ensures that a process using a particular device has a lock on the data read from that device, and another process or another processor does not interfere. Schemes like this give rise to enhanced or modified instruction sets.

The *multiprocessor scheduling* system needs to be enhanced to handle some additional functions. One of these functions is to determine which processor a process should run in. Most implementations handle this through a common process table and a processor profile. These help in determining the loading of processors in relation to their capacities, and help in load balancing the system. They also help in matching the processor to the desired application. This approach requires substantial modifications to the kernel routines that run under the *swapper* process.

Most multiprocessor systems feature sophisticated hardware level *interprocessor communication* capabilities. Additional code changes will be required for additional interprocessor communications system calls; and for changes in the handling of common message queues, semaphores, and shared memory across all processors.

6.3.2.2 Machine Dependable Code

The *C* level routines that interface directly with the hardware, as we noted earlier, are contained in the modules called *machdep* and *macherr*. The *machdep* module contains *startup* code that identifies the operating system, displays real and available memory sizes, and sets up the map from the memory mapping register. This module also includes code to start the clock; send an interrupt to a process; copy a number of bytes from one physical memory location to another; clear sections of physical memory; create a duplicate of a process; change protection codes of text (code); check size of data, text, or stack of a process; manipulate page tables; and set up initial memory. The second module, *macherr,* has routines to check the CPU state, and to process memory parity, CPU timeout, or bus errors.

These two modules along with the assembly language routines are required to be rewritten completely for multiprocessor operation. The rewrite becomes more involved if byte ordering and memory management of the target system are significantly different from that of the *porting source* machine.

6.3.2.3 Kernel Port

The *kernel port,* unlike a full uniprocessor port, is not a straightforward port. All the subsystems—memory management, I/O management, disk filesystem management, and process management—need substantial enhancement to adapt them to a multiprocessor architecture. It is important to note that the inherent architecture of the UNIX system is conducive to such enhancement.

6.3.2.4 *C* Libraries

The *C Libraries* may require some change for the port to the target system due to hardware and device handling differences in a multiprocessor system. The port may be carried out using a translator that translates known and well defined code segments from the *source* system to the *target* system. Special devices or special memory management techniques may require re-writes of some system calls.

6.3.3 UNIX System on Compatible Host Kernels

A port of this nature, while not very common, has been actually used for some computer systems. The port of the AT&T UNIX System V to the Cray Timesharing system, where the UNIX subsystem operates as a subpartitioned CTSS user process, is an example of such a port. If the host operating system is similar in concept (and that is usually the case if it is based on the MULTICS concepts) a port of this nature becomes feasible. Architecturally the port appears as shown in Figure 6-1. While the concept presented here is an architecturally simple concept, in reality the port may be

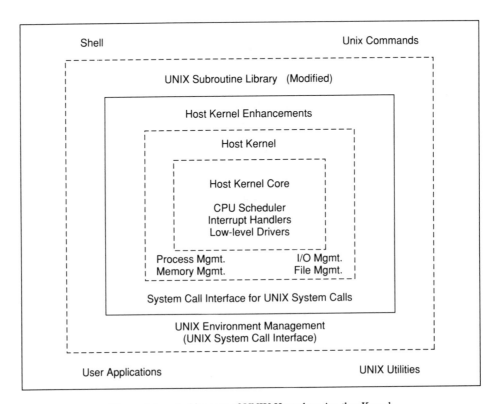

Figure 6-1. Architecture of UNIX Hosted on Another Kernel

much more complex if the host machine has very powerful real time capabilities, such as a Cray 1.

Any operating system based on the *MULTICS* concepts has some common features with the UNIX system, including protected kernel layers, management of multiple processes, memory management, file system management, device management. A compatible layer structure makes mapping of layers feasible.

The architecture described in Figure 6-1 is designed to make a user process running a UNIX environment give the appearance of a full UNIX system to that user. It supports all UNIX system calls (to the extent the host system supports them or can emulate them), provides UNIX shell user interface, and provides a range of utility programs. The UNIX process competes with the other processes running in the host system. Typically, a number of UNIX processes can be started up, all operating as processes of the host kernel. A key issue in the design of such a system is to provide interprocess communications among UNIX processes in a manner that faithfully emulates a native UNIX implementation.

6.3.3.1 System Call Interface Layer

The system call interface, as we have seen earlier, is one of the three entry points to the UNIX kernel, and it is the only interface between a user process and the kernel. The kernel switches from the user mode to kernel mode on executing a trap instruction. This single point of interfacing with the kernel routines presents an ideal location for the placement of a *system call interface* layer. This layer consists of routines that translate the UNIX system call to equivalent host kernel system call. The translation involves setting up the equivalent of a user structure for the host kernel, and any other tables or data structures required by the host kernel. The translated call is then vectored to the appropriate kernel mode entry point or the kernel service routine of the host kernel.

This interface is probably the most complex design component due to potential differences between host and UNIX system calls, and system call set up. The integrity of the UNIX kernel emulation depends on how closely the original system calls are emulated, and the predictability of their operation. The C libraries may also require design modifications to provide the basic functions unchanged or to provide a very close emulation of the basic functions.

6.3.3.2 Process Management

The system can be set up such that all UNIX processes present a combined appearance of a UNIX system. That is, they can perform interprocess communication and can send and receive UNIX *signals*. Communications to processes of the host system can be set up via interprocess communications.

The management of processes is really a function performed by the host kernel. The host kernel may or may not provide all of the functions required for UNIX process management. This can be addressed by setting up the system call interface such that it emulates all functions required by UNIX and provided by the host. In addition, it filters functions that the host kernel does not support and provides a response appropriate for the successful completion of the system call. Examples of some calls that may fall in this category include calls such as those that allocate memory or change process priority, i.e. calls that the host kernel may not support, or that may be supported in a very different manner. A successful completion response may satisfy the user application requirements, even though no action really took place. Very often, the impact of the call not actually being processed impacts only performance, and is not noticed unless performance is a major issue.

6.3.3.3 Support of UNIX Functions not Available in Host

There may be some functions or system calls essential for the operation of the UNIX operating system, that may not be provided by the host kernel. The host kernel has to be extended in that case to provide the kernel services for these functions. It is assumed that the source code and the expertise to modify the host kernel are available before embarking on a port of this nature.

There may also be some existing system calls in the host kernel that may not quite operate in a manner consistent with the requirements of the UNIX System. These calls may have to be modified or extended to support the required UNIX functionality, or they may have to be duplicated and modified, and then set up under a different name and even a different calling sequence.

6.3.3.4 Support of Host Functions not Available in UNIX

The host kernel may support a number of functions not supported under UNIX. In very rare cases the application programs require to be changed. For the most part these functions can be ignored if they have no real bearing on the normal operation of a user application program. In some cases, the C library or even the system call interface layer may have to convert a single UNIX System call into a sequence of systems calls for the host kernel. The design goal should be to minimize changes (ideally, to have no changes at all) required to be made in user application programs to run in this pseudo-UNIX environment.

6.3.3.5 Error Management

The management of errors returned from the kernel—user errors, system errors, etc.—can be another complex design issue. However, due to a clean system call interface layer, the key design issue is to ensure that the host kernel always returns an error to the system call interface layer, when an error is encountered that needs to be returned to the user process or application program. The host kernel may require some modifications to achieve this. Most UNIX system user errors are returned in the user structure. The system call interface layer may also require the design of an *error translator routine* to ensure that the error returned to the user has the appearance of a UNIX error, and that it is the appropriate error to be returned for the error encountered in the kernel.

6.3.3.6 Porting Strategy

In a port of an existing kernel, the system utilities including compilers, linkers, and loaders already exist for the language supported by that system. If that system does not support a *C* compiler, then the UNIX *portable C* compiler has to be *bootstrapped* on the host system. The UNIX portable *C* compiler has been ported to a number of computer systems and is designed to be highly portable. This compiler is highly compatible with Kernighan & Ritchie's definition of the *C* language. Only about 30 percent of the code of this compiler is machine dependent.

The first major task, generally, is to convert the assembly language code templates from the source system (e.g., a VAX), to the target language code templates. All other machine dependent issues are handled at this time. Using these templates, a simple code generator utility is developed on the host system. The code generation utility is then used to port a minimal *C* compiler using the assembler code as intermediate (*meta*) code from the source system to the code in the language of the target system. The minimal *C* compiler is used to port the full *C* compiler over to the target host system. With an operational *C* compiler, the rest of the UNIX system can be ported.

Since the host system has its own kernel and the device drivers are most likely a part of the host system kernel, no device drivers need be ported. The host system device driver may, however, require some enhancements. Due to a clean break at the system call interface layer, only the user mode component of the device driver needs to be ported. In addition, some form of system call dispatch table may have to be developed.

The process management, memory management, file system management, and device management functions are provided by the host system. The port of the user mode code requires additional work to adapt system call sequences, parameters, inputs to the system call, and the like to the requirements of the host kernel.

This port strategy, given a compatible host kernel with full process management capabilities, provides a single user UNIX process operating as a process under the host kernel. But due to the fact that all of the user mode code is UNIX, it appears to the user to be UNIX. A number of such UNIX processes can be started under the host kernel giving the semblance of a UNIX machine.

There are numerous benefits from this port strategy for systems that are being used for complex or proprietary applications, and that need, additionally, to be able to support UNIX based processes.

6.3.4 Other Operating Systems on UNIX Host Kernels

A number of implementations of this nature have been completed, most noticeably the support for MS-DOS as a UNIX process. In this case the target operating system may be similar in concept or it may be very different. As long as UNIX can support all the functions, or at the very least the key functions of the target operating system, a successful port can be performed. Architecturally the port appears as in Figure 6-2.

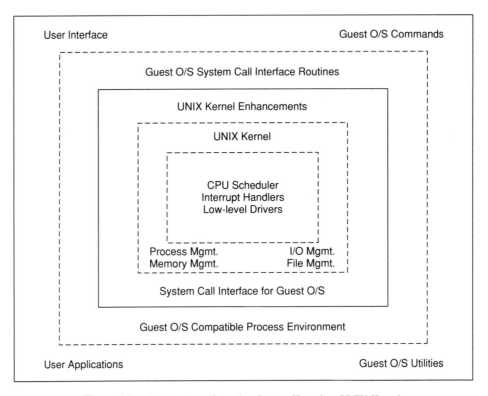

Figure 6-2.   Architecture of Another System Hosted on UNIX Kernel

6.3.4.1 System Call Interface Layer

Even single user and single threaded operating systems, e.g. MS-DOS, use system calls to provide user applications an interface to the operating system functions. These system calls are also often mapped to a *C language interface*. A system call layer not very different from that described in the previous section can be designed to convert a system call of the guest operating system to that of a UNIX System. The interface layer performs the functions of setting up the call exactly as the corresponding system call library routine would, and then executing the *trap* instruction.

6.3.4.2 Process Management

The management of a process becomes an issue only if the guest system has the capability to spawn processes. If not, the guest system environment can be overlaid on a UNIX process (using the *exec* system call), and the management of this process is carried out in the kernel as for any other UNIX process.

If the guest system does spawn processes, then special handling is required to set up sub-processes and to provide the expected interprocess synchronization and communication.

6.3.4.3 Support of UNIX Functions not Available in Host

There are two kinds of functions that must be considered. Some functions are features of the UNIX system not supported by the guest system. These will never be called by the guest system and can be ignored. The other category of functions are those that are not supported by the guest system, but that may get executed on its behalf by some other process (albeit erroneously). Alternatively, a function executed by another process may require a response from the guest system for a function that the guest operating system does not typically support. An example of this is a *signal,* e.g. SIGKILL. The system call interface layer has to be made intelligent enough to respond to such requests and to take appropriate action for functions that require an action.

6.3.4.4 Support of Guest Functions not Available in UNIX

There may be some guest functions that are typically not supported by UNIX. Each function needs to be studied to determine how it should be handled. The options available for handling these functions include the following:

1. Modify the host function library to perform a return without performing any operation.
2. Provide valid returns from the UNIX kernel but the kernel service routine performs no function.
3. Provide a valid successful completion return with pre-defined return values. The function always succeeds though no operation takes place.
4. Implement a new kernel service routine and modify the UNIX kernel to support the function in an acceptable manner.

    The last item here is also the manner in which a special new system call can be added to the UNIX system for specific application requirements. In the last three cases, a modification to the kernel service routine table in sysent is required.

6.3.4.5 Error Management

Error handling is performed by the system call interface layer. We saw in Section 3.3 that the UNIX system call errors are returned in register *0* and the carry bit is set in the PS. The system call interface layer checks the PS on return and if an error is encountered, it sets up the error return for the guest operating system and starts the guest user process. The system call interface layer also handles normal system call returns.

6.4 SUMMARY

Due to the ease of portability and the availability of the UNIX source code, the UNIX system has been ported to a large number of different hardware systems and over kernels of other operating systems. Other operating system environments have also been ported over UNIX Systems. This chapter described the issues and the procedures for performing these different types of ports.

6.5 EXERCISES

1. Compare the system calls of the UNIX operating system with the calls in another operating system available to you. What are the differences? How would you adjust for these differences to host one operating system over the other?

2. What kinds of data format and data translation problems would arise in the ports described in Exercise 1?

3. How would you address file system differences in the ports described in Exercise 1?

7

Implementation Differences and Application Portability Issues

The UNIX operating system was created in 1969 and has been nurtured for two decades. During this period it has evolved from an esoteric engineering system to a widely used commercial time-sharing operating system. While it competes with MS-DOS, OS/2, and a number of proprietary operating systems, the competition within its own community is very intense. The UNIX system is viewed by many as the ultimate *open system* that has the potential to provide object code level portability across hardware from different vendors. To that end, there are competing groups such as Open Systems Foundation (OSF), Open Systems Architecture (OSA), and IEEE P1003 Committee, involved in defining standards. OSF and OSA are also involved in producing standard source code. The competing source bases include AT&T UNIX System V (Releases V.3 and V.4), Berkeley UNIX 4.3bsd, Sun Microsystem's implementation of Berkeley UNIX, and a number of other variants including DEC Ultrix and IBM AIX.

AT&T System V in its newest release (System V.4) has embodied a number of new features to address key differences with Berkeley UNIX (including NFS support) in an attempt to regain its role as an industry standard. In an environment with a variety of operating system implementations, and a potential for portability across systems, adapting to implementation differences plays a key role in building new applications. Let us first review how the UNIX system arrived at this variety of implementations, and then determine how to build portable applications.

7.1 THE UNIX LINEAGE

The root of all current implementations of the UNIX Operating System can be traced back to Version 6, an internal Bell Laboratories implementation released in 1977. Figure 7-1 describes the family tree of the UNIX operating system.

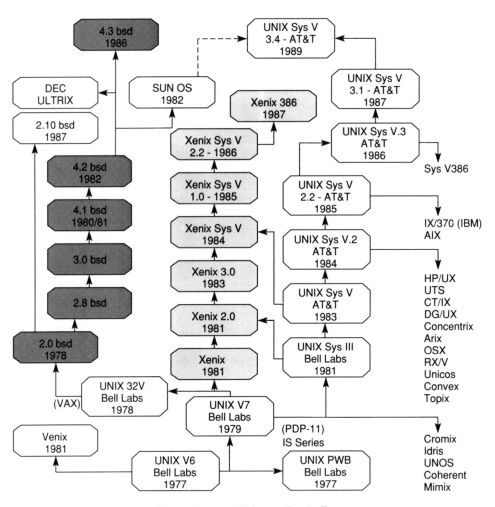

Figure 7-1.   UNIX System Family Tree

The USG 1.0 release in 1973 was the result of a research effort carried out within Bell Laboratories under the auspices of the UNIX Support Group. The first Digital Equipment VAX 11/780 implementation was carried out at the University of California at Berkeley, and the successors to this implementation were tagged with the acronym *bsd* for Berkeley Software Distribution. The family tree traces the series of releases that led to the current implementations of the UNIX Operating System.

AT&T UNIX System V

AT&T UNIX System III was the first commercial release of UNIX with professionally finished manuals and a more reasonable commercial source code licensing price structure. AT&T UNIX System V was the first major enhancement to that release and increased reliability and added some important new features. AT&T UNIX System V Release 2 (and the update to it System V Release 2.1) caught up partially with the major new components of Berkeley UNIX 4.2bsd. The key enhancements of AT&T UNIX System V through Release 2.1 include the following:

1. Interprocess communications (semaphores, shared memory, and message queues).
2. Demand paged virtual memory.
3. Larger disk blocks (but not as large as 4.2bsd).
4. VI Editor (visual editor).
5. Curses and terminfo package for screen management utilities.
6. Advisory and mandatory record and file locking.
7. Improved file system reliability (file hardening).
8. Loadable device drivers (automatic configuration check).

Two flavors of file and record locking scheme were introduced in this release. The *Advisory Cooperating* flavor requires lock requests by all processes so that a process accessing the record or the file can be advised of the lock (or use) status. In this flavor, access is not denied even if the record is locked and it is really up to the application to manage record or file lock controls. In the *Mandatory* flavor, non-cooperating processes are denied access to locked records by the I/O subsystem calls. In addition, exclusive *write locks* can be set to restrict write access to only one process at a time. *Shared read locks* provide multiple read accesses but no write access.

File system hardening was carried out to eliminate the interval during which the system crashes may leave the file system in an inconsistent state due to incomplete disk writes of modified buffers. Three features were added to achieve better reliability. *Bad block handling* provides dynamic reassignment of bad blocks. *Ordered writes* were implemented to ensure consistency, i.e. buffers are written to disk in the sequence in which they are modified. *Synchronous writes* to disk ensure that the kernel returns to the writing process when the disk write is complete, not when the data has been transferred to the buffer. *Periodic buffer flushing* is performed on the basis of a tunable parameter set at system generation time. This feature performs a periodic sync. *Mount protection* allows marking the file system clean before *umounting*. If the *clean* parameter is not set, the *fsck* is required to be run.

AT&T UNIX System V Release 3

AT&T UNIX System V Release 3 continued the effort at making UNIX a better distributed computing base. Key features included in this release are Streams communications facility and transport layer interface, and shared libraries.

The Streams interface is described in Chapter 3 and the reader is encouraged to go back and review it.

AT&T UNIX System V Release 4

With System V Release 4, AT&T has made the effort to deliver a product that combines the key features of the UNIX System variants. These key features included in System V Release 4 are the following:

1. *Open System.* Provides hardware independence with portability and interoperability across a wide range of system architectures.
2. *Open Look Graphics User Interface.* Toolkits are included to allow developers to create user interfaces that combine customized windowing and graphics.
3. *Application Binary Interfaces* (ABI). Vendors whose hardware architecture conforms to the ABI specification experience a binary level compatibility, that is, applications require just recompilation to run on another platform.
4. New and changed commands with enhanced features.
5. *Real-time Scheduling.* Provides capabilities to run process control applications.
6. *POSIX* compliance.
7. *ANSI C* standard compliance.
8. *Enhanced Communications.* This release supports NFS and the client/server model, and provides socket compatibility for NFS.
9. Security enhancements and new system administrator interfaces have been added to this release.

Berkeley UNIX 4.2bsd

Release 4.1bsd was the first major redesign of UNIX carried out at Berkeley. Its predecessor was Berkeley 3bsd that was derived from 32V. Berkeley 3bsd featured memory paging, VI text editor, and *C Shell* as the major enhancements. Release 3bsd was followed by Release 4.1bsd. With that release the Berkeley Computer Systems Research Group was in full operation. Funded by the U.S. Department of Defense Advanced Research Projects Agency (DARPA), major networking enhancements were incorporated in 4.1bsd and were followed on in Berkeley 4.2bsd. Some key highlights of changes incorporated through Berkeley 4.2bsd include the following:

1. Memory demand paging.
2. Use of 4K byte disk blocks.
3. Fast file system access.
4. Local area networking support—full TCP/IP support.
5. Reliable signal mechanism.

Berkeley UNIX 4.3bsd

Release 4.3bsd built on the success of the earlier release. It is faster and more reliable and provides additional networking protocols, including the Xerox (XNS) protocol suite.

Sun UNIX (4.2bsd)

The Network File System (*NFS*) was implemented by Sun Microsystems and was released with Berkeley 4.2bsd as Sun UNIX 1.0. The NFS implementation was designed to be user transparent. User transparency was achieved by adding a new interface to the kernel that separates the generic file system operations from specific file system operations. The *file system interface* consists of two parts: the Virtual File System (*VFS*) interface defines the operations that can be done on a file within *a* file system, while the *vnode* interface defines the operations that can be done on a file within *that* file system. This architecture allows addition of new file systems in much the same way as new device drivers are added to the kernel. Figure 7-2 presents the NFS architecture.

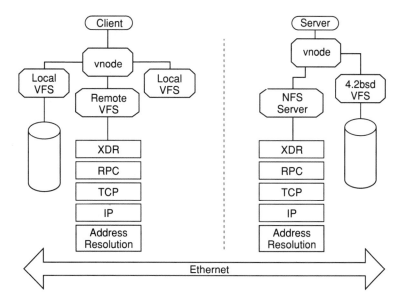

Figure 7-2.   Sun NFS Architecture

7.2 UNIX INTERFACE STANDARDIZATION

The UNIX operating system has become the operating system of choice for workstations. Initially, the market for UNIX included engineering workstations only. However, the kinds of hardware and the range of applications have proliferated. Applications like desktop publishing, electronic spreadsheets, distributed databases, and imaging have found a good operating base in UNIX.

With this kind of proliferation, vendors of application programs and end-users have experienced the need for portability from one hardware base to another, and have a heightened sense of the need for standardization.

Ideally, there should be one standard UNIX system. Realistically, AT&T UNIX System V and Berkeley 4.3bsd have retained separate identities; and have retained some level of kernel differences, even though they are converging functionally. The Open Systems Foundation (OSF) is likely to come up with a third source code base. It is unlikely that a single kernel porting source would emerge out of the standardization efforts.

On the other hand, a single standard interface definition has a better chance of becoming reality. The interface standards (or recommendations for standards) include the following:

1. ANSI/X3.159—1988 Programming Language C Standard.
2. 1984 /usr/group Standard.
3. AT&T UNIX System V Interface Definition (SVID).
4. IEEE 1003.1 POSIX Standard.

The AT&T SVID is the first effort by AT&T in setting the lead for defining a standard. However, it does not have the industry backing and the required support from IEEE, ANSI, or ISO. The U.S. Department of Defense (DOD) uses it frequently to define a standard interface, an effort hotly contested by competitors of AT&T UNIX System V. Pushed by the user community, especially U.S. DOD, the IEEE organization set up the POSIX standards committee.

The /usr/group has continued its efforts to gain further consensus in other standardization areas to eventually bring these areas under the auspices of the IEEE committees. The /usr/group has the following standards sub-committees in the area of distributed file systems:

1. Network interface.
2. Graphics.
3. Internationalization.
4. Performance measurements.
5. Real-time.
6. Super-computing.

Some of the work has already moved under the auspices of IEEE POSIX committees. Let us now take a closer look at the IEEE POSIX standard and see how it compares with current ANSI, SVID, and Berkeley 4.3bsd.

7.2.1 POSIX Interface Standard

The POSIX Standard, also known as the IEEE 1003.1 POSIX Standard, is the result of the 1003 Working Group sessions under the auspices of IEEE. The operating system interfaces described in this standard are primarily derived from the 1984 */usr/group* Standard. Both the 1984 /usr/group Standard and the follow on work done by the 1003 Working Group are largely derived from UNIX Version 7, AT&T UNIX System III, and AT&T UNIX System V. Compatibility to other systems has been provided to the extent feasible. The POSIX standard can be obtained from the Publications Department of the Computer Society of IEEE.

In addition to developing a standard interface, some effort has gone into overcoming shortcomings of the current operating system, especially in areas like *signals* and *interprocess communication,* command interface, file locking and database management, networking, operating system security, input/output, and terminal control.

As defined, the standard consists of standard terminology and the description of each system call grouped by functional area of the operating system. Each system call is described in detail and each description consists of a synopsis, a description of the call and the parameters, the returns from the call, and possible errors returned from the call.

In addition to the IEEE 1003.1 Working Group, there are eight other working groups considering related standards:

1. IEEE 1003.0 Application Portability group is chartered with defining standards for operating system interfaces to ensure application portability.

2. IEEE 1003.2 Shell and Tools group is defining a standard interface and environment for applications that require the services of a shell command interpreter, and a set of common utilities and programs. System V Interface Definition (*SVID*) and the *X/Open* Portability Guide are used as input sources for these standards.

3. IEEE 1003.3 Testing and Verfication group is defining a standard methodology for testing conformance of POSIX interface implementations. The verification suite may be produced by an agency like the National Bureau of Standards (NBS). Any verification suite developed would require verification.

4. IEEE 1003.4 Transaction Processing group is defining acceptable changes to the UNIX kernel to make the UNIX system a real-time operating system. These changes would translate into syntactic and semantic changes to system calls to handle timers, priority scheduling, shared memory, contiguous files, IPC name space, and asynchronous event notification.

5. IEEE 1003.5 ADA Language Bindings group is defining the ADA language bindings. The role of this group expanded to other programming languages.

6. IEEE 1003.6 Security Standards group is defining standards for encryption and other security features.

7. IEEE 1003.7 System Administration group is defining standards for system administration.

8. IEEE 1003.8 Networking group is defining standards for process-to-process communications across networks, directory services, network management, transparent file access, remote procedure call mechanisms, and remote file access.

7.2.2 POSIX and ANSI C Comparison

The ANSI C (X3J11) Committee defined the complete C functions, while the IEEE 1003.1 Working Group dealt only with operating system specific functions. The POSIX standard assumes that programs always operate in a standard C execution environment on top of a host operating system with multiple processes (typically, UNIX). The ANSI C standard, on the other hand, provides for free standing—i.e. no host operating system—single process implementations. ANSI C also provides for a separate *text* mode for files, while POSIX maintains only the traditional *binary* mode. In some areas, POSIX has compromised to retain compatibility with historical variants of C compilers. ANSI C did not operate under such constraints.

It should be noted that there is very significant overlap between the two standards and that the committees coordinated and helped each other to a great extent.

7.2.3 POSIX and SVID Comparison

POSIX is more closely related to SVID than to any other standard or specification for UNIX operating systems. While POSIX used SVID as the base, it did not retain the full scope of SVID. The notable areas where POSIX narrowed its scope include system administration, interprocess communication, and networking functions. Other IEEE 1003 working groups are standardizing these areas. Additionally, POSIX has not retained all commands and utilities of SVID and, in some cases, replaced them or added to them from Berkeley 4.3bsd commands and utilities. Actually 4.2bsd was used for this purpose.

7.2.4 POSIX and Berkeley 4.3bsd Comparison

As we just noted, POSIX is derived largely from SVID. Some features were derived from Berkeley 4.2bsd. We also noted earlier in this chapter that Berkeley 4.3bsd is very similar to Berkeley 4.2bsd (the newer release provides better performance and additional networking features).

Key features included in POSIX that are derived from Berkeley 4.2bsd include supplementary groups per process, reliable signals, and the job control facility.

There are a number of features that are part of the POSIX standard, but that are not supported in Berkeley 4.3bsd. The notable features include FIFO special files— note that FIFO files were not supported in Version 7 of UNIX; file locking—note that this feature was included in AT&T UNIX System V Release 2; some internationaliza- tion functions; and the new UNIX System V terminal interface—note that Berkeley 4.3bsd supports curses instead of terminfo.

Some key Berkeley 4.3bsd features are not supported in POSIX. These include long file names up to 255 characters in length—they are supported but not required for compliance with the standard; symbolic links; sockets for local or network wide interprocess communication; networking; and precise timers—Berkeley 4.3bsd pro- vides for a precision of 1 millisecond on timers.

7.3 PORTABILITY—HOW TO ACHIEVE IT

The definition of portability is subjective. It can vary from a system that is portable at execution level to one that requires relinking or re-compilation, to one that requires code changes. Portability along bloodlines and across bloodlines is another important issue. Portability across bloodlines is not as good. Typically, it requires changes to programs that use the special features of one specific architecture. However, the changes are small in scope and are usually done by hand.

7.3.1 Portability Along Bloodlines

Portability at execution level implies that the executable object program can be loaded in the target system without any change and that it runs normally. Portability to this level is found very rarely, and is almost always within the bloodline and on the same hardware. Portability within the bloodline is usually very good for forward compatibility, i.e. code developed for a particular release will almost always run on the next release without changes, and generally, only with a re-compilation and re-link. Backward compatibility is not so good, i.e., code developed for the latest release may require modifications for compilation and successful running on a previous release. Both AT&T and Berkeley have made efforts to provide compatibility in their later releases to allow programs written for previous releases to be recompiled and run without source code changes. Berkeley UNIX 4.2bsd provided a compatibility mode for 4.1bsd programs to ease transition to the new release. AT&T UNIX System III programs also ported easily to System V and its follow-on releases. In most cases, the additional capabilities provided added new features without adversely affecting portability of old programs to new releases.

7.3.2 Portability Across Bloodlines

Portability across bloodlines and across different hardware is dependent on a number of factors. Almost invariably, portability across bloodlines is also associated with a hardware change. The factors that are commonly encountered are either bloodline related or hardware related. The hardware related issues are almost always encountered along with bloodline related issues because the ports are done to different types of hardware.

7.3.2.1 Bloodline Related Issues

The bloodline related issues are primarily a result of extensions performed by the developers to overcome real or perceived problems, or to achieve different levels of functionality as compared to the original base. There are a number of bloodline related issues, such as,

1. *C* compiler issues:
   a. Bitfields implementation
   b. Pointers
   c. Character set
   d. Shift operations
   e. Identifier lengths
   f. Register variables
   g. Type conversions
   h. Evaluation order.
2. Terminal and screen management.
3. Signals.
4. Interprocess communications.
5. I/O controls.
6. Memory addressing (Berkeley UNIX 4.2bsd).

There are two primary reasons for *C* compiler issues. Most of these issues are a result of a difference between the porting base and the target hardware. Other issues, e.g., identifier lengths, are a result of desired enhancements made at the time of the port.

Terminal and screen management are carried out using the *curses* package in UNIX 4.2bsd and the terminfo package in AT&T UNIX System V. Sun Microsystems enhanced the Berkeley package with the SUNtools package. Microsoft XENIX added on a windowing package. There is some standardization effort under way. However, there are enough different implementations that porting software based on any of these specialized window and screen management packages requires special attention.

The Berkeley implementation extended the original implementation of signals considerably and made signals more reliable.

While the basic mechanisms for interprocess communications—shared memory, message queues, and semaphores—have remained fairly unchanged across UNIX implementations, both Berkeley and AT&T added their own versions of communications packages to achieve network level communications. Berkeley added the sockets interface to support TCP/IP and AT&T added the Streams interface to support Streams based networking.

I/O Controls have been significantly enhanced in AT&T UNIX implementations and the enhancements made to AT&T UNIX System V, e.g. use of *ioctl* routines instead of *setty,* have not been carried over to the Berkeley UNIX 4.2bsd. The System V derived implementation of Microsoft XENIX is very similar to the AT&T product.

Memory addressing and memory issues have been the major bone of contention between the two major bloodlines of UNIX—AT&T System V and Berkeley 4.2bsd. Berkeley used demand paging in 4.2bsd while AT&T System V was a swapping system. AT&T has since improved the memory management on its later (point) releases of UNIX so that it now uses a combination of swapping and demand paging for memory management. For the most part, this did not affect application level portability except for code that attempted to access memory using the extended memory management system calls provided in Berkeley UNIX.

7.3.2.2 Hardware Related Issues

The hardware related issues are primarily those involved with data representation, data conversion, and storage differences across systems. These include issues such as,

1. Byte size and word size.
2. Byte alignment.
3. Byte ordering in word.
4. Sign extension.
5. Most/least significant bit.
6. Address space.

Byte length for most machines is 8 bits. There are some special cases of 9 bit bytes or bytes of other sizes. There is a lot more variation in the word size. Word size has varied from 2 bytes to 8 bytes depending on the hardware. 2 or 4 byte words are the most commonly encountered sizes.

Byte alignment becomes an issue in the definition of structures or unions within structures and unions. Some hardware such as the PDP11 and the Motorola M68000 require data items longer than one byte to be aligned on even byte address boundaries. Other hardware such as as VAX 11/780 or MicroVAX have no such requirement. The manner in which structures and unions are used is significant in determining their portability.

The byte order differs across hardware and is even more of an issue in systems that have multiple bytes per word. Programs developed such that the byte order information is used for accessing data require modifications for adjustment to the new byte order. The portability can be improved by anticipating portability requirements and setting up define statements for bytes such that changes can be achieved at the global level. Byte ordering in character strings may also occasionally cause problems.

Two very significant coding issues are *sign extension* and the definition of *short* and *long* integers. The type conversion flexibility in *C* can create problems in a port. Both, the *sign extension* and the bit length of an integer may run into unforeseen problems when type conversions to *char* take place. Byte ordering in character strings may also occasionally cause problems.

Programs that require moving data as a sequence of bits may encounter problems with the most significant or least significant bit definitions.

7.3.3 Writing Portable Code

There are some key steps to writing portable code that will work wih different implementations of UNIX as well as with different hardware implementations. Three key steps are the following:

1. Selecting target implementations and hardware.
2. Building a list of differences for target hardware systems.
3. Following a set of rules to avoid specialized implementations.

7.3.3.1 Selecting Target Implementations and Hardware

Essentially all implementations in use are offshoots of either AT&T UNIX System III or of Berkeley UNIX 4.1bsd. Using a common subset of system calls ensures portability across implementations. This approach ensures that the special features of an implementation are eliminated, e.g., the extended signals capability or the memory addressability of the Berkeley UNIX 4.2bsd. If it is important to retain these special features, conditional compilation can be used by employing the implementation type as a switch.

The application programs can be set up for specific and selected hardware, or it may be set up to be general enough that some compile time parameters can accommodate almost any available hardware.

7.3.3.2 Building a List of Differences in Hardware Implementation

Once the target hardware has been selected, the parameters listed in the previous section (and any other that may apply) are noted. Different hardware issues also can be dealt with by using conditional compilation. Switches can be defined for each primitive, e.g. byte ordering, *int* size, etc., or a set of flags can be set for specific hardware implementations.

7.3.3.3 Programming Rules and Program Checking

Programming rules set up to avoid any implementation differences are extremely useful for writing portable code. These rules specify the usage of #*if* and #*ifdef* conditional compilation codes.

The use of utilities like *lint* ensures that the program is error free, and has no special structures or constructs that may be non-portable.

7.4 SUMMARY

The portability of applications to UNIX implementations on different hardware systems has been the greatest impetus to the popularity of UNIX. In this chapter, we looked at four perspectives on this issue. We looked at the genesis of UNIX and its evolution. We also compared the two most common distributions of UNIX, and then we looked at the standardization efforts being carried out to promote application portability. Finally, we looked at some recommendations for writing portable code.

7.5 EXERCISES

1. Compare system calls in the most recent releases of AT&T UNIX System V and Berkeley 4.3bsd. Describe the differences.
2. Describe the differences in the implementations of the file systems between the most recent releases of AT&T UNIX System V and Berkeley 4.3bsd.

8

Potential Areas For System Improvement

The UNIX operating system, unlike many other operating systems which are designed to perform specific functions in pre-defined application environments, grew from an experimental personal operating system to a commercial time-sharing operating system that is restricted neither to any specific hardware, nor to any specific class of applications. Almost every major port to a new class of system hardware has resulted in a major enhancement to the UNIX operating system. With the release of UNIX as a full-fledged supported commercial operating system, and its use in an increasingly larger class of applications, the demands on UNIX have kept increasing. On the one hand, there has been the effort to standardize the UNIX system call interface. On the other hand, its kernel is modified frequently to support the special application requirements of system integrators.

The UNIX system call interface needs to be standardized to ensure portability. The only major reason for not modifying the UNIX kernel is the inclusion of new features distributed in later releases and the overall maintenance issues related to customized kernel code. The discussion in this chapter is centered around the changes that can be made to the UNIX kernel to enhance it for different application classes. It is assumed that the system call interface remains largely unchanged and is closely tied to the original porting source base. Some of the changes noted here have already been made for some special implementations. It is hoped that eventually there will be a common UNIX source base that provides these and other enhancements or features as configurable options or as conditional assembly/compilation options.

8.1 PROCESS SCHEDULING FOR REAL-TIME APPLICATIONS

UNIX has been implemented as a time-sharing system. There have been various attempts to develop proprietary implementations of UNIX that are designed to provide some real-time capability. There are also investigations in progress by the standardization committees of IEEE and the /usr/group to develop a standard interface for a real-time implementation of UNIX.

There are two important aspects of performance in a real-time system. One has to do with the sheer processing power of the system that results in a fast response. The response time in such a system needs to be short enough to ensure no loss of data. The second aspect is customization of the operating system to meet the requirements of a particular application. The customization may include scheduling algorithms, modification of time slices, control of process priorities, and the like.

Most of the features needed are provided by both AT&T UNIX System V recent releases and the Berkeley UNIX 4.3bsd. However, UNIX does not provide sufficient control on process scheduling and switching, and the time it takes to respond to an interrupt. Nor does it provide a means of locking down processes in memory. The clock interrupt that normally controls re-scheduling cannot be controlled by the user either.

8.1.1 Real Time Processes

Some of the time-sharing operating systems that provide special real-time functions use the features of preemptive scheduling and memory locked processes. Additionally they provide the user with a capability to define certain processes to be real-time and to adjust priorities of these processes to allow them to interrupt any other process that is not real-time.

In real-time applications, for example factory automation, detection systems, air traffic control systems, and process control applications, it is important that a critical event be attended to immediately. The scheduling algorithm in UNIX does not provide a means of preempting a running kernel process or superceding other kernel processes and placing this event to the head of the run queue. It is also important that a real-time process once started not be interrupted until it completes the operation.

The system can be improved to handle real-time applications by enhancing the scheduling algorithm such that the user can tune the system to the application requirements. The user should be able to define one or two processes as being real-time such that they always operate at the highest priority level and can preempt any other process at any time except during critical system functions. The *nice* system call is not capable of achieving this.

8.1.2 Preemption of Kernel Processes

Preemption of a kernel process is not allowed in the current distributions of the UNIX operating system. A high-priority process cannot preempt a low priority process that is executing a system call in the kernel mode. Redesigning this mode of operation would require a more involved process scheduler and CPU scheduler. The saving of the process context and the state of the machine will also be more complex. In this kind of a kernel, a high priority process that is locked in memory will have a much better response capability to the needs of a process control device in a manufacturing environment.

8.1.3 A Biased Scheduler

A biased scheduler is one that does not treat all processes equally. The normal UNIX scheduler uses a clock interrupt or another higher priority interrupt as triggers for re-scheduling. Instead, the scheduler could be set to continue scheduling all processes as before, but can provide for a *timer* interrupt where the timer can be set by the user to re-schedule only the processes defined as being real-time by the user. This would allow the scheduler to respond to the real-time processes at a predefined interval. By keeping the total number of real-time processes very low, e.g. only one or two, the scheduling check can be made very fast. If there is no real-time process ready with data, control returns to the interrupted process.

8.1.4 Virtual Memory vs. Real Memory

The UNIX System is designed to support a large number of users on systems limited in their real memory capability by using virtual memory techniques. The code and data for any process that is currently not active, or is waiting for an input/output event to complete, is stored temporarily in a swap area on disk. It is loaded in memory when it gets unblocked and has moved to the head of the priority queue. For the operation of a real-time process that must respond in a fraction of a second, it needs to remain in real memory at all times so that it can be scheduled very rapidly. This requires a new capability that would allow a process to be programmatically locked in memory for the duration it has to be able to respond quickly. AT&T UNIX System V has a *plock* system call that provides for locking of a user process in memory.

8.1.5 Single User Version

For systems that are designed primarily for process control, the real-time requirements are even more stringent. They also need to operate as single user systems but with multi-tasking capability. A full implementation of UNIX as a single-user system, without the overhead of process scheduling, that is fully resident in memory is desirable for most process control applications. In a kernel preemption mode described above, adequate response could be provided for most real-time applications. The process actually serving the process control device or a communication line can be made high priority.

8.1.6 Implementation Recommendation

To summarize, process scheduling for real-time applications requires some key modifications to the UNIX kernel. These include the following:

1. Definition of processes as being real-time (high priority).
2. Definition of memory resident processes (locked in memory).
3. Scheduling algorithms that favor real-time processes.
4. Preemption of processes in kernel mode.
5. Operation of UNIX as a single user system with reduced overhead.

Some of these functions have been implemented in some commercial real-time implementations of UNIX and have made possible the use of UNIX for process control, communications, and other real-time applications.

8.2 THE UNIX FILESYSTEM

The UNIX file system was developed to provide a simple, yet flexible data storage system. The disk may be viewed as a randomly addressable array of 1K byte blocks (AT&T UNIX System V) or 4K bytes (Berkeley UNIX 4.2bsd). A file is an array of bytes and UNIX does not impose any structure on the data within the file. The first block, block *0*, on the disk is always the *boot block* and the second block, block *1*, contains the *superblock*. The next sequential block of storage is used for the inodes. The disk blocks required for inodes are based on the configured number of the inodes. The rest of the disk is available for files.

On creation, a file in AT&T UNIX System V starts with 13 disk blocks. These disk blocks may be contiguous in a relatively unused disk. In a disk that has become fragmented after repeated writes and deletes, the blocks may be dispersed across the disk.

The Berkeley UNIX 4.2bsd has a different file system architecture that specifically addresses some of these issues. The Berkeley UNIX System uses larger block sizes and the inodes are located on the same physical drive as the file.

8.2.1 Contiguous Disk Files

Contiguous files are supported by many large timesharing operating systems to provide fast access storage for index files of a database, or for other pre-defined fixed length data. Creation of contiguous files or extension of contiguous files on a highly fragmented disk are the most common problems encountered. UNIX does not currently support contiguous files. Adding that support could significantly increase the performance of some applications. The algorithms used to access free blocks on disk would become more complex but the benefits of contiguous files probably outweigh that complexity.

8.2.2 Fast File I/O

Even faster file transfer may be achieved by using configurable or dynamically definable block sizes for disk input and output. AT&T UNIX System V uses 1K byte blocks and Berkeley UNIX 4.2bsd uses 4K byte blocks. Neither of the two are ideal for all disk accesses. Faster disk I/O may be achieved if block sizes can be set to 1K, 4K, or 16K bytes or any other appropriate value according to the size of the data being accessed. This kind of change will also require a change in the manner the UNIX buffer pool is set up and used.

8.2.3 Network File System Integrity

Networked UNIX systems are becoming the norm rather than the exception. The UNIX distributions have no special features to ensure the integrity of the networked file systems, nor are there any features to ensure security other than the normal permissions checks. User *ids* and *permissions* on two systems may be set to be the same for two different users and a network request by a user on one node may be serviced by another node as long the *id* and *permissions* are okay. Mis-identification of this nature is not prevented. The UNIX system requires enhancements so that the level of security can be increased on a conditional basis. Node identification can be added to ensure that there is no breach of network security.

8.3 DEVICE DRIVERS

The procedures for adding device drivers to UNIX not only differ from one implementation to another, but are also fairly involved for most users, and frequently require re-compilation and/or re-linking of the operating system. A badly written driver can impact other users and can potentially hog the system. The different schemes used by different implementations of UNIX for adding user-written device drivers include the following:

1. Re-linking the operating system with the new driver.
2. Replacing dummy driver stubs with new object code.
3. Replacing existing drivers with new code.

Besides the complications of the approach taken, the concept of user level drivers is misused in the sense that the process scheduling flow in the UNIX kernel is often substantially altered by adding the driver. The drivers do give the users the capability to lock out all interrupts and get control of the machine—a feature used often for building real-time capability in the operating system.

A common and more user friendly approach to writing device drivers would be a significant improvement to the operating system. The general device driver structure is good. What may be needed is the simplification of the process of adding device drivers such that re-linking of the entire operating system is not necessary. The availability of configurable standard (or dummy) drivers may also be good for most users.

8.4 UNIX SYSTEM SECURITY

The National Computer Security Center has established criteria for the evaluation of security levels in computers for government agencies. These classifications are as follows:

- A1 —Design Verified and Certified
- B3 —Security Domains
- B2 —Structured Protection
- B1 —Labelled Security Protection
- C2 —Controlled System Access
- C1 —Discretionary Security
- D —Minimal Protection

Current implementations of UNIX are generally rated at the the C1 level and some implementations with special security enhancements have been certified at the C2 level. The UNIX system has the basic features that provide security but requires a number of enhancements to move up the security classifications list.

The UNIX system security is embodied in the *login* process that requires a password in the concept of *file permissions* that specify owner/group/world privileges to read, write, or execute files, and in the use of the encryption capability. This level of security is adequate for most installations. However, it does require very careful initial set-up and constant policing due to the potential of a user finding the *root* password or achieving superuser privileges by executing an *su* call and providing a superuser password. Either of these methods gives the user full access to alter the system security from any workstation, or even from a remote login.

Where security is an important consideration, a feature that would provide additional security would be a system manager defined switch that restricts *superuser* privilege to the designated boot console or terminal only; that prevents users from reading the *passwd* file; that actually restricts the *superuser* privilege to the *root* only; that sets up a default *UMASK* value and requires specific user action to change it; that prevents modifications to the *profile* files by users; and that ensures that the *PATH* variable is set up properly. Further restrictions that may be useful include restricting modification of the *passwd* file at the boot console only. It is assumed that the system boot console is in a secure area. This feature would make UNIX considerably more secure and it would also make security set up less tedious.

Another feature that may be added is what may be called a *limited superuser* privilege. This feature would allow superuser access to files that belong to the group only instead of to the entire file system. An example of this is where the supervisor may have superuser access to the files created by the subordinates only. This provides the needed superuser feature, but in a more secure manner.

8.5 USER INTERFACE

The User Interface to the UNIX System is embodied in the command line interfaces like the *Bourne shell* (AT&T UNIX System V) and the *csh* (c-shell in Berkeley UNIX 4.3bsd). There are a number of other implementations of shells such as the *Korn* shell. Some factors that measure the effectiveness of a user interface are the following:

1. Adaptability to user expertise.
2. Consistency in usage across functions.
3. Context-based help functions.
4. Context-based error management.

The command line interfaces have remained popular with programmers due to the speed of operation and accessability of all operating system functions. They are an excellent tool for an experienced programmer but not for a casual user.

The development of the *curses* package, consisting of a set of screen management routines, was the first attempt by Berkeley at providing a better User Interface than the cryptic shell interface. The *curses* package was complemented by Sun Microsystems with the SUNTOOLS package that was used as the base for the *desktop* interface. Other implementations provide menu-driven user interfaces with the shell as an alternative for system programmers. Object-oriented user interfaces based on *desktops* with pull-down menus, pop-ups, dynamic window management, and pointing devices like mice, light pens, pads, and the like are now available with some implementations. A *curses* like package, *terminfo,* is also available with the AT&T UNIX System V distribution.

New techniques based on the use of expert systems are starting to emerge that will conceptually change user interfaces. They attempt to gauge the skill level of the user by evaluating such factors as user response time, the nature of help function usage, and the use of some key system functions. These user interfaces are designed to adapt to the user expertise level dynamically. They can be set to wait for the user to enter a command line and if none is entered in a pre-defined time period, to display a menu or a pop-up appropriate for that context. Consistency is important for all level of users, but even more so for the expert users because they tend to only glance at the screen, and very often type ahead. They expect to find the same type of information in the same place. This applies to the use of arguments, command modifiers, use of windows, and error responses. Expert systems can assist in providing a consistent response that takes into account the context.

Context-based help functions are another significant area where expert systems can make a special contribution. They not only provide the help function for the current context, but the help information provided is adjusted to the user expertise level. For example, an expert user is presented more in-depth descriptions of the system function, potential side-effects, and the like, while a casual user is provided help on the basic functionality only. As stated earlier, the determination of expertise level is performed dynamically. The system should allow the user to switch to the in-depth or general level of information from the menu screen. This action in itself is a determinant of the user expertise level and the frequency and direction of help function level changes are used in the expertise level compilation.

The display of error messages only tells the user what went wrong. Very often, the user has no inkling of the context in which the error occurred and how to recover from it. An expert system approach, is again well applied here if the expert system can not only determine the context in which the error happened and can display that, but can also guide the user to recover from the error condition. Again, based on the user expertise level, it can set a time delay to allow the user to start the recovery without prompting.

A user interface that can adapt all aspects of the interface to the user expertise level will be a very significant step in the evolution of the UNIX operating system, a step that retains its charm for the experienced system developers and makes it easy to use for applications users.

An important standardization effort will be the definition of a screen management tools package that is based on a standard graphics interface standard. A number of standards are in contention, ranging from windowing standards e.g. *Xwindows,* and *NeWs* to the graphics interface standards like *GKS, PHIGS,* etc.

8.6 INTERPROCESS COMMUNICATION ACROSS SYSTEMS

Interprocess communications across systems has not kept pace with the natural evolution of networked systems. UNIX is used very frequently for large networked systems. The implementation of features like remote procedure calls has demonstrated the need to provide capabilities for managing processes across systems on a local area network. Neither the AT&T nor the Berkeley distributions of UNIX support features like semaphores, shared memory, messages, or any other means of interprocess communications between processes operating on different systems on a local area network. Obviously, the kernel would require changes to support a network-wide semaphore or shared memory capability. There are already multiprocessor implementations that have proprietary UNIX kernels designed for network-wide shared memory.

A network-wide semaphore capability will be useful. This would allow seamless communications among processes running on different systems, a prerequisite for distributing synchronized applications among processors in a distributed computing network.

8.7 NETWORK BRIDGES AND INDUSTRY STANDARD PROTOCOLS

The use of UNIX systems has traditionally been in the areas of engineering workstations and communications. However, starting with the 1983 liberalization of the distribution policy, UNIX has made inroads in a number of traditional data processing areas. Until recently, a majority of the UNIX systems communicated mostly with other UNIX systems or with systems for Defense projects. The Transmission Control Protocol (*TCP*) and Internet Protocol (*IP*) were used early on for file transfer and terminal emulation. The simplicity of the TCP/IP protocols, their ease of implementation in software as well as in intelligent controllers, low overhead, and wide-ranging support have made them the most common networking protocols for UNIX. AT&T addressed the networking issue by releasing the Streams Interface for UNIX System V releases.

The increasing use of UNIX systems for data processing and office automation applications has made obvious another significant area for the enhancement of UNIX. The data processing and office automation environments have traditionally used SNA and ISO protocols. Most major manufacturers support protocols like SNA, X.25, MAP, and the emerging ISO Open Systems architecture. Neither Streams, nor TCP/IP map directly to the layers of the other protocols. A major enhancement to UNIX would be to provide a set of generic layered interfaces that provide a reasonably good mapping to these protocols.

8.7.1 AT&T Streams and Network Objects

Networking in the AT&T UNIX System V first appeared as the *Streams* and the Remote File System (*RFS*) implementations in System V Release 3. The AT&T Streams architecture is a layered architecture where the streams are the interfaces between the protocol layers and the UNIX kernel. This provides the capability to implement different protocols to operate with the same Streams interface. (See Figure 8-1.)

ISO Layer	AT&T UNIX System V.3	Network Objects
Application	RFS Application using Streams	File Transfer Terminal Emulation Application interface
Presentation	Stream Modules (Transport Library)	Library Routines
Session	New System Calls for Streams	Socket Interface
Transport & Network	Protocol Modules for TCP/IP, XNS, SNA, OSI, etc.	Protocol Modules
Data Link & Physical	Ethernet (IEEE 802.3), Token Ring, SNA, etc.	Data Link Object

Figure 8-1.   AT&T Streams and Network Object Mapping

The interfaces are implemented as a set of new system calls and as a set of Streams interface modules. Every attempt has been made to make the interfaces generic enough to handle the common industry protocols. The concept needs to be enhanced further through the use of the concept of objects. Objects at each layer, in that scheme, remain totally independent from objects at any other layer and interface through clearly defined interfaces only. This would, for example, allow a TCP/IP protocol object to communicate via an SDLC data link object.

8.7.2 TCP/IP to ISO

The ISO protocol set has found a large number of supporters including, among others, General Motors, Boeing, and Digital Equipment Corporation. The ISO protocol set is based on the Open Systems Interconnect 7-layer model. The increasing use of the ISO protocol set will require compatibility between TCP/IP and the ISO Protocol set for the systems to communicate on the same network. If an ISO protocol needs to communicate with a system that supports TCP/IP only, then the TCP/IP should be able to respond to it by emulating the required functions. Use of a protocol translator is useful for such requirements. A protocol translator is defined as a layer of code that converts the data created under one protocol to data created under (or that can be read by) another protocol. (See Figure 8-2.)

The table on page 250 shows a good level of compatibility at the different protocol levels between TCP/IP and ISO. Each layer for each protocol set has two characteristics that define that layer. These characteristics are the interface to that layer and the services provided by that layer.

ISO Layer	Berkeley UNIX 4.2bsd	ISO Protocol Set
Application	FTP, TELNET, rlogin Application using Sockets	File Transfer Access Method Virtual Terminal Protocol (VTP) X.400
Presentation	Library Routines Serving User Processes	Presentation Protocol
Session	New System Calls to Implement Sockets	Session Protocol
Transport & Network	TCP IP	Transport Protocol (TP4) CLNS Internet Protocol
Data Link & Physical	Ethernet (IEEE 802.3)	Address Resolution Protocol Ethernet (IEEE 802.3)

Figure 8-2. TCP/IP to ISO Protocol Set Mapping

One or both of these may be different for the different layers of the two protocol sets. Where differences exist, bridging modules are required to convert from one protocol set to the other. The implementation of such bridging modules is not integral in any implementation of UNIX. Implementation of such modules will make UNIX a powerful network operating system.

8.7.3 TCP/IP to MAP

Manufacturing Access Protocol (MAP) was developed for process control applications for manufacturing control systems. UNIX is increasingly being used for manufacturing systems and for engineering workstations that interface with manufacturing systems.

8.7.4 TCP/IP to X.25

The X.25 is a three-layer protocol standard developed under the aegis of the CCITT. The AT&T Streams interface was designed to handle it as a protocol module. In the case of TCP/IP, the X.25 protocol essentially replaces the Internet Protocol (IP) and provides the functions for the Network layer, Data Link Control layer and the Physical Link layer. This requires mapping the interface and services of the Internet protocol layer. The issues involved in this mapping include the following:

1. Address translation.
2. Virtual circuit management.
3. Packet fragmentation and reassembly.
4. Internetwork routing.

The enhancement to the UNIX kernel would again consist of an interface and services protocol translation module that provides a smooth translation from one protocol to the other. This enhancement would make support for X.25 integral with the UNIX operating system.

8.7.5 SNA Support

AT&T Streams interface has been designed to support SNA modules. However, SNA layers do not fall neatly into the ISO model and some layers overlap. SNA also has a number of layers that require their own level of support. This support is not inherent in UNIX at this time, but will be required for the use of UNIX systems in data processing and office automation. (See Figure 8-3.)

Layer	AT&T UNIX System V.3	SNA
Application	RFS Application using Streams	Application Layer
Presentation	Stream Modules (Transport Library)	Presentation Services Transaction Services
Session	New System Calls for Streams	Data Flow Control Connection Point Manager
Transport & Network	Protocol Modules for TCP/IP, XNS, SNA, OSI, etc.	Transmission Control Path Control NCP
Data Link & Physical	Ethernet (IEEE 802.3), Token Ring, SNA, etc.	Data Link Control (SDLC) SNA Physical Data Channel

Figure 8-3.   AT&T Streams and SNA Mapping

As currently set up, SNA can be interfaced only at the Network and Transport layers through the Streams Interface. The UNIX system needs to be enhanced to integrally support all layers of SNA such that it can communicate as a node in an SNA network.

8.8 SUMMARY

This chapter concludes the discussion of the UNIX operating system by highlighting areas of the system that may be enhanced to support special features required most frequently. These requirements are due to the increasing use of UNIX for real-time applications, as a workstation system for office automation, data processing applications, and as a networked system. This chapter is also intended to provoke some thinking on the part of the readers to consider adaptability of UNIX for their specific needs.

APPENDIX A

System Control Structures and Tables

The UNIX System uses a number of databases and data structures to keep important user, process, file, and status information on disk and in memory. This appendix describes the variables and parameters that make up some of the more significant control structures and tables, and the use of these control structures and tables in the operating system architecture for performing the different functions within the kernel.

PAGE TABLE ENTRY

The memory management architecture of the UNIX system is based on dividing the total physical memory in segments of equal size called pages. The typical size of these pages ranges from 512 bytes to 16K bytes depending on the implementation. The page table entries specify the usage of the memory pages. The components of a page table entry include the following:

- Page frame number.
- Type of page.
- Page modified bit.
- Page protection:
    Kernel mode readable only
    Kernel mode writable only
    User mode writable
    Kernel mode writable, user mode readable
    User and kernel mode readable only.
- Page valid bit.

VIRTUAL ADDRESS STRUCTURE

This structure consists of the following three entries:

- Byte offset within page.
- Virtual page number.
- Memory region:
  System/user
  Text
  Data
  Stack.

USER STRUCTURE

The User Structure is a database used by the kernel to locate all required information about a user process while the process is swapped into memory. The kinds of information contained in the User Structure include the following:

- Save information for exchanging stacks.
- I/O flag.
- Return error code.
- Effective user ID.
- Effective group ID.
- Real user ID.
- Pointer to proc structure.
- Pointer to argument list.
- SYSCALL return values.
- Base addresses for I/O.
- Bytes remaining for I/O.
- Offset in file for I/O.
- Pointer to inode of current directory.
- Root directory of current process.
- Current pathname component.
- Pathname pointer.
- Current directory entry.
- Inode of parent directory of pathname pointer.
- File pointers of open files.
- Per process flags of open files.
- Arguments to current system call.
- Text size (code size).
- Data size.

- Stack size.
- Label variable for quits and interrupts.
- Label variable for swapping.
- Signal disposition.
- Process user time.
- Process system time.
- Sum of children's user times.
- Sum of children's system time.
- Address of user saved R0.
- Buffer base.
- Buffer size.
- Program counter offset.
- Program counter scaling.
- System interrupt flag.
- Flags for I & D separation.
- Controlling TTY pointer.
- Controlling TTY device.
- Mask for file creation.
- User login data.

PROCESS TABLE ENTRIES

The following describes the kinds of information located in the process table entry (*proc structure*). This information is used by the kernel to determine scheduling priorities and readiness to run. It also defines the resource requirements for the process to run.

- Process states:
    Awaiting an Event
    Abandoned
    Running
    Intermediate state in process creation
    Intermediate state in process termination
    Being traced.
- Process flags:
    In core
    Scheduling process
    Process cannot be swapped
    Being swapped out
    Being traced.
- Process priority.

- Resident time for scheduling.
- CPU usage for scheduling.
- Nice routine for CPU usage.
- Signals (an inclusive OR of all signals) pending for this process.
- User ID.
- Name of process group leader.
- Unique process ID.
- Process ID of parent.
- Address of swappable image.
- Size of swappable image.
- Event awaiting.
- Pointer to user structure.
- Pointer to linked list of running processes.
- Time to alarm clock signal.

SHARED MEMORY PAGE TABLE STRUCTURES

The per process page table consists of *page table structures* that include the following components:

- Page frame number.
- Type of page.
- Page modified flag.
- Page protection flag.
- Valid page flag.

SHARED MEMORY HEADERS

The *shared memory* headers are used for identifying shared memory segments and their current usage parameters. The contents of the shared memory header structure *shmid_ds* includes the following:

- Operation permissions structure:
    Creator user ID
    Creator group ID
    User ID
    Group ID
    Mode.
- Segment size.

- Pointer to associated page table.
- ID of process that performed last shared memory operation.
- Current number attached.
- In-memory number attached.
- Last shared memory attach time.
- Last shared memory detach time.
- Last shared memory change time.

MESSAGE QUEUE HEADER

The message queue header structure includes the following:

- Operation permissions structure:
       Creator user ID
       Creator group ID
       User ID
       Group ID
       Mode.
- Total number of messages in queue.
- Maximum number of bytes in queue.
- ID of process that last sent message.
- ID of process that last received message.
- Pointer to first message on linked list.
- Pointer to next available message slot.
- Pointer to last message slot in linked list.
- Time of last message send.
- Time of last message receive.
- Time of last message change (control).

MESSAGE HEADERS

Message headers form a linked list. The following describes the components of the message header structure:

- Pointer to next message header.
- Message type.
- Message byte count (text size).
- Message pool allocation spot.

SEMAPHORE STRUCTURES

The *semaphore structure* defines the semaphore itself and consists of the following:

- The value of the semaphore.
- Process id of last operation.
- Number of processes awaiting semaphore value to become greater.
- Number of processes awaiting semaphore value to become *0*.

SEMAPHORE DATA STRUCTURE

The semaphore data structure consists of the following components:

- Semaphore id.
- Operation permissions structure:
  Creator user ID
  Creator group ID
  User ID
  Group ID
  Mode.
- Pointer to semaphore arrays—base address (lists).
- Number of semaphores in this set.
- Time of last operation.
- Time of last message change (control).

SEMAPHORE UNDO STRUCTURE

The semaphore undo structure pointer consists of the following parameters:

- Semaphore set id.
- Semaphore number.
- Adjustment (decremented).

SUPERBLOCK

The superblock is always block 1 of the logical disk of a UNIX file system. It contains information that defines the current state of the file system. This information includes the following:

- Size in blocks of i-list (inode list).
- Size in blocks of the file system.

- Number of free blocks in the file system.
- A list of the free blocks available on the file system.
- The free inodes list.
- Inode lock flags.
- Flag to indicate that the superblock has been modified.
- Flag to indicate that the file system has been mounted for *read-only*.
- Time and date of the last superblock update (time offset).
- Total free blocks in the file system.
- Total free inodes in the file system.
- File system name.
- File system disk name.

DISK INODES

A file is identified internally in the UNIX System via its inode number. The inode is copied into memory for every file that is being accessed. The inode includes the following information about the file:

- File type and mode (ordinary, directory, special, etc.).
- Number of links to the file.
- Owner's user ID.
- Owner's group ID.
- File access permissions.
- File size in bytes.
- 3-byte addresses of up to 13 disk blocks.
- Time and date of last access.
- Time and date of last modification.
- Creation time and date (relative time offset).

IN-CORE INODE

The in-core inode is built by copying the disk inode and then adding more fields for additional information. The additional fields are the following:

- Inode access status flags:
    Inode is locked (modification in progress)
    A process is waiting for inode to become unlocked
    The file information in the in-core inode is modified,
        i.e. it may differ from the disk inode
    File contents changed, in-core inode modified,
        i.e. it may differ from the disk inode

The file is a *mount'*ble device.
- Reference count acquired from file table entries.
- Device ID where disk inode resides.
- Disk address for file pointer.
- Last logical block read (file position).

FILE STRUCTURES (OR FILE TABLE ENTRIES)

While the inode is used on a per file basis, a file table entry is used on a per file open basis, i.e. a separate file entry is used if the same file is opened by another process. This takes care of the file being accessed under different access permissions. The file table entry consists of the following:

- File access flags.
- Reference counts.
- Pointer to inode table entry.
- READ/WRITE pointer.

BUFFER HEADERS

The UNIX System uses a number of internal buffers that form the buffer cache. The headers attached to these buffers provide information about the availability and use status of the buffers. Unlike inodes that have only information but no data, buffers have data and the header information is necessary for determining their current usage. The buffer header includes the following fields:

- Status flags (current state of the buffer).
- Device queue pointer (device table).
- Forward and backward pointers on free list.
- Forward and backward pointers on hash queue.
- Available queue pointer (position on free list).
- Device #—major/minor (device to which buffer is currently attached).
- Transfer size (data size).
- Low order core address.
- Words for clearing.
- Superblocks.
- Inode list.

- Block number on disk.
- High order core address.
- Error information (words not transferred).
- Request start time.

DRIVER I/O BUFFERS

The driver I/O buffers are dedicated to device drivers for data input. The information included in the headers used for these buffers is as follows:

- Status flag (same as for data buffer).
- Device ID.
- Controller busy flag.
- Error data.
- Device register data.
- Temporary storage.

BLOCK DEVICE SWITCH TABLE

This table is indexed by major device number. Each device has an entry that includes the following information:

- Device *open* routine.
- Device *close* routine.
- Device *strategy* routine.
- *Buffer* allocated.

CHARACTER DEVICE SWITCH TABLE

This table is indexed by major device number. Each device has an entry that includes the following information:

- Device *open* routine.
- Device *close* routine.
- Device *read* routine.
- Device *write* routine.
- I/O control routines.
- Address of terminal structure.

C-LISTS

C-lists consist of a linked list of cblocks used for storing character I/O and raw I/O data temporarily. The C-list header consists of the following information:

- Character count.
- Pointer to first cblock data entry.
- Pointer to last cblock data entry.

Cblocks are (ususally 24 to 32 bytes long) buffers and consist of the following components:

- Pointer to next header.
- Position of first character in buffer.
- Position of last character in buffer.
- Buffer data.

Typically two or more c-lists may be used for I/O to any device. Separate C-lists are used for input and output.

TTY STRUCTURE

A TTY structure is needed for each UNIX character device that is used for normal terminal I/O. It consists of c-list addresses, addresses of input and output, line discipline routines and other parameters required for character I/O. The TTY structure includes the following:

- C-list structure for raw I/O.
- C-list structure for canonical queue.
- Input buffer structure.
- C-list structure for output queue.
- Pointer to routine to start output.
- Pointer to routine to start input.
- Destination channel for a multiplexor.
- Device address.
- Device number.
- Mode flags settable by *ioctl* call.
- Internal state (timeout, device open, busy, etc.).
- Process group name.
- Number of delimitters in raw queue.
- Line discipline.

- Printing column of device.
- Erase character.
- Kill character.
- Input speed (receive).
- Output speed (transmit).
- Character input since a *ttwrite* for TTYs.
- Local mode word.
- Local state bits.
- C-list structure for control queue.

APPENDIX B

Glossary of UNIX Terms

Block Devices Block devices are devices like disk drives or magnetic tapes that store information in fixed length blocks and require fixed length block transfers. The system provides special system buffers for temporary data storage.

Buffer Pool Also called the buffer cache, this is a configurable system area that is set aside for system buffers. These system buffers provide temporary local storage for disk blocks that may be required frequently.

Cache Memory The dictionary describes cache as a hidden reserve. The term cache memory is used for additional memory, generally located on a processor board or a controller board, used for temporary storage of disk blocks or program instructions. The temporary storage performs two functions: it allows devices like disk drives to operate effectively by storing disk blocks read in until the processor is ready to copy them into system buffers and, it allows program instructions to be fetched from memory and stored in fast memories on the processor board for quicker access and consequently better performance.

Character Device Character devices include terminals, teletypes, plotters, and printers that transfer variable length character information.

CPU Scheduler (Swapper) The CPU scheduler performs the tasks of swapping processes in and out, locating memory for a process to run, and of scheduling the CPU for a process to run.

Demand Paging *Demand paging* systems do not swap a complete process in. They copy the minimum needed to run the process and use the concept of *page faults* to indicate the need to bring in another page of the process from virtual memory on disk to physical memory. Every process is partially in memory at all times.

Device Drivers Device drivers are used to provide a link between the user and a peripheral device. Resident in the UNIX kernel, they provide an interface for system call kernel service routines to interact with devices.

Device Handlers Device handlers are low-level driver routines that perform the tasks of starting and stopping devices, checking status, and performing data transfers. An interrupt from a device is vectored to its device handler.

Directory Files Directory files manage the cataloging of the file system. Directories associate names with the files themselves and separate files into groups that typically reflect the structure of the user's application. Directories may be created for each user, or for each project. The user's directory may be created as a *sub-directory* under the project directory. Further levels of sub-directories may be created, e.g. for source files, data files, and program files. The UNIX System creates directory files as ordinary files but gives them special write protection privileges such that only the system can write into them. Read access is available to users under normal access control.

Event Polling Event polling can support multiple tasks or multiple users by scheduling them in a round robin, or pre-set order, or by pre-set priority. The task that has an event posted (e.g. a keyboard input, printer completion, etc.) is scheduled. Once scheduled, the task continues until it is blocked for an event, e.g. input from keyboard or a communications line, printer becoming free, etc. Even though there are some disadvantages of this scheme for multi-user systems, this scheme has been used even for large multi-user systems due to its inherent simplicity and resulting processing speed for specific applications.

FIFO Files (Pipes) These are treated as first-in-first-out files and are used for pipes. They are used to provide communication between two processes when an array of bytes needs to be communicated.

File Links The directory entry for a file consists of the filename and a pointer to a data structure called an *inode* that describes the disk addresses for the file data segments. Since the file itself does not 'reside' in a directory, or 'belong' to a directory, the association between a directory and a file is generally called a *link*. A file may be linked to a number of directories.

File System A UNIX file system consists of four sections. The first section (or block) is called the *boot block* (used for system bootstrap), and the second section (or block) is called the *superblock*. The superblock is used to maintain current user status of the file system. The third section is a contiguous sequence of disk blocks containing sequential inode records. The relative position of the record in the sequence is the inode number. The system always allocates the next available inode to a new file. The total number of inodes is a configurable parameter and is set when the file system is created (*mkfs*). The last section consists of data blocks that make up the files. The data blocks are allocated on a random basis and space is allocated only when it is written into. The exception to this rule is the initial space allocation for a file that is created. It is allocated 13 contiguous blocks (differs on implementations) where the first 10 blocks are contiguous data blocks and the other three blocks provide indirect block addressing (up to three levels of indirection) to address very large files. More than one file system may be resident on one disk.

Inodes Files are identified internally by a number called the inode number, and the system maintains an inode table on disk that it copies into memory if the file is opened. This table associates filenames with inode numbers. (Please refer to the description of file systems above for further details).

Interrupt Driven Interrupt driven systems overcome the disadvantages of the event polling systems by providing the capability to respond to device interrupts quickly. These systems also provide priority and state driven scheduling of processes on an interrupt basis.

Kernel The UNIX kernel has always been recognized as the base operating system that supports user programs and utility programs like compilers, linkers, source code control, nroff, etc. The utility programs and UNIX commands are not considered a part of the UNIX kernel. The kernel consists of the layers closest to the hardware that are, for the most part, protected from the user, and the layer above it that provides user processes an environment in which to operate.

Kernel Mode A process operates in kernel mode when it is executing system code. This typically happens when a user application program executes a system call and requires execution of system code to perform an operating system level function.

Kernel Service Routines Kernel service routines (for the purposes of this text) refer to the routines in the UNIX kernel (system code) that service system calls. Every system call is vectored to its kernel service routine for call execution.

Kernel Space The kernel space is the space in memory where all kernel services are provided via kernel processes. It is a privileged area and the user has access to it only through the system call mechanism. Users have direct access to neither machine instructions nor devices. The kernel space, however, does have direct access to both.

Kernel Stack Every process has associated with it a kernel stack that is used when the process operates in kernel mode (execution of a system call).

Memory The term memory is used rather imprecisely. It generally refers to the *physical memory,* but is frequently used for *swap* or *virtual memory.* Memory, physical as well as virtual, is used for all processes, and physical memory is required for the system code as well as the current (and resident) processes.

Memory Management The term memory management refers to the allocation and de-allocation of physical and virtual (swap) memory in swapping systems, and additionally, management of page faults in demand paged systems.

Mounted File Systems File systems can be temporarily attached under a directory of another file system. This is used frequently in UNIX Systems to combine file systems for easier access. The *mount* system call is used for such attachment.

Multiprocessing Multiprocessing is defined as the execution of multiple processing elements performing a number of concurrent tasks in a system with the intent of maximizing overall throughput from the system. The multiple CPUs pool resources and are used on an as needed basis to share the load.

Ordinary Files Ordinary files are files that contain the information entered into them by the user, an application program, or a system utility program. The UNIX system treats ordinary files as a sequence of bytes or words. An ordinary file can contain *text* information as a string of characters (bytes) or *binary* information as a sequence of words. The UNIX kernel imposes no format or structure to the internal sequencing of the bytes or words in a file.

Parallel Processing Parallel processing is the concurrent execution of multiple tasks of the same application. There is no architectural difference between multiprocessing systems and parallel processing systems, and the two are used interchangeably throughout this book. The architectures for multiprocessing and parallel processing have been developed in a number of flavors. The common theme in these architectures is that most applications perform a number of parallel tasks and the performance of the overall system can be improved either by a more powerful CPU or by distributing these tasks across a number of processors. A highly effective performance is achieved by distributing tasks across a number of processors. Figure 4-2 describes the typical architecture of a parallel processing system. The major impetus to the development of this technique is the cost advantage gained by using lower speed components that pool the resources of the CPUs for a much greater overall throughput.

Preemptive Preemptive interrupt driven systems are generally required for critical real time applications (e.g. process control) where the interrupts or higher priority processes that become unblocked must be able to preempt a kernel process to provide a rapid response to a peripheral device.

Process A UNIX process is portrayed as the execution of an image (or the current state) of a virtual machine environment. The environment consisting of *memory, priority, user interface* device if needed, and access to other system resources, is associated with the process. A user identification is also associated with the process.

Process Management The operating system requires an orderly procedure for scheduling the CPU among the operating system, system peripherals, user applications, and system functions called by the user application programs. There are a number of schemes used by operating systems for scheduling CPU resources. Schemes used for managing multiple processes are called process management schemes.

Process Scheduler The process scheduler performs the functions of maintaining status of processes and changing their status to make them runnable if they are not blocked or an event happens that they are *sleep*ing on. It calls the *CPU scheduler* (also called the *swapper*) to allocate memory and swap processes in and out.

Programming Interface The programming interface provides user programs access to system functions. UNIX has a very well defined System Call interface. There are over 75 system calls (some implementations have a much larger number) that perform the various functions that manage the system resources like memory, disk storage, and peripherals.

Root Device On system initialization, only the root device, the device that contains the root directory '/', is known to the system. This name is built into the system. Other directories are created under the root directory. Other storage devices or file systems are attached by *mounting* them under the *root,* under the *current* directory, or under any directory that is currently known to the system.

Shell The Command Language Interpreter is a separate program in UNIX, commonly referred to as a shell.

Special Files Special files are used to access peripheral devices; and each I/O device is associated with a special file. Please refer to Section 3.6 for a detailed description of how special files are used.

Superblock The superblock contains all information that defines the current state of the file system. The third section is a contiguous sequence of disk blocks containing sequential inode records. The relative position of the record in the sequence is the inode number. The system always allocates the next available inode to a new file.

Swap Device A swap device is used to temporarily store processes that are swapped out of physical memory. It is usually an area of contiguous storage on the system disk and is used as virtual memory.

Swapping Swapping systems swap in or swap out complete processes (text, data, stacks, and other system tables needed to manage the processes while they are in main memory). A process resides on disk until it is ready to run again. It is then swapped in to main memory and gets scheduled based on priority. The larger the size of available main memory, the larger the number of processes that can stay resident in memory.

System Call A system call is used by a user program to invoke an operating system function, for example, to read or write files, access peripherals, read system date and time, change priorities, etc.

System Call Interface The system call interface layer converts a process operating in the user mode to a protected kernel mode process so that the program code can invoke kernel routines to perform system functions.

System clock The system clock is used to track real time and provide system date and time information. The clock handler services the clock interrupt (at clock tick or every second for most implementations) and wakes up the scheduler to reschedule processes and the CPU.

Unlinking The concept of 'deleting' a file is called unlinking in the UNIX system. 'Deletion' from a directory results in the removal of the entry for that file in the directory, a process called *unlinking*. The file is inaccessible after the last link is removed and its inode is added to the free list. The disk space used by the file is reclaimed for use.

User Interface The user interface is typically the program that interacts with the user and provides the user with access to the operating system functions. The typical user interface for UNIX Systems is called a *shell*. More recent implementations include windows, pointing devices, pop-up and pull-down menus.

User Mode A process executing user code (not system code) is considered to be in user mode. Any user process not executing a system call is in user mode. The process uses memory in user space while it is in user mode.

User Space The user space is the space in memory where user processes run. This consists of memory starting at the top of memory used by the kernel and includes all available memory above that.

User Stack The user stack is the stack used for a process while it operates in user mode. The stack is used for passing parameters for sub-routine calls and as temporary storage for variables.

User Structure The user structure consists of information about a process that is required while the process is resident in memory. The user structure is swapped out with the process if the complete process is swapped out.

Virtual Machines Modern multi-user interactive operating systems implement a collection of virtual machines. These virtual machines are similar to the base machine except some (hardware dependent and potentially hazardous) instructions are not available. In a sense, for the user they are an image of the base machine.

Virtual Memory The theme common to all solutions for more memory is the use of a part of the disk as an extension to main memory. Called *virtual memory*, this storage provides memory space for all users and can be expanded as needed if the number of users the system is configured for increases. Since the CPU can use only main memory for executing code and accessing data, the code and data components of a process have to be copied in to main memory for execution.

Index